580/C-32
coffee saucer

American Porcelain

1770–1920

AMERICAN PORCELAIN

1770–1920

Alice Cooney Frelinghuysen

THE METROPOLITAN MUSEUM OF ART
Distributed by Harry N. Abrams, Inc.
New York

This book has been published in conjunction with the exhibition *American Porcelain: 1770–1920*, held at The Metropolitan Museum of Art, New York, from 8 April 1989 until 25 June 1989.

The exhibition has been made possible by Lenox China.

Additional support for the book was provided by The William Cullen Bryant Fellows of The American Wing at The Metropolitan Museum of Art.

Published by The Metropolitan Museum of Art, New York, and distributed by Harry N. Abrams, Inc., New York.

John P. O'Neill, Editor in Chief
Barbara Burn, Executive Editor
Teresa Egan, Managing Editor
Mary-Alice Rogers, Editor, The William Cullen Bryant Fellows Publications, The American Wing
Bruce Campbell, Designer
Helga Lose, Production

Typeset by Columbia Publishing Co., Inc., Baltimore, Maryland
Color reproductions by Reprocolor International s.r.l., Milan, Italy
Printed and bound by Dai Nippon Printing Co., Ltd., Tokyo, Japan

LIBRARY OF CONGRESS CATALOGING-IN-PUBLICATION DATA

Frelinghuysen, Alice Cooney.
American porcelain, 1770–1920/Alice Cooney Frelinghuysen.
p. cm.
Bibliography: p.
Includes index.
ISBN 0-87099-540-5.—ISBN 0-8109-1887-0 (Abrams)
1. Porcelain. American—Exhibitions. I. Title
NK4405.F74 1989 88-36886
738.2'0973'07401471—DC19 CIP

Cover-jacket: Century vase, 1876. Union Porcelain Works, Greenpoint, New York. The Brooklyn Museum, Gift of Carll and Franklin Chace in memory of their mother, Pastora Forest Smith Chace, daughter of Thomas Carll Smith (43.25)

Frontispiece: Vase, 1828–38. William Ellis Tucker, Tucker and Hulme, Tucker and Hemphill, or Joseph Hemphill, Philadelphia. Philadelphia Museum of Art, Gift of Eliza Amanda Tucker, in memory of Thomas Tucker (31-55-1)

Contents

Lenders to the Exhibition

Bryce and Elaine Bannatyne, in association with P. G. Pugsley and Son, San Francisco, California

Florence I. Balasny-Barnes

The Bennington Museum, Bennington, Vermont

The Brooklyn Museum, New York

The Carnegie Museum of Art, Pittsburgh, Pennsylvania

Arthur V. Colletti

The Colonial Williamsburg Foundation, Virginia

Detroit Historical Museum, Michigan

Martin Eidelberg

R. A. Ellison

Everson Museum of Art, Syracuse, New York

Anne M. Ewing

Ann Willets Lapham Frazer

David and Barbara Goldberg

T. E. Goodwin

Mrs. Kenneth C. Heath

High Museum of Art, Atlanta, Georgia

Historic Hudson Valley, Tarrytown, New York

Historic New Orleans Collection, Louisiana

Betty and Robert A. Hut

Mr. and Mrs. George M. Kaufman

Lenox, Inc. (Archives of Lenox China)

Museum of the City of New York

John H. Nally

National Museum of American History, Smithsonian Institution, Washington, D.C.

The Newark Museum, Newark, New Jersey

New Jersey State Museum, Trenton, New Jersey

Alfred and Michiko Nobel

Ohio Historical Society, Museum of Ceramics at East Liverpool, Ohio

Philadelphia Museum of Art, Pennsylvania

The Art Museum, Princeton University, Princeton, New Jersey

Mary M. Rowan

The State Museum of Pennsylvania / Pennsylvania Historical and Museum Commission, Harrisburg, Pennsylvania

University City Public Library, Missouri

Wadsworth Atheneum, Hartford, Connecticut

Wyck Association, Philadelphia, Pennsylvania

Private collectors (six)

A hundred years ago, Walter Scott Lenox, founder of Lenox China, expressed the motivation that has guided his company since its inception: "It has always been my ambition to see china painting take the place it deserves among the arts."

Today, as Lenox celebrates its centennial, it is pleased to be associated with The Metropolitan Museum of Art in the recognition and display of American design and craftsmanship in porcelain.

Ever mindful of its proud heritage, Lenox remains dedicated to continuing its contribution to the tradition of excellence in American ceramic arts.

Safford P. Sweatt
President
Lenox China & Crystal
April 1989

Foreword

A*merican Porcelain: 1770–1920*, both as exhibition and publication, is a wholly appropriate exemplification of The Metropolitan Museum of Art's prevailing concern for the display and study of the finest examples of American decorative art. Approximately a hundred and thirty objects of porcelain, of which about a fifth are from the Museum's own holdings, have been brought together to present the most important examples in that medium to have been fashioned in this country. Until now, the extremely diverse nature of American porcelain and its history as an art form have been largely unexplored. In this book, the public is presented with new and carefully weighed scholarship on the medium in highly accessible form.

Although this comprehensive review of the subject is appearing only now, the Metropolitan can claim a long-standing interest in American porcelain, since one of its founding trustees, William C. Prime, was an early and eager collector of ceramics, including American pottery and porcelain. One object in this exhibition, a small bowl by the Jersey Porcelain and Earthenware Company, was prominent in the Prime collection. Subsequently, Joseph Breck, the Museum's Curator of Decorative Arts in the early decades of this century, added major pieces to the American ceramics holdings, including some remarkable porcelains by the artist-potter Adelaide Alsop Robineau. A great boost in building the collections in this area came in 1970 with the landmark exhibition *19th-Century America*, which helped both to celebrate the Metropolitan's centennial and, under the leadership of the late Berry B. Tracy, to focus attention on American decorative art, including porcelain. Building on these foundations, the Department of American Decorative Arts in the last decade made numerous acquisitions of fine examples of American porcelain, some through gifts, others through purchases made possible by funds generously given by the Friends of The American Wing.

I would like to acknowledge with thanks Alice Cooney Frelinghuysen, Associate Curator, who conceived the exhibition, selected its contents, and wrote the catalogue. Thanks also to Mary-Alice Rogers, Editor, Bryant Fellow Publications, who edited the book; Frances Bretter, Research Consultant, who ably assisted Mrs. Frelinghuysen; David Harvey, of the Design Department, who is responsible for the exhibition installation; and John K. Howat, the Lawrence A. Fleischman Chairman of the Departments of American Art, and Lewis I. Sharp, Curator and Administrator of The American Wing, who gave the project their full support.

To both the public and private lenders of the porcelains displayed, we extend our warmest thanks; without their cooperation the exhibition could not have been mounted. We are greatly indebted to the William Cullen Bryant Fellows for their substantial sponsorship of this publication, as well as to the Clara Lloyd-Smith Weber Fund and the American Ceramic Circle for underwriting the scholarly symposium held jointly with the exhibition.

Our deepest appreciation and thanks go to Lenox China and its officers and staff for embracing the concept of the exhibition and for providing the major funding that made it come to fruition.

Philippe de Montebello
Director

Introduction

The exhibition and catalogue here devoted to the handsome display and careful study of American porcelain are the product of the philosophy that guides the activities of the Departments of American Art. The Department of American Decorative Arts, which is the parent of this current project, and the Department of American Paintings and Sculpture, working together within The American Wing, share a primary goal of mounting exhibitions and preparing publications that present in an attractive and scholarly manner the finest, most beautiful, and most interesting of American historic art. We aim thereby to attract a broad public, many of whom have a new interest in American art, and to present that public with a rich menu of aesthetic pleasure and art-historical knowledge.

Integral constituents of our activities, which are increasingly of a specifically educational nature, are the Erving and Joyce Wolf Galleries, where most of our special exhibitions, such as this one, are presented, and The Henry R. Luce Center for the Study of American Art, where the reserve collections of the Wing are permanently on view. Through special exhibitions we are able to show works of high quality in thematic and evocative ways that demonstrate the history and development of this country's various forms of artistic achievement.

This beautiful catalogue, offering a new and comprehensive examination of American porcelain in especially distinguished examples, belongs to a sizable and growing series of publications on all aspects of American art underwritten in substantial part by the William Cullen Bryant Fellows. Our hope is that the readers of the book will be inspired by it not only to explore the field of American porcelain but to go further into the other realms of American art.

John K. Howat
The Lawrence A. Fleischman Chairman
of the Departments of American Art

Acknowledgments

The idea for this exhibition and catalogue grew out of the installation in 1981 of the permanent collection of American ceramics on the balcony of the Charles Engelhard Court in the new American Wing. During the course of the preparation, a surprising paucity in scholarly writings on the medium became apparent, as did the need for building up certain areas of the Museum's collection. One result of the reevaluation of our American porcelain holdings was the concept for the exhibition, which was approved by Philippe de Montebello, Director of The Metropolitan Museum of Art, and the in-house exhibition committee in January 1983. *American Porcelain: 1770–1920* was mounted for the purpose of bringing together representative examples and presenting a complete accounting of the history of the medium during the period under review.

John K. Howat, the Lawrence A. Fleischman Chairman of the Departments of American Art, gave me the opportunity to organize the exhibition and to write its catalogue. Without his encouragement and advice, the project would never have been realized. Lewis I. Sharp, Curator and Administrator of The American Wing, saw me over many a hurdle along the way. I am grateful to the Museum for awarding me a professional travel grant in 1985, which enabled me to visit several important collections of American porcelain throughout the United States. I deeply appreciate the generosity of Lenox China, whose support in its centennial year made possible the exhibition that this catalogue accompanies. In particular, I would like to thank Lenox President Safford P. Sweatt; Peter R. Cheney, Vice President of Advertising and Marketing Communications; Marjorie Exton, Special Events Coordinator; and Alice J. Kolator, Director of Public Relations. I am also indebted to Thérèse Caruso, in charge of the Lenox account at Edelman Public Relations, for her help. I express my particular gratitude to Robert J. Sullivan, Consultant for Lenox China and formerly Vice President, Advertising and Promotion, for his tireless enthusiasm for the project from the earliest discussions of it five years ago. The scholarly symposium, held in conjunction with the exhibition in May 1989, was made possible through the generosity of the Clara Lloyd-Smith Weber Fund, with additional funding provided by the American Ceramic Circle.

We are fortunate in having secured important loans from more than forty public and private collections throughout the United States. The Museum thanks the lenders for their willingness to part with their treasures for an extended period of time, never an easy thing to do.

The exhibition and the catalogue could not have been completed without the support, advice, and encouragement of many individuals. I express my utmost gratitude to the many scholars who selflessly gave me their help, suggestions, and counsel: John C. Austin, Curator of Ceramics and Glass and Senior Curator, The Colonial Williamsburg Foundation; Regina L. Blaszczyk, Museum Specialist, Division of Ceramics and Glass, National Museum of American History, Smithsonian Institution; Michael K. Brown, Curator, Bayou Bend Collection, The Museum of Fine Arts, Houston; Jean Burks, formerly Assistant Curator, Department of American Art, Philadelphia Museum of Art; Joan B. Connelly, Assistant Professor of Fine Arts, New York University; Suzanne Corlette Crilley, Curator, Cultural History, New Jersey State Museum; Antoine d'Albis, Manufacture National de

Céramique at Sèvres; Laurens d'Albis; Bert Denker, Decorative Arts Photographic Collection, The Henry Francis du Pont Winterthur Museum; Ulysses G. Dietz, Curator of Decorative Arts, The Newark Museum; Martin Eidelberg; Paul Evans; Beatrice B. Garvan, Curator of American Art, Philadelphia Museum of Art; William C. Gates, Jr., Curator of History, Ohio Historical Society, formerly Curator, Museum of Ceramics at East Liverpool; William H. Gerdts, Professor of Art History, The Graduate School and University Center of The City University of New York; Robert L. Giannini III, Associate Curator, Independence National Historic Park; George Gurney, Associate Curator of Sculpture and Painting, National Museum of American Art, Smithsonian Institution; Eugene R. Kosche, Curator of History, The Bennington Museum; Sandra MacKenzie Lloyd; John A. Mahé II, Curator, Historic New Orleans Collection; David Revere McFadden, Curator of Decorative Arts, Cooper-Hewitt Museum, Smithsonian Institution; Ellen G. Miles, Curator of Paintings and Sculpture, National Portrait Gallery, Smithsonian Institution; Susan H. Myers, Curator, Division of Ceramics and Glass, National Museum of American History, Smithsonian Institution; Christina Nelson, Curator of Decorative Arts, The Saint Louis Art Museum; Kirk Nelson, formerly Curator of Decorative Arts, The Bennington Museum; Barbara Perry, Curator of Ceramics, Everson Museum of Art; Alan Salz; Marvin D. Schwartz; Kevin L. Stayton, Curator of American Decorative Arts, The Brooklyn Museum; Kenneth R. Trapp, Curator, The Oakland Museum; Robert Tuggle, Director of Archives, Metropolitan Opera Association; and Susan R. Williams, formerly Curator of Household Accessories and Tablewares, The Strong Museum. I am particularly indebted to Ellen Paul Denker, Arlene Palmer Schwind, and Diana and J. Garrison Stradling, who gave freely of their knowledge, perspective, and intelligence. Their expertise has added much to present scholarship, and their knowledge, combined with their enthusiasm in giving advice and answering questions, have helped me immeasurably.

In addition, a number of institutions and their staffs have been of great assistance to me in providing access to their collections, answering numerous inquiries, and facilitating the requests for the loans and photographs of their objects. For their help I thank in particular Linda Ballard, Reference Librarian, University City Public Library; Alberta M. Brandt, Photographic Services Supervisor, The Henry Francis du Pont Winterthur Museum; Marigene H. Butler, Chairman, Wyck Association; Susan Finkel, Assistant Curator, and Maxine Friedman, formerly Registrar, Department of Cultural History, New Jersey State Museum; Robert Fryman, Curator, Museum of Ceramics at East Liverpool; Kathleen Eagan Johnson, Registrar, Historic Hudson Valley; Phillip M. Johnston, Director, The Carnegie Museum of Art; Melodie Kosmacki, Collections Manager, 1876 Exhibition, Smithsonian Institution; Jack L. Lindsey, Assistant Curator of American Art, Philadelphia Museum of Art; Laura C. Luckey, Director, The Bennington Museum; Kristan H. MacKinsey, Curatorial Assistant, Decorative Arts, The Saint Louis Art Museum; Randy Niederer, The Riverview and Harbourton Cemeteries, Trenton, New Jersey; Donald Peirce, Curator of Decorative Arts, High Museum of Art; Allen Rosenbaum, Director, and Betsy Rosasco, Associate Curator, The Art Museum, Princeton University; Helen Stenger, Riverview Cemetery Association, East Liverpool, Ohio; and Deborah Dependahl Waters, Curator of Decorative Arts, Museum of the City of New York.

The study of actual porcelain objects has no substitute. A number of private collectors and dealers have graciously allowed me to examine, photograph, and borrow their works of art and research materials and have benefited me greatly with their knowledge: Norlyne K. Atwood; Bryce Bannatyne, Jr.;

Florence I. Balasny-Barnes; Deborah P. Blumenthal; Margaret Caldwell; Arthur V. Colletti; Debe Cuevas, of Sotheby's; Bob Ellison; Jack Feingold and Bruce Aldini, of Gem Antiques; Mr. and Mrs. Stuart P. Feld; Thomas C. Folk; David and Barbara Goldberg; Robert A. and Betty Hut; Francis E. and Henrietta Judson; George M. and Linda Kaufman; Jay and Emma Lewis; Richard Margrave; Nancy McClelland, of Christie's; Letitia Roberts, of Sotheby's; Marco Polo Stufano; and J. William Widing III. John H. Nally, to whom I will always be indebted for his generosity, knowledge, help, and infectious enthusiasm, died while the exhibition and catalogue were in preparation. I am unutterably saddened by his loss and bitterly regret that he did not live to see the realization of an undertaking to which he contributed so much.

I owe much gratitude to the descendants of the potters and decorators who acquainted me with and allowed me to borrow some of their ancestors' creations, at the same time providing me with much valuable historical and familial information: on James Carr, Helen Carr Drennen and Cyd Marie Law; on Charles Cartlidge, Anne M. Ewing, Mary M. Rowan, and William Cartlidge Vestal, Jr.; on William H. Morley, Mrs. Kenneth C. Heath; on Elijah Tatler, Mrs. William D. Tatler; and on the Willets Manufacturing Company, Ann Willets Lapham Frazer.

The only porcelain company still in operation from the period of the exhibition is Lenox China (formerly Lenox, Incorporated), which opened its archives, original catalogues, design drawings, and porcelain collection to me. For their aid in facilitating my use of these materials, I particularly thank Ellen Paul Denker, Consulting Curator, and Eliza McCoy Yermack, formerly Senior Staff Attorney.

Throughout the project, I have been fortunate in being able to call on the staffs in various departments of the Metropolitan Museum for assistance, information, and administrative counsel. Their specialized knowledge and unfailing willingness to consider my questions have been of the greatest value: in the Director's office, Mahrukh Tarapor, Assistant Director; in the Development Office, Emily Kernan Rafferty, Vice President, Nina McNeely Diefenbach, Associate Manager, and Richard Maxwell, formerly Associate Manager; in Archives, Jeanie M. James, Archivist; in Objects Conservation, John Canonico, Associate Conservator, Shinichi Doi, Assistant Conservator, and Yale Kneeland, Assistant Conservator; in Public Information, John Ross, Manager, and Matthew Austin, Assistant Public Information Officer; in the Registrar's office, John Buchanan, Chief Registrar, Herbert M. Moskowitz, Registrar, and Nina S. Maruca, Associate Registrar; in the Thomas J. Watson Library, William B. Walker, Arthur K. Watson Chief Librarian, Doralynn Pines, Associate Museum Librarian; Katria Czerwoniak, Library Associate, and Patrick F. Coman, Supervising Departmental Technician; in the Primitive Art Department, Julie Jones, Curator; and in the Design Department, David Harvey, who has designed a thoughtful and beautiful installation. In its final form, this catalogue represents the work of many people whose thoroughness and skill are deeply appreciated. John P. O'Neill, Editor in Chief, gave invaluable advice and lent his keen eye to aesthetic decisions, and members of his staff also contributed to the successful completion of the book: Teresa Egan, Managing Editor; Helga Lose, Production Associate; Kendra K. Ho, proofreader; and Susan Bradford, indexer. The majority of the superb photographs were the masterly work of Schecter Lee, with the assistance of Rodrigo Shopis. Bruce Campbell was responsible for the book's elegant design.

I am most grateful to my colleagues in The American Wing for their unstinting contributions of much appreciated help. A number of interns and volunteers performed many necessary tasks, from Xeroxing to reading microfilms of nineteenth-century newspapers and city directories. For their assistance, I thank them all: Heather Fabricand; Kay Freeman; Bess Frelinghuysen; Arlene Nichols; Rebecca Reynolds; and Louise Robbins. Special thanks go to Ellen Lynch and Linda Shulsky. For their cheerful handling of numerous administrative tasks, I acknowledge Ellin Rosenzweig, Administrative Assistant; Seraphine Wu, Administrative Assistant; and Barbara A. Whalen, former Administrative Assistant. Departmental technicians George Asimakis, Gary Burnett, Don E. Templeton, and Jason J. Weller, provided dependable handling of the delicate objects, not only for the installation but also for the photography many months before. I greatly appreciate the insights and suggestions of Doreen Bolger, Curator; Donna Hassler, Research Associate; Kathleen Luhrs, Editor; Oswaldo Rodriguez Roque, Associate Curator; and Catherine Hoover Voorsanger, Research Associate. Jordana Pomeroy, Research Assistant, conscientiously checked hundreds of footnote references as well as performed many other tasks.

Particular thanks go to Frances Bretter, Research Consultant, who handled a myriad of organizational details with great devotion and precision and, perhaps more important, contributed an unfailingly objective perspective.

I cannot adequately express my gratitude to Mary-Alice Rogers, Editor of the William Cullen Bryant Fellows Publications, whose skill, insight, and dedication benefited the book to an incalculable degree.

I express my most affectionate thanks to my family for their thoughtfulness, encouragement, and forbearance throughout the project.

Alice Cooney Frelinghuysen
New York, 1989

Notes to the Reader

The marks and inscriptions cited at the catalogue entry headings have been confirmed where possible. The dimensions are given to the greatest degree and to the nearest sixteenth of an inch. The credit lines have been checked with the lenders and appear according to the wishes of the individual institutions and private collectors. Full details of the publications referred to in the notes by an author's surname and a date will be found in the Bibliography, which begins on p. 303. All available dates indicating the span of a person's life or the duration of a manufactory are listed at the appropriate entry in the Index, which begins on p. 310.

American Porcelain
1770–1920

Figure 1. Pickle dish, 1770–72. American China Manufactory (Bonnin and Morris), Philadelphia. W. 4½ in. (11.4 cm.). Philadelphia Museum of Art, Gift of Mrs. Benjamin Rush (50-32-1)

In the realm of ceramics, porcelain occupies the place of honor. Its manufacture, traceable for well over thirteen centuries in China and cultivated in the Orient, in Europe, and in England, has been the focus of scholarly and public attention for many generations. In America, however, the delicate medium has been overshadowed in importance by the stoneware and red earthenware made in rural potteries throughout the nineteenth century and, more recently, by the individuality of the objects produced as part of the Arts and Crafts movement. The exhibition devoted to American porcelain that this catalogue accompanies brings together a selection of treasures that spans a century and a half of native achievement and reflects the influence of concomitant historical, stylistic, and technological developments. Though the wares made at the major potting centers (the cities of New York, Trenton, Philadelphia, and East Liverpool) are the primary theme, objects from other regions today virtually unknown are also presented. In this book, information on largely unrecognized loci of porcelain production will be discussed for the first time in the hope that it will provide impetus for further study.

Porcelain is a wondrous, miraculous, and sometimes mysterious material having the singular properties of pure white color, extreme hardness and smoothness even before being glazed, translucence when seen through transmitted light, and resonance when struck. The two principal ingredients of oriental porcelain—the root from which many branches emerge—are a white china clay called kaolin, which constitutes its body, and petuntse (a china, or feldspathic, stone), which furnishes it with its translucence.

Because raw materials for making true oriental porcelain were not available in eighteenth-century England, factories there used local ingredients to make what has been called soft-paste porcelain. In the new century, with advances in technology and with innovations in the formulas for pastes and glazes, numerous hybrids evolved. Except for parian and Belleek, they do not fit into neat subcategories, yet because they adhere to the properties peculiar to porcelain, they will be so designated for the purposes of this study. Not under consideration, however, are such period terms as whiteware, cream-colored graniteware, stone china, opaque porcelain, or semivitreous ware.

Porcelain can be formed on a potter's wheel, cast in a plaster mold, or hand-molded in a variety of shapes limited only by the potter's imagination, but it must be fired in a kiln at an extraordinarily high temperature—between twelve and fifteen hundred degrees Celsius (2,192–2,732 degrees Fahrenheit). Its uses are as diverse as the techniques of its fabrication and ornamentation. For effect, many of the potters represented in this book relied on the purity and whiteness that radiated from the undecorated form. Others used the smooth surface as a vehicle for under- or overglaze embellishment that encompassed the variety of techniques utilized in American porcelain throughout its history: designs achieved with transfer-printed patterns, colored enamels, gilding, or colored glazes, all of which attained a luminosity and brilliance not possible on coarser ceramic mediums. As the nineteenth century turned into the twentieth, yet another decorative technique came to the fore: the art of carving, a strikingly impressive means of creating dramatic shadows in the porcelain's chaste surface. In that era, there were practitioners so skilled that they could pare an object down to a fragile, translucent shell.

First made in China as early as the Tang dynasty (A.D. 618–907), porcelain became known in the West through early explorers such as Marco Polo, who in the late thirteenth century wrote of a material he described as resembling *porcellana* (a cowrie seashell), perhaps giving porcelain its name. In Europe, after a protracted search for the secret of its manufacture, the formula was discovered in Meissen in the early years of the eighteenth century by Johann Friedrich Böttger, a chemist at the court of Augustus the Strong, Elector of Saxony, now part of Germany. In 1708, Böttger developed a clay that produced a white, translucent body when fired; in the following year, his patron founded the Royal Saxon Porcelain Manufactory. From Saxony, the formula passed to the Austro-Hungarian Empire and thence to France. The middle of the eighteenth century saw porcelain manufactories springing up throughout Europe and spreading to England.

In America, still closely allied with the mother country, experiments with the medium had begun by 1738. Tentative efforts from the period clearly illustrate the reigning English style. The few extant porcelains from the short-lived factory of Gousse Bonnin and George Anthony Morris in Philadelphia virtually duplicate English shapes; their decoration of underglaze blue-and-white painted or transfer-printed designs is in the prevailing rococo and chinoiserie modes (Fig. 1).

By the early 1800s, allegiance had shifted to the French Empire style. The simplicity of those neoclassical shapes made them ideal for showing off the gilded ornament then in vogue as well as the naturalistic landscape, portrait, and overglaze floral compositions in polychrome enamels also characteristic of the period. In some of the masterly versions produced in Philadelphia at the factory established by William Ellis Tucker, American subject matter found its way onto domestic porcelains for the first time.

In the mid-1800s, native manufacturers catered to the preference for foreign imports that had plagued them from colonial days by employing immigrant craftsmen who were beginning to bring to America the expertise and artistic direction of their cultural heritage. Though Continental porcelains continued to exert considerable influence, particularly those from the Limoges region of France, the parian porcelain that had been developed in England in the 1840s was taken up by American factories employing English-trained workmen in greater numbers. Predominant at the time was the Rococo-revival style, though now lacking the grace of its eighteenth-century origins. The new manufacturing techniques that had developed with increasing mechanization produced porcelain forms often clumsy in shape and overloaded with relief ornament. While overall concepts were borrowed from England, American motifs were sometimes introduced into the designs. Industrialization, in combination with the new transportation routes opening up the country, lowered the cost of porcelain production and provided access to larger and wider markets. Factories, increased substantially in size and number, now extended as far north as Bennington, Vermont, and as far west as East Liverpool, Ohio.

In 1876, the Centennial Exposition in Philadelphia was the watershed in the development of American porcelain. Potteries such as the Union Porcelain Works in Greenpoint (Brooklyn), New York, and the firm of Ott and Brewer in Trenton, New Jersey, hired experienced sculptors and artists to design works for display at the national celebration. What they turned out was flamboyant, even gaudy. Though the objects adhered loosely to classical prototypes, they were altered and overlaid with explicit patriotic themes. The ceramics gathered from all over the world and shown in one place were a source of fresh inspiration for American artists and craftsmen, and there emerged from the country's birthday party an unmistakable American style.

The Centennial and subsequent international exhibitions brought the ceramic achievements of the world into the national consciousness. As a new breed of collectors acquired porcelains from older, foreign cultures and brought them back to this country, the influence of the Near and Far East reverberated throughout the land for the first time. New hordes of British and European artists and artisans left their homelands and crossed the Atlantic to seek more favorable working conditions and higher wages. The wares that were produced and decorated in those post-Centennial decades were remarkably similar to foreign counterparts. In the early 1880s, Ott and Brewer's was the first American manufactory to develop a porcelain that copied

Figure 2. Adelaide Alsop Robineau. Covered vase, 1914. H. 6⅝ in. (16.8 cm.). Everson Museum of Art, Gift of Dr. Ethel T. Eltinge (82.33.2)

the eggshell medium created at Belleek, Ireland. Potteries in Trenton, which remained the center for production of artistic and commercial porcelain, pioneered in the manufacture of highly decorated objects modeled after those made in England at Worcester, Derby, and Minton. The preference of the time for painted decoration executed by highly skilled craftsmen who had learned their profession on the other side of the Atlantic was a legacy not just from England but from Germany and Austria as well.

In the late nineteenth century, the artist-potter emerged as an artistic entity. An intrepid few, mainly women, took up the challenge of creating their own forms from porcelain of their own making. For decoration, they abandoned painting in favor of carving and enlivened their surfaces with new types of glazes they had discovered (Fig. 2). Those ambitious and highly informed artists continued to find inspiration in oriental porcelain, but they also took heed of new trends in contemporary European design, especially in Danish, French, and German interpretations.

From the first courageous experiments in the 1770s to the artistic objects individually worked by hand in the 1920s, these porcelains represent many invisible and now almost forgotten difficulties, setbacks, financial reverses, and personal heartbreaks. The beautiful, creative, and extraordinary objects celebrated in this exhibition and catalogue survive as expressions only of triumph.

The Eighteenth Century (cat. nos. 1–3)

In light of the difficulties encountered by those who attempted it, the manufacture of porcelain in colonial America can be characterized as a highly ambitious pursuit. Although the necessary raw materials were available in several colonies, including Georgia, South Carolina, and Delaware, processing them was beyond the colonists' means. Expertise and workmen were hard to come by; firing the forms, especially under such rudimentary conditions, was hazardous; and the few who succeeded in mastering the process found their prices undercut by the considerably lower cost of imported wares.

The first documented porcelain of American origin was a kilnful, drawn in Savannah, Georgia, about 1738, by one Andrew Duché, which contained the first recorded piece. It was described in a report made that year by William Stephens, American Secretary to the London-based Trustees of Savannah, as "a small Teacup . . . [which] when held against the Light, was very near transparent."[1] Duché, who began his ceramics career in Philadelphia working as a stoneware potter with his two brothers and his father, Anthony, was living in South Carolina by 1735. The following year, he moved to Savannah, and shortly afterward began to experiment with the making of porcelain.[2]

In 1739, encouraged by his initial success, Duché petitioned the Trustees in London for additional money and supplies, claiming that he had "found out the true manner of making porcelain or China Ware."[3] Stephens, already offended by Duché's subversive activities and uncooperative manner, was further annoyed by the potter's failure to comply with the request that he send sample porcelains to England for the Trustees' inspection. Despite their differences, Stephens scrupulously recorded in his journal in May 1741 that reports about town credited Duché with having "accomplished his Intention of making China Ware; that he had baked several Cups and Basins, which were transparent . . . but [the process] was still such a secret that he did not allow any to see it."[4] The following month, Stephens noted: "I took Occasion to call upon Mr. Duchee, to see some of his Rarities . . . but it happened not to be at a right Season . . . I understood all his fine Ware was baking a second time, as it ought to be, with proper Glazing; But he shewed me a little Piece, in Form of a Tea-Cup . . . which he said had passed through one Baking, and was yet rough; but upon holding it to the Light, as it was, without any Coloring on it, I thought it as transparent as our ordinary strong China Cups commonly are."[5] Though neither the teacup nor

Figure 3. Sauceboat, 1770–72. American China Manufactory (Bonnin and Morris), Philadelphia. H. 4 in. (10.2 cm.). The Brooklyn Museum, Dick S. Ramsay Fund (42.412)

any other Duché piece has survived and there is no evidence that he continued in his manufacturing venture,[6] his initial kilnful can be dated to 1738, at least six years before the first porcelain of English manufacture was registered.[7]

The chronology of Duché's career has led to speculation that he was responsible for having specimens of American clays sent to England and that those materials went into the first porcelain manufactured at the Bow factory. That claim has since been disproved.[8] Nevertheless, necessary materials *were* being sought in the southern colonies by the mother country. In 1744, the first Patent for English porcelain stated that "a new method of Manufacturing a certain material whereby a ware might be made of the same nature or kind, and equal to, if not exceeding in goodness and beauty, China or Porcelain ware imported from abroad" had been invented. One of its principal ingredients was "an earth, the produce of the Chirokee nation in America, called by the natives unaker [a reference to the nearby Unicoi mountains]."[9]

The next May, William Cookworthy, a chemist in Plymouth, England, recorded the discovery of "CHINA EARTH. . . . It was found on the back of VIRGINIA, where [an unnamed man] . . . discovered both the *Petunze* and *Kaolin*," the main ingredients of porcelain.[10] In 1749, an American named John Campbell reported finding in Edgecombe County, North Carolina, "clay [that] resembles what I saw at Bow for their china ware."[11] Apparently, large quantities of china clay were present in the hills of America, but there is no proof that it was exported to England in any quantity.[12]

The mid-1760s saw further unsubstantiated references to American-made porcelain. In England, the *Bristol Journal* of 24 November 1764 reported: "This week, some pieces of porcelain manufactured in Georgia was imported; the materials appear to be good, but the workmanship is far from being admired."[13] The notice may have been referring to the pursuits of Samuel Bowen, who in 1766 had received a gold medal from the English Society for the Encouragement of Arts, Manufactures, and Commerce "for his useful observations in china and industrious application of them in Georgia."[14]

For their tableware, eighteenth-century Americans relied almost exclusively on pottery imported from England: inexpensive delftwares, the newly developed salt-glazed stonewares, and, beginning in the 1760s, a cream-colored earthenware called Queen's ware, made at the factory of Josiah Wedgwood. Porcelain specified as Bow China is known to have been imported as early as 1754.[15] In addition, the colonists were being offered such luxury items as "curious fine China in Statuary [figural works]" and "Ornamental China for chimney pieces."[16]

By the late 1760s, two of this country's most vocal patriots—the noted physician Benjamin Rush and the statesman and inventor Benjamin Franklin—were examining the possibility of establishing native factories to produce porcelain made of domestic clays. Franklin, known for his encouragement of American industry, appears to have been fascinated by the medium. On his travels in England and France, he visited several factories. Writing to his wife from London, he told her that he was sending her a large case, in which was a small box containing "English China; viz. Melons and Leaves for a Desert of Fruit and Cream, or the like; a Bowl remarkable for the Neatness of the Figures, made at Bow, near this City; some Coffee Cups of the same; a Worcester Bowl, ordinary."[17] Letters he wrote sometime later show that the project was still close to his heart: in one, he acknowledged receipt of "Colours suitable for Painting which you have found in different Parts of our Country."[18] In another, he said: "I show'd the Specimens you sent me to an ingenious skilful French Chemist, who has the Direction of the Royal Porcellane Manufacture at Seve near Paris, and he assured me that one of those white Earths would make a good Ingredient in that kind of Ware." He added, "If we encourage necessary Manufactures among ourselves, and refrain buying the Superfluities of other Countries, a few Years will make a surprizing Change in our favour."[19]

Around that same time, Rush was in Edinburgh completing his medical training. Passionately interested in the destiny of his country, he realized that the colonists would have to create their own industries if they were ever to overcome their dependence on England. Writing to Thomas Bradford, a patriot printer, in April 1768, he adjured him: "Go on in encouraging American manufactures. . . . I have made those mechanical arts which are connected with chemistry the particular objects of my study, and not without hopes of seeing a china manufactory established in Philadelphia in the course of a few years."[20] Two months later, he told Bradford of his renewed optimism in the prospect: "From late intelligence I have had from America, I am now fully convinced of the possibility of setting up a china manufactory in Philadelphia."[21]

Franklin and Rush soon saw their hopes realized. The partnership of Gousse Bonnin, who had come to Philadelphia from England, and George Anthony Morris, a native Philadelphian who probably supplied initial funds, continued the experiments with American clays that Duché had begun three decades earlier. In January 1770, undaunted by their lack of experience, they issued a bold announcement in a local newspaper: "New China Ware. Notwithstanding the various difficulties and disadvantages, which usually attend the introduction of any important manufacture into a new country, the proprietors of the China Works, now erecting in Southwark [Philadelphia], have the pleasure to acquaint the public, they have proved to a certainty, that the clays of America are productive of as good Porcelain as any heretofore manufactured at the famous factory in Bow, near London."[22] To find workers for their firm, which they named the American China Manufactory, they published advertisements in which they stressed that only the most expert workmen need apply: "None will be employed who have not served their apprenticeship in England, France, or Germany."[23] Skilled domestic talent was probably not forthcoming. Bonnin, traveling to England to seek capital in February 1770, shortly after the partnership had been formed, may also have seized the opportunity to lure English workmen to Philadelphia: that October, a Pennsylvania newspaper printed that "nine master workers have arrived here for the porcelain manufactory of this city."[24] The partners also published their need for raw materials. They sought animal bones, which, presumably, would be reduced to bone ash to add to the clay, pearl ashes (refined potash), as well as zaffer, which provided the underglaze blue color. They used clay obtained from the banks of the Delaware River "between Newcastle and Wilmington and it was mixed with calcined bones."[25]

The American China Manufactory, which was the only successful producer of porcelain in colonial times, drew its first kiln of wares in late 1770; notice of its "first Emission of Porcelain" appeared in a newspaper dated 10 January 1771.[26] From the very beginning, the manufactory was patronized by the city's elite. A description of the factory written sometime later concluded: "A number of beautiful articles particularly of tea ware well shaped and painted were in use among the best families in America."[27] Patrons included John Cadwalader and Thomas Wharton.[28] Deborah Franklin, Benjamin's wife, sent Bonnin and Morris porcelains to her husband in England. In acknowledging them, he wrote, "I thank you for the Sauceboats, and am pleased to find so good a Progress made in the China Manufactury. I wish it Success most heartily."[29]

Based on surviving examples, shards found at the factory site, and other documentary evidence, the Bonnin and Morris wares were surprisingly ambitious in concept and sophisticated in technique. Extant objects closely resemble the popular English blue-and-white porcelains imported in the colonial era from factories at Bow, Liverpool, Lowestoft, and Worcester, though their quality is generally inferior: the paste is porridgelike in texture and the glaze is often unevenly applied and not entirely free of impurities. The factory offered everything from basins, bowls, and plates in assorted sizes, to more elaborate pieces such as sauceboats (Fig. 3), fruit baskets, and pickle stands (cat. nos. 1, 3), to multiple forms such as breakfast sets, "compleat sets for the dining and tea table together," and, for the ladies, "complete sets of Dressing Boxes."[30] The decoration—primarily underglaze designs painted in blue—also followed the English fashion: borders featuring either rococo-style floral and scroll ornament or oriental diapering, the larger areas painted with bouquets and butterflies or with simple chinoiserie landscape scenes. Marks that appear on some of the objects—the initial *P*, for Philadelphia, or the initial *S*, for the Southwark section of Philadelphia—are painted in underglaze blue (Fig. 4).

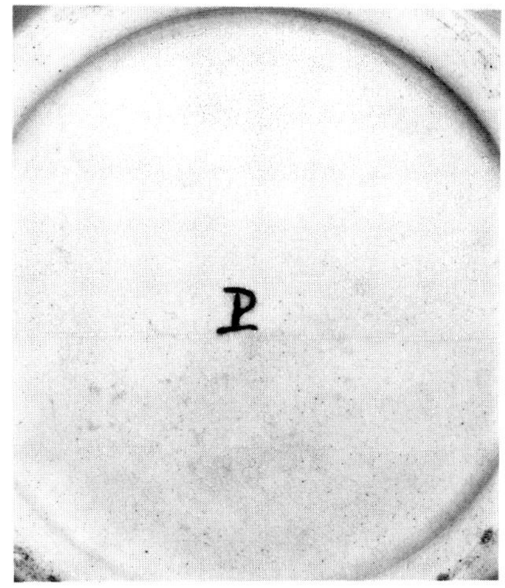

Figure 4. Detail (mark), fruit basket, 1770–72. American China Manufactory (Bonnin and Morris), Philadelphia. Collection of Mr. and Mrs. George M. Kaufman (see cat. no. 1)

The proprietors, in producing enamel-painted wares, may well have intended to copy the overglaze polychrome enameling so fashionable in England. Advertising in January 1772, probably for decorators, the firm assured any applicant: "The greatest Encouragement will be given to all Painters, either in blue or enamel."[31] Several of the discovered shards reveal designs painted in iron red under the glaze, perhaps documenting that the advertisement was answered.[32] The factory also used

Figure 5. Fruit basket, 1770–72. American China Manufactory (Bonnin and Morris), Philadelphia. H. 2¾ in. (7 cm.). The Henry Francis du Pont Winterthur Museum (59.57)

transfer-printed decoration, as demonstrated by one reticulated basket (Fig. 5) descended directly from Morris's uncle John Morris. Notable among the molded forms produced by Bonnin and Morris were shell dishes, English-type floral rosettes used to adorn the firm's fruit baskets, and the "Quitted [Quilted] Cups" known today only through fragments and historical references.[33]

The aspiring young partnership lasted just under two years. Its end was announced on 14 November 1772 in a local newspaper: "Public Notice is hereby given, that the China Manufactory with all the buildings, kilns, mills and other implements, will be peremptorily sold, by Public Auction, to the highest bidder, on Monday the 21st day of December next."[34] The premises had not been sold by May of the following year, as the partners revealed in an advertisement: "Any Gentleman inclining to engage in the China Business, may now enter on very advantageous terms, as these works are completely fitted, and a young man of sobriety and integrity in town, from Germany, who is completely skilled in the whole process of compounding the materials, upon a plan fully equal to the best in England, and who would readily undertake the management, upon reasonable terms, either in partnership or otherwise. . . . The purchaser may enter into possession within three days after sale."[35] Morris died suddenly in October 1773 and the sheriff seized the property from Bonnin, now almost bankrupt. It was purchased, probably as a real-estate investment, by two local promoters who within the year were offering it as suitable for the establishment of almost any manufactory or even for conversion to tenements and a livery stable.[36] The building eventually turned into "a sailor's brothel and riot house on a large scale."[37]

Because of the outbreak of the revolutionary war and perhaps because the demise of the Bonnin and Morris firm was widely publicized, there were few attempts to manufacture American porcelain in the latter part of the century, and nothing has been documented to any one venture. Nevertheless, isolated references concerning efforts in the medium continued to appear in the 1780s and 1790s. Reportedly, in August 1783, "A porcelain fabrick was about to be established at Philadelphia by a French regimental surgeon. The clay brought from Maryland for the purpose is fine and smooth, and some small specimens of porcelain had been fused out very successfully. However, many difficulties are yet to be overcome and the price of the finished porcelain must be greatly more than for European ware."[38] The surgeon's identity has never been established, probably an indication that he had failed to overcome those many difficulties. Two years later, Peter Lacour, a "French gentleman, now at New-York," advertised that he was "desirous of being employed in raising and conducting a China and Earthen Ware manufactory."[39] His impressive qualifications included his having been educated at the Academy of Sciences in Paris and his being "well skilled in making China and the best Earthen Wares," having had "the direction of a principal manufactory of those articles in France."[40] He then vanishes from contemporary accounts without a trace. Equally ephemeral is the Samuel Faulkner listed in the Philadelphia city directories in 1795 and 1796 as a "china manufacturer," at 91 North 6th Street.[41] Those references notwithstanding, the porcelain industry in America apparently remained dormant until the second decade of the nineteenth century.

The Early Nineteenth Century (cat. nos. 4–19)

In 1810, after a hiatus of almost forty years, attempts to establish an industry began again when kaolin was discovered at Monkton, Vermont, and a company was "chartered for the manufacture of fine porcelain for it."[1] In January 1812, John Murray, a founder of the newly incorporated Monkton Argil Company, wrote an urgent letter to Congressman Abijah Bigelow, of Vermont, asking him to use his influence to obtain financial backing for the company, either from public funds or from private sources, so that plans "to manufacture ware from the Porcelain earth found at Monkton" could proceed.[2] Although Murray's letter said that buildings had been erected and preparations were under way to begin operations that spring, no evidence supports his story.[3] (Years later, references to the "porcelain earth" of Monkton reappear: in 1839, it was described as "very pure and it is said that it will make the very best of china ware. The bed is inexhaustible.")[4] In 1815 and 1816, the *Niles Weekly Register*, a Baltimore newspaper of wide circulation, reported the establishment in Maine of "a manufactory of fine porcelain, which turns out large quantities of ware." The clause that follows: "which good judges are not able to distinguish from the best *Liverpool Ware*," suggests that the medium was not porcelain but a refined white earthenware.[5]

The earliest porcelain actually produced in nineteenth-century America was that being made from possibly about 1813 through 1824 at the New York City factory of Dr. Henry Mead. The only surviving example of Mead attribution is a vase (see cat. no. 4) that once carried a paper label specifying its place of manufacture and its date: New York, 1816. Mead, who took his degree in scientific studies at Columbia College in 1794, practiced as a physician in New York, retaining his title of doctor long after he abandoned his medical career.[6] In 1813, he purchased property on Lewis Street between Delancey and Rivington streets and founded a short-lived copper manufactory. By 1816, probably to obtain capital for building a porcelain factory, he sold the land, though he continued to lease it, and, with New York City merchant Nicholas Matthieu Delonguemare, who had purchased a share in the fledgling enterprise, went into business.[7] While the Mead Vase is dated to 1816, the earliest documented reference to the doctor's porcelain production does not appear until three years later, when the *Niles Weekly Register* of 27 February 1819 announced: "The manufacture of China Ware, or porcelain, Equal in firmness to the French, has been commenced in New York."[8] Examples of the pottery's production, said to be made of "domestic materials," had been presented for inspection at the monthly meeting of The New-York Historical Society held a few days earlier and had been judged satisfactory in all respects.[9] The identity of the men who provided Mead with the required technical expertise is unknown, though an advertisement he published that October suggests their nationality: "A Manufactory has, on a small scale, been commenced, and some first rate workmen imported from France."[10] Despite his hopeful beginnings, Mead could not solve the problems imposed by his lack of capital and his inability to find suitable workers.[11] In December 1824, a New York newspaper reported the end of his brave porcelain endeavor.[12] (A listing dated 4 November 1825 in the account book of a New York brick seller, which reads, "Dokter Mead for the Chiney facktory 200 fire brick," implies that the works lasted well into the following year.)[13]

About 1825, probably around the time Mead vacated the property, two Frenchmen, Louis François Decasse and Nicolas Louis Edouard Chanou, formed a partnership and established a porcelain manufactory on the same site. Decasse, in 1819 or 1820 a partner of Delonguemare,[14] probably supplied the capital; Chanou, who arrived in America in 1822, having served a six-year apprenticeship at the Sèvres factory, was the technical expert. Detailed information on the Decasse and Chanou factory is as yet undiscovered, but the known objects of its production compare favorably in paste and quality with wares of French origin. A saucer (Fig. 6)

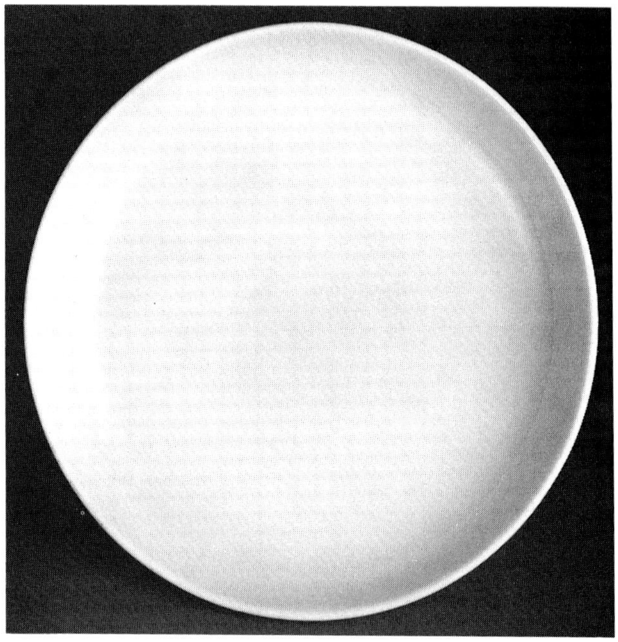

Figure 6. Saucer, ca. 1825. Decasse and Chanou, New York City. Diam. 5 in. (12.8 cm.). Musée National de Céramique, Sèvres, France (inv. no. MNC.911)

now at Sèvres, in the collections of the Musée National de Céramique, was presented by Chanou as a specimen of porcelain made of native materials in 1826 to Alexandre Brogniart, technical director at the Sèvres factory from 1800 to 1847.[15] Exceedingly white, translucent, and well formed, it is consistent in quality with the firm's other sole surviving examples, a tea set (see cat. no. 5) whose most ornate decoration—that of two plates, or stands (Fig. 7)—refers directly to the design vocabulary of the day. The firm's production ended on 27 July 1827, when the factory was leveled by a disastrous fire, a fate that haunted the porcelain industry.[16] Although Decasse continued to occupy the site, all operations were probably soon discontinued, and of Decasse and Chanou, little else is known. When the complex was rebuilt, it was as a firebrick manufactory, by 1830 renamed the Salamander Works, which added factory-molded yellow earthenwares to its products about 1836.[17]

On 10 December 1825, the Jersey Porcelain and Earthenware Company was founded in Jersey City, New Jersey, directly across the Hudson River from Manhattan.[18] According to a New York newspaper of August 1826: "About twenty artists, of

Figure 7. Two plates, or stands, from tea service, 1824–27. Decasse and Chanou, New York City. L. 7⅞ in. (20 cm.), W. 6¼ in. (15.9 cm.). Collection of Mr. and Mrs. George M. Kaufman

first rate skill and experience, were procured from England and France—principally the latter—who have now for several months been engaged, and have produced kilns of ware, equalling in all respects, the finest French China ware of the same description." The workmen had been brought to America by the Jersey City firm.[19]

That October, the wares the factory submitted to the annual exhibition of the Franklin Institute in Philadelphia (an establishment founded to promote products of American manufacture) were awarded a silver medal. A visitor to the manufactory recorded his findings: "The ware [made under the direction of William W. Shirley, a company founder trained in the potting business in England] is much superior to anything we had expected to find there. The principal articles which we saw, were either of white biscuit, or of white and gold in the French style. The texture, and the colour, are equal to that of the china imported from France; the surface clear and regular, and the gilding in general well done."[20] The sole example attributable to the firm (see cat. no. 6), though modest in scope, confirms that description. A contemporary account alludes to more ambitious forms: "The finished work . . . richly painted and gilded ware of many descriptions, including elegant chimney ornaments, was the best evidence that the artists, in each department, were perfect masters of their business."[21] Presumably because it could not compete with imported porcelains, the Jersey Porcelain and Earthenware Company sold its factory on 29 September 1828 to David Henderson, a manufacturer of white and yellow earthenwares and fine stonewares, who established the American Pottery Company on the site.

In Philadelphia, William Ellis Tucker came to porcelain manufacture through his familiarity with the importing side of the business. His father, Benjamin Tucker—a key figure in the development of the factory—owned and operated a china store in Philadelphia at 324 High Street from 1816 until 1823. During that time, William worked at the store and also decorated plain white imported ceramics, firing them in a small kiln built on the property. In 1826, he opened his own factory, leasing what had been the old city waterworks building. Initially, he was backed by Charles Bird, a local merchant who purchased a partnership for John Bird, his son. The earliest experiments made in the summer of that year yielded products of Queen's ware, now a generic term for fine white earthenware. In October, Tucker and Bird showed samples of their Queen's ware at the annual Franklin Institute exhibition, apparently not yet prepared to include examples of porcelain.[22] That same month, in a daybook he conscientiously maintained, Tucker recorded porcelain formulas for the first time.[23] He obtained his kaolin from the farm of Israel Hoopes in Chester County, Pennsylvania, reportedly the source for that used at the Jersey Porcelain and Earthenware Company.[24] Entries in the Tucker daybook show that he was procuring additional clay from other sources in Pennsylvania, as well as in Delaware, New Jersey, and New York.[25] Because sufficient quantities were not always available, he attempted in 1830 to buy up the Decasse and Chanou kaolin left at the New York site after the fire. His father, in a letter to Isaac T. Hooper, addressed as "Dear Friend," solicited Hooper's aid: "From the saturated state of the ground in consequence of heavy rains in the [Pennsylvania] neighborhood from which my son obtains one of the ingredients for making his porcelain . . . he has for some weeks been deprived of getting it, and . . . he has been induced to think of obtaining from New York, if he possibly can a quantity, which some time ago was taken there in a vain attempt to make china: and is now in the possession of the Proprietor of the Salamander Works . . . where formerly Shanmur's [Chanou's] factory stood which was burnt down."[26]

The end of Bird's partnership, by 5 January 1827 dissolved for undisclosed reasons, all but coincided with the drawing of William Ellis Tucker's first kilnful of porcelain, probably sometime that February.[27] The first documentation of actual specimens is contained in a letter Benjamin Tucker wrote to his friends Isaac and Hannah Jones on 16 February 1827 to accompany his gift of two porcelain pitchers from William's "first kiln of china," which Benjamin was presenting in gratitude for the Joneses' care

Figure 8. Tea or coffee service, ca. 1838. Tucker factory, Philadelphia. H. coffeepot, 8⅞ in. (22.5 cm.), sugar bowl, 3½ in. (8.9 cm.), cream pitcher, 6¼ in. (15.9 cm.), cup, 2⅞ in. (7.3 cm.); Diam. saucer, 5½ in. (14 cm.). The Metropolitan Museum of Art, Rogers Fund, 1963 (63.88.1, 7–10, 18)

of his infant daughter, Elizabeth, during his wife's temporary incapacitation.[28] Pitchers appear to be the first porcelain forms Tucker made. Offered in one of William's rare advertisements were "a Few pair of American China Pitchers . . . being a part of his first kiln."[29] Porcelain pitchers—"1 pr. horse pitchers, one pair star pattern, & one large Eagle pattern"—were among the shipment made in June of that year to the Baltimore merchant Marcus C. Stephens.[30] Their quality must have merited a re-order; in the following month, "six pairs of Porcelain Jugs" were sent to Stephens.[31] They were priced at three dollars a pair. By the fall of that year, the factory was producing a greater range of vessels to submit to the Franklin Institute exhibition. Tucker sent not only pitchers but also cups and saucers and fruit baskets. Though the Committee on Porcelain and Earthen Ware felt compelled "to remark that greater attention to dressing the bottoms &c after the last fireing would render them more agreeable to handle and less injurious to tables &c on which they are placed," it found that "the body of the ware is strong and sufficiently vitrified—the glaze is generally very good, and the gilding is done in a neat and tradesman like manner."[32] Until 1838, when the factory closed down, Tucker submitted specimens (in 1828, as many as a hundred pieces) to each consecutive Franklin Institute exhibition, and each panel of judges found them praiseworthy. In the report for 1828, Tucker's painted decoration, mentioned for the first time, was compared with the best specimens of French china and found "superior in whiteness." Two years later, according to the judges' report: "Much improvement was appar-

Figure 9. Tucker Pattern Book 1, nos. 63, 64. Library, Philadelphia Museum of Art, Rare Book Collection

Figure 10. Tucker Pattern Book 1, no. 1. Library, Philadelphia Museum of Art, Rare Book Collection

ent, especially in the painting and other ornamental parts . . . and the forms are generally chaste, and copied from the best models."[33]

The "models" copied by the Tucker designers were porcelains imported in large quantities from France and England, the shapes generally ovoid and based on classical prototypes, in the style of the day. Although a few examples were left unadorned (see cat. no. 9), most were embellished at least with simple gold ornament, sometimes accompanied by initials. One coffee service (Fig. 8) so decorated bears the initials *MET*, presumably those of Mary Earp Tucker, who married Thomas, William's brother, in 1838; still other forms featured landscape scenes or views of Philadelphia painted in black, sepia, or polychrome. Because the majority of the pieces are unmarked and because they resemble unmarked French porcelains in style, some confusion in attribution is inevitable.[34] Other objects, though similar to their transatlantic counterparts, are signed by the factory or can be documented by their presence in the Tucker factory pattern books (Figs. 9, 10)—one devoted to shapes, one devoted to ornamentation—which have survived to this day.[35] The book of shapes includes vessels from tapered spill vases to ornate urns of varying sizes; twelve different pitcher forms; a reticulated fruit basket in four variations; ogival, straight-sided, and paneled cups, with and without handles; tea sets in both English and French styles; a *veilleuse-théière* (a teapot and its cylindrical warmer); butter coolers; plates, platters, bowls, covered dishes, and compotes; a "spitting box" and a funnel. In the book of ornamentation, one pitcher, designated as "vase shape," is illustrated with eleven different decorative schemes, from simple gilding and rosebuds to an elaborate floral design (Fig. 11) shown here both in the drawing and in the porcelain example (Fig. 12).

While English white earthenwares made for export to this country were decorated with transfer-printed views of American cities and American patriots and imported French vases were painted with American scenes and notable American personages, the Tucker factory was probably the first domestic firm to embellish its porcelains with native themes.[36] These could be views of Philadelphia (see cat. nos. 13, 14, 17) or patriotic heroes (cat. no. 16). Portraits of the Marquis de Lafayette and President Andrew Jackson grace the two vases of a pair; on the reverse (Fig. 13) of the Lafayette vase is the American eagle with the Stars and Stripes and arrows and olive branches in its claws. President Jackson, in office during the Tucker factory's period of operation, was a logical subject. In 1830, in an effort to gain the president's patronage, William Tucker sent him a gift of porcelain accompanied by a request for financial support. The response from the White House was an order for a porcelain service and the president's compliments: "I was not apprised before of the perfection to which your skill and perseverance had brought this branch of American manufacture. It seems to be not inferior to the finest specimens of French porcelain."[37] In addition to the president of the United States, the elite of Philadelphia patronized Tucker's enterprise, as they had the manufactory of Bonnin and Morris in the previous century. Only the very wealthy could enjoy the luxuries Tucker offered, such as the dinner services and other porcelains inscribed in gold with an owner's initials.

Financial instability dogged the factory throughout its existence. The manufacture of porcelain was a costly undertaking, not least because of the wages demanded by the required highly skilled workers. From the beginning, though William Tucker preferred to remain solely in charge, he had to allow many others to invest in the business. Undoubtedly wanting to make his own decisions, he refused to let his father join the firm. In the spring of 1828, however, he was forced to accept John Hulme, son of a wealthy Philadelphian, as a partner. A number of examples carry the names of Tucker and Hulme (see cat. nos. 7, 10, 11), but by early June, the partnership had dissolved. Tucker's plea to President Jackson was by no means unique. He also sought government aid from the senators and congressmen of Pennsylvania, but, like the president, they did not accede. Only Representative Joseph Hemphill, a respected Philadelphia jurist, showed any personal interest. In May 1831,

Figure 11. Tucker Pattern Book 1, nos. 58, 59. Library, Philadelphia Museum of Art, Rare Book Collection

Figure 12. Pitcher, 1828–38. Tucker factory, Philadelphia. H. $9\frac{5}{16}$ in. (23.7 cm.). Collection of Mr. and Mrs. Stuart P. Feld

Judge Hemphill bought a partnership in his son's name for the sum of seven thousand dollars. That particularly generous declaration of faith, coming when it did, may have ensured the factory's survival for six more years.

Though Benjamin Tucker was not an official part of the company, he remained a vital influence, freely giving advice and money until the very end. In the firm's early years, he persuaded a reluctant William to accept his younger brother Thomas as an apprentice employee. In a letter dated 29 April 1828, Benjamin entreated William to encourage Thomas's natural talents, pointing out that he had the capacity for "painting more important and imposing figures." (Thomas had likely been engaged in simple decorating as the first part of his factory training.) Benjamin pressed his case: "Thomas has shown a very commendable disposition, by contentedly pursuing the first rudiments for one year."[38] Subsequently, Thomas was appointed chief decorator at the firm. Later, when William was in obvious ill health, Benjamin entreated him to instruct Thomas in every part of the business: "Thou art obliged to initiate thy brother Thomas into all the mysteries and the art of a perfect porcelain manufacture, with an engagement to take him into the concern."[39] Benjamin's foresight was vindicated in 1832, when William died at the age of

Figure 13. Pair of vases (reverse sides), 1830–38. William Ellis Tucker, Tucker and Hemphill, or Joseph Hemphill, Philadelphia. H. Lafayette vase, 11⅜ in. (28.9 cm.), Jackson vase, 11⅝ in. (29.5 cm.). The White House

Figure 14. Pitcher, 1830. Smith, Fife and Company, Philadelphia. H. 6⅛ in. (15.6 cm.). The Henry Francis du Pont Winterthur Museum (83.172)

thirty-two, leaving Judge Hemphill, through his son, the factory's legal owner. Wisely, the judge kept Thomas on, appointing him plant superintendent, and Thomas directed operations until 1837, when Judge Hemphill sold out of the business. That October, Thomas leased the factory for a period of six months. Because of the prevailing economic instability and in the absence of any tariff on imported goods, he could neither compete with the prices of foreign wares nor afford to maintain the manufactory, and he had to retire when his lease expired. Nevertheless, Thomas's talents, combined with William's commitment to excellence and Benjamin's determination to succeed, had secured for the family business an impressive twelve-year production and an assured place in the history of American porcelain.

During one of the factory's many financial crises, perhaps that of early 1830, some employees probably left the company. The similarity of three pitchers, each marked by Smith, Fife and Company of Philadelphia (Fig. 14; cat. no. 19), to a Tucker example of Grecian shape suggests that the Smith, Fife workers had come from the Tucker factory and used Tucker molds in their production. Little is known about the Smith, Fife venture. In 1830—possibly the only year that the firm was in business—two pitchers it entered in the Franklin Institute exhibition (where they were in competition with Tucker factory examples) won the judges' approval. In a letter of 20 December 1830, a disgruntled William Tucker mentioned the firm's closing to John F. Anderson, of Louisville, Kentucky, a prospective member of the porcelain fraternity with whom he was then corresponding: "This is to inform you that Smith & Fife have absconded from this city without giving any intelligence where they were going, leaving their debts unpaid." He added that the sheriff had seized the firm's assets, which included its molds.[40]

The porcelain entrepreneurs of the early nineteenth century, facilitated in their endeavors by a wider knowledge of the medium and refinements in the technique of its manufacture, set the stage for the remarkable achievements of the next period, which was to be extraordinarily productive.

The Mid-Nineteenth Century (cat. nos. 20–34)

As the nineteenth century approached its middle years, increased technology and industrialization brought the making and decorating of porcelain out of the hands of individual craftsmen and into the machine age. With the reduction in cost of manufacturing and the lowering of retail prices, porcelain became available to the American middle-class consumer for the first time. In that era, public taste altered. The restrained, smooth neoclassical shapes gave way to the exuberant relief-molded designs of the prevailing Rococo-revival style, its naturalism and abundant adornment reflecting the optimism abroad in the nation. During the period from the 1840s to the 1860s, large numbers of immigrants entered the United States. The craftsmen among them, many from the Staffordshire area of England, were welcomed at domestic manufactories in need of their advanced skills. For their American employers, those experts constructed new, advanced kinds of porcelain kilns and formed, fired, and ornamented the wares in an assured and professional fashion. Concurrently, French influence resurfaced in the styles coming out of Limoges, a burgeoning porcelain center whose sales to the American market were increasing in volume. Expanding methods of transportation throughout the heartland of the developing nation facilitated moving raw materials to the potteries and finished wares to the retailers. In that period, the great porcelain-producing centers—the cities of Brooklyn, Trenton, and East Liverpool—gained supremacy in the field.

With growing population, urbanization, and methods of travel came a proliferation of hotels, boardinghouses, and saloons, all requiring dinnerware for their tables, basins and other toilet utensils for their bedchambers, and vessels for their bars. Factories lost no time in making those items a specialty. Stouter, squatter shapes, their broad surfaces well suited for manifold relief-molded designs—flowers, foliage, scrolls, and figural compositions—came into vogue. In 1853, the Crystal Palace Exhibition of the Industry of All Nations was held in New York (America's first world's fair) for the purpose of broadening America's knowledge of foreign achievements and, in turn, of displaying domestic technical prowess, if not yet artistic excellence.

At the Crystal Palace, the gospel of the rococo style was proclaimed on porcelains from England, France, and Germany. Specimens from Sèvres and Limoges included commercial wares shown by the Haviland Brothers company, a china shop in New York City praised for its "rich and attractive display."[1] Of the American participators, including several newly founded New York firms, the United States Pottery Company of Bennington, Vermont, made the greatest impression. The showing of Charles Cartlidge's Greenpoint pottery (which had four large kilns in operation and was employing about sixty workers) earned that factory a "first premium on account of superior excellence of body and glazing."[2] Its display, described as "Porcelain tea, table, and fancy ware," testifies to the scope of Cartlidge porcelain production.[3] A large cup and saucer (Fig. 15) whose molded shape, polychrome floral painting, and gold highlights relate more closely to European porcelains than to English was undoubtedly made about 1850. Its inscription, "To Mrs. Godfrey from C. C.," implies that it was a wedding gift from Cartlidge to his daughter Maria, who married Jonathan Godfrey on 21 October 1850.[4]

Charles Cartlidge's training began in Staffordshire, England. He came to this country in 1832, setting up shop at 103 Water Street in Manhattan as agent for the Staffordshire potteries of William

Figure 15. Cup and saucer, ca. 1848–56. Charles Cartlidge and Company, Greenpoint (Brooklyn), New York. H. cup, 3½ in. (8.9 cm.); Diam. saucer, 7 in. (17.8 cm.). The Brooklyn Museum, Gift of Mrs. Henry W. Patten (65.201.1)

Ridgway, then enjoying a healthy trade with America.[5] In 1841, he took as partner Herbert Q. Ferguson, who would marry Cartlidge's daughter Eliza six years later, and put him in charge of a Ridgway agency in New Orleans. In 1848, having lost his post when Ridgway went out of business, Cartlidge purchased land in the Greenpoint section of Brooklyn, an area handy to river transportation, and, bringing Ferguson back to New York, embarked with him on the manufacture of porcelain. Since the first sample made of American materials by Charles Cartlidge and Company was fashioned before the factory was ready for full-scale production, it had to be fired at David Henderson's American Pottery Company, in Jersey City, New Jersey.[6]

With his plant in operation, Cartlidge set out to produce porcelain buttons (Fig. 16), which were then replacing the more expensive ones made of mother-of-pearl.[7] For his rapidly enlarging market, he began to fabricate "door and room signs [Fig. 17], number plates for church pews, shutter, door, window, curtain and drawer knobs, bell pulls, door and number plates, keyhole escutcheons, furniture castors, stair carpet plates, speaking tubes and rosettes."[8] The manufacture of both buttons and door and furniture trimmings utilized a new, English-developed machine process whereby damp clay was pressed into a series of steel molds, or dies, and subjected to great pressure before being fired.

The variety of forms offered by the Cartlidge factory included both mundane and highly specialized items: "Inkstands, wafer trays, paper weights . . . knife handles, shawl pins, umbrella and cane handles, wine labels, candlesticks, spittoons, shaving or soap boxes . . . sets of piano keys,"[9] as well as snuff boxes, a variety of smokers' paraphernalia, and "mortuary portrait frames" for affixing to tombstones.[10] As a supplement to those sometimes exotic items, Cartlidge produced tablewares and pitchers. The favorites among the latter, which gradually came to dominate his output, were two having relief-molded motifs either of corn and cornstalks or oak leaves and acorns. Those he turned out in several different sizes. The moderate price and heavy grade of Cartlidge porcelain made it eminently suitable for commercial use. Several Cartlidge pitchers are marked with the names of men whose business address was given as "Arbor," Saloon, or Porterhouse; one is inscribed "Union Hotel," another, "Claremont" (see cat. no. 21). The words "American Porcelain" found inside some of the spouts and visible when the pieces were in use constitute an early form of enterprising, if subtle, advertisement. Numerous pitchers carry names or initials that can be traced to the original owners through old city directories, where their listed occupations identify them as tradesmen in a variety of fields. Most of them either worked or lived in Brooklyn or Manhattan, close to the Cartlidge factory. The majority of the names are men's, but those of two women, a seamstress and a dressmaker, also appear. Such patriotic motifs as the shield of the United States or the American eagle, either painted or in relief, were often added to the pitchers. The relief decoration was probably conceived by the Englishman Josiah Jones, Cartlidge's brother-in-law and chief designer.[11]

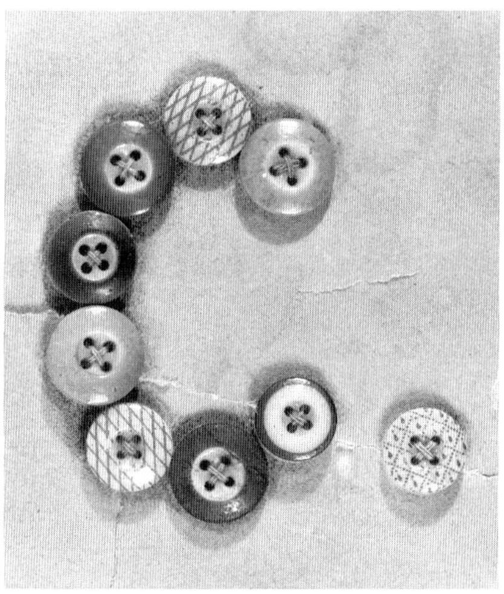

Figure 16. Porcelain buttons, on original card, ca. 1848. Charles Cartlidge and Company, Greenpoint (Brooklyn), New York. The Brooklyn Museum, Gift of Mrs. Henry W. Patten (65.201.3–11)

Figure 17. Doorplate, 1848–56. Charles Cartlidge and Company, Greenpoint (Brooklyn), New York. H. 1¼ in. (3.2 cm.), W. 2½ in. (6.4 cm.). Collection of Mary M. Rowan

The names of only four of the several decorators employed by the firm are known: George Washington, Frank Lockett (Fig. 18), Daniel Smith, and Elijah Tatler, all of them English-trained.[12] The designs they executed embraced the highly naturalistic, vibrantly colored flower painting made popular by English porcelains. The most common embellishment was simple gilding used for highlighting relief ornament, for banding, and for inscriptions. More elaborate decorative devices were coats of arms, landscape scenes, and city views, notably those executed by Tatler (see cat. no. 24). Also utilized were transfer-printed designs created by a pattern engraved on copper and then transferred to the object. As the procedure has been described: "The designs were printed in outline, both over and under the glaze, and the coloring was afterwards filled in by women."[13]

Cartlidge probably attempted to sell his porcelains far afield, perhaps drawing on some of the contacts he had made during his Ridgway tenure. He tried to enter the Canadian market through Andrew Hayes, of Montreal, agent there for John Ridgway, Bates and Company of Staffordshire. In 1851, Hayes advertised Cartlidge's porcelains in a local newspaper: "Charles Cartledge & Co./Sole Manufacturers of American Porcelain/Door Furniture, &c. &c."[14] The medium was said to be particularly suited to the Canadian market because of its ability to "withstand the rigours of the severe Winters of the North."[15]

In the 1850s, Cartlidge invested some of his profits in other, more speculative ventures, including a new steam-boiler apparatus. His forays into unknown territory undermined his resources and threatened the stability of his business. In the latter

Figure 18. Door finger plate, 1848. Charles Cartlidge and Company, Greenpoint (Brooklyn), New York, decorated by Frank Lockett. H. 11½ in. (29.2 cm.), W. 3⅛ in. (7.9 cm.). On the back, on a paper label, is the legend: "Manufactured & Decorated/at the porcelain works of/Charles Cartlidge in 1848./Greenpoint, N.Y. (Kings Co.)/Decorated by Frank Lockett/Loaned by Mrs. Annie/Tyndale of Media, Pa./Oct. 1894." Collection of Anne M. Ewing

half of 1854, in an attempt to recoup his losses, he dissolved the firm of Charles Cartlidge and Company and reorganized it as the American Porcelain Manufacturing Company. The original factory never marked any of its wares (though a number of surviving examples, having descended in the Cartlidge family, serve to attribute certain of its other objects), but one pitcher, a presentation piece to an as yet unidentified recipient (Fig. 19), is inscribed with the name of the successor firm. The new company lasted less than two years, closing its doors in 1856, but the Cartlidge manufactory is still memorable for being instrumental in nurturing the commercial porcelain industry in America. Former Cartlidge workers contributed much knowledge and experience to other young manufacturing loci: the potters Charles Hattersley, William Young, Richard Millington, and John Astbury all became major influences in the growing pottery center of Trenton, and Enoch Barber and Charles Leake went on to practice their trade in Bennington, Vermont.

The porcelain trimmings that had been a specialty of the Charles Cartlidge company were also the mainstay of the firm William Boch and his two brothers, Anthony and Francis Victor, founded in Greenpoint on Fifth (later Eckford) Street, near Greenpoint Avenue, sometime around 1844. (William's sons William junior and Nicholas entered the firm at a later date.) When the Boch brothers exhibited at the New York Crystal Palace in 1853, their display, which included "stair rods, and plates of decorated porcelain; plain and gilded porcelain trimmings for doors, shutters, drawers, &c," must have resembled Cartlidge products.[16] In 1855, Boch wares advertised in the Brooklyn city directory (Fig. 20) confirm the similarity of the two companies' repertoires: "All kinds of house, lock, & furniture trimmings; porcelain pitchers, mugs, vases, and other fancy wares. Also, porcelain lambs, images, and other decorations for graveyard monuments, constantly on hand and made to order."[17] The prodigious number of relief-molded pitchers made by William Boch and Brothers, like those of their neighbor and competitor, utilized

Figure 19. Pitcher, ca. 1853–56. American Porcelain Manufacturing Company, Greenpoint (Brooklyn), New York. H. 12½ in. (31.8 cm.). Collection of John H. Nally

designs borrowed directly from the eighteenth-century rococo, many of which were to remain popular with the middle-class market for decades. Molds from both factories may have been in circulation throughout the period; some of them may even have been acquired by the proprietors of the successor to the Boch brothers firm. The Boch pitchers and mugs that are impressed with the firm's mark have Bacchus as their theme. (The indistinct appearance of the grapes and vines surrounding the god of wine is caused by a shallow molding covered with a thick glaze.)

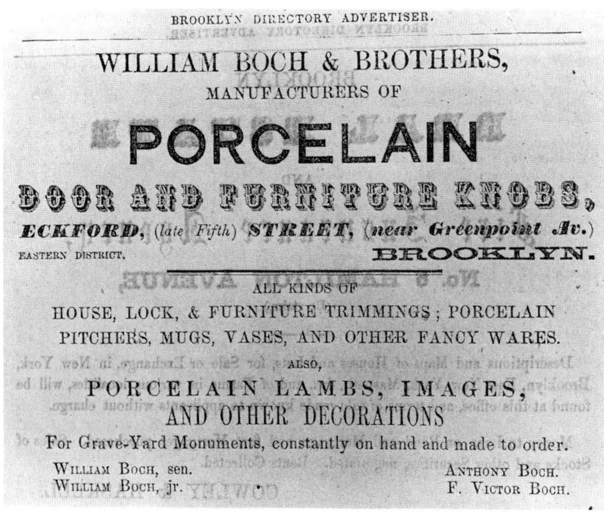

Figure 20. Advertisement, William Boch & Brothers, *Smith's Brooklyn Directory*, 1855–56, facing p. 129. The Brooklyn Historical Society

In about 1861, Thomas Carll Smith, who had already enjoyed a career as a businessman and an architect, joined the Boch brothers as an investor and soon became sole owner. The firm he established on the premises, the Union Porcelain Company (later the Union Porcelain Works), produced a Bacchus-and-grapevine pitcher (Fig. 21) that is marked with the new company's name and the address of its New York City office, 82 John Street. The Union company maintained an emphasis on porcelain house trimmings, which it copiously illustrated and described in a hundred-and-sixty-four-page catalogue it issued in 1861 (Fig. 22). Among the wares also offered were "pitchers, spittoons, cups and saucers for coffee, tea and chocolate, preserve plates, heavy oval dishes, mugs with handles, milk and cream pitchers, bowls, mustard cups, shaving mugs, tumblers, ice cream saucers, plates, porcelain images, ice picks, toddy sticks, lemon squeezers."[18] Pitchers of capacities from one to four quarts were available in four patterns—one, listed as Embossed, was possibly the Bacchus design; the others were Plain, Corn, and Oak Leaf, the two last probably made from Cartlidge molds in Smith's possession.

William Young and Company, of Trenton, New Jersey, was the first earthenware and porcelain manufactory established in what was to become the center of large-scale production in those mediums.[19] The firm was founded by Charles Hattersley, who had left Cartlidge's employ by 1852 (about the time of Cartlidge's major financial crisis). He was later joined by a group of the factory's Staffordshire-trained potters—Richard Millington, John Astbury, and William Young and his three sons, Edward, John, and William junior. He purchased land in Trenton, a city ideally situated between the urban markets of Philadelphia and New York and having direct access to major transportation routes, and by the middle of the following year had erected a factory for the manufacture of porcelain doorknobs. By the end of 1853, the senior Young had acquired Hattersley's lease and founded his own firm. Porcelain pitchers documented to the Young factory are decorated with relief designs of a tree trunk and vine (see cat. no. 28), demonstrating the continuing influence of the Rococo-revival style. They may have been among the specimens of the pottery's produc-

Figure 21. Pitcher, ca. 1865. Union Porcelain Company, Greenpoint (Brooklyn), New York. H. 8 13/16 in. (22.4 cm.). Collections of Henry Ford Museum and Greenfield Village (57.63.7)

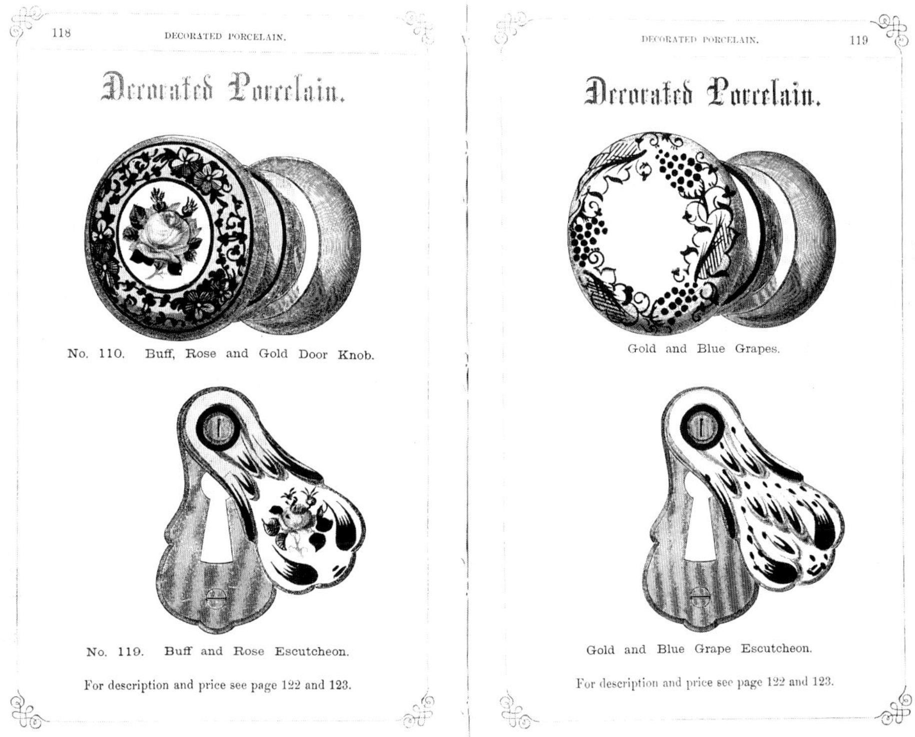

Figure 22. *Union Porcelain Co.'s Price List of House Trimmings* (New York: Francis & Loutrel, 1861), pp. 118–19. Library of Congress (TR818.U6)

tion exhibited at the Franklin Institute in Philadelphia in 1854, along with "door knobs, escutcheons, door plates, harness furniture, and many other articles."[20] The Trenton press, possibly puffed up with pride in the first porcelains of local origin, reported: "Many of these were splendidly ornamental in gold and colors. The color was pure white, and the enamelling was surpassingly brilliant."[21]

In Philadelphia, porcelain manufacture was revived about 1851 by the Staffordshire-trained potter Ralph Bagnall Beech, who that autumn exhibited at the Franklin Institute Fair "1 Lot of Porcelain Flower and Scent Vases."[22] Nothing is known of their appearance, but, presumably, they were English in style.[23] Beech, who was listed in the Philadelphia city directories as a porcelain manufacturer between 1852 and 1857, though not identified with any known firm, may have been the professional adviser to a pottery built on North Front Street in about 1852 or 1853 by two German chemists, Charles Kurlbaum and John T. Schwartz, or Schwartze, neither of whom had any knowledge of the porcelain business.[24] According to historian Edwin AtLee Barber, the factory decorators were all German-trained, as was the manager, whom Barber did not identify.[25] (He may have been William Reiss, Sr.) In view of the national background of all the men associated in that enterprise, it is not surprising that what was produced reveals a definite European influence, especially the shapes of a documented tea set (see cat. no. 32), which emulate porcelain counterparts manufactured at Limoges for Haviland Brothers and Company. When the Kurlbaum and Schwartz wares were shown for the first time at the Franklin Institute, in 1853, they were found comparable to the best French porcelains;[26] when the firm exhibited at the institute in the following year, the quality of its plain and decorated porcelain was judged favorably with the "finer European ware."[27] Both Kurlbaum and Schwartz are listed in the city directories as porcelain manufacturers through 1859.[28]

Another firm named the American Porcelain Manufacturing Company (totally unrelated to the failed Cartlidge enterprise) was established in 1854 in Gloucester, New Jersey, across the Delaware River from Philadelphia. Information on the firm is scarce, except that the founding partners were John C. Drake, Abraham Bechtel, George B. Keller, Peter Weikel, and Martin H. Bechtel, all from Philadelphia, the senior William Reiss, from Gloucester, and Matthew Miller, Jr., George Setley, and George Bockins, from nearby Camden, New Jersey.[29] Only a few porcelains can be documented to the factory's manufacture (see cat. nos. 29, 31). The partners seem to have had little potting experience, though the German-born Reiss is thought to have had a factory in Wilmington, Delaware, and later to have managed the Kurlbaum and Schwartz porcelain works.[30] According to Philadelphia city directories, Abraham Bechtel, whose occupation is given as "porcelain manufacturer," may have run the manufactory; the Bechtels and Drake (business associates from at least 1850) and Keller were all dry-goods merchants; the others, listed at their own business addresses, may have participated only as investors.

In 1854, at the annual exhibition at the Franklin Institute, "Three Cases White and Decorated Porcelain, by the American Porcelain Manufacturing Company," were shown.[31] The specimens were compared favorably with the porcelain submitted by Kurlbaum and Schwartz, though there were "trifling differences in body and glaze."[32] In 1857, the company, reorganized and with a new set of partners, became the Gloucester China Company. That December, a report on the factory's production appeared in a local newspaper: "A large quantity of the china manufactured is on exhibition at their office, Second and Walnut streets, in this city. The ware is pure white and very clear and strong."[33] The Gloucester company was apparently having problems with glazing and firing, however, for the surfaces of their wares were "blistered and rough."[34] The factory closed in 1860.

The mid-century also saw a porcelain industry opening up in the Middle West through the influence of William H. Bloor, a Staffordshire potter who came to America in 1842. Bloor was a wanderer who worked at many different American factories during his lifetime. In 1848, with William Brunt, he manufactured doorknobs in East Liverpool. By 1854, he had moved to Trenton, where he was associated for about three years with the potters Henry Speeler and James Taylor. The partnership's experiments must have included porcelain. In 1856, at the Franklin Institute, the firm of Speeler, Taylor and Bloor exhibited objects of graniteware, earthenware, and "china." A surviving parian-porcelain pitcher incised with the firm's name is a further indication that the partners were producing in the medium in the 1850s. By the end of that decade, Bloor had relocated in East Liverpool, where by August 1860 he had purchased a section of the local Phoenix Pottery and was remodeling it to produce "porcelain and parian."[35] By the end of the following March, he had drawn his first kiln of whiteware, porcelain, and parian at the factory, which was called the East Liverpool Porcelain Works, or, the United States Porcelain Works.[36] Bloor's price list encompassed an impressive variety of plates, dishes, oval baking dishes, coffee cups (French and plain, with handles or without), ice cream dishes, teawares available in regular, restaurant, or hotel quality, soup and sauce tureens, compotiers, pickle dishes in leaf, shell, fluted, or scrolled patterns, ewers, basins, and other toilet wares, and chamber candlesticks. Among the forms offered in parian were fancy matchboxes and cigar pats, paperweights, vases, jugs, and statuettes.[37]

In 1862, Bloor, unable to find qualified workers and in financial trouble, was forced to close down after barely two years in operation. He then migrated back to Trenton, where he continued in the manufacture of parian and porcelain at the Etruria Works he established with John Hart Brewer and Joseph Ott. The Etruria Works was to become one of the most enduring of the Trenton porcelain firms, continuing in growth and dominating the industry through the end of the century.

Parian (cat. nos. 35–53)

Parian, a medium developed in England in the early 1840s and quickly copied in America, is a type of porcelain having the appearance of marble. No properly furnished Victorian parlor was without it in one form or another. In this country, where its popularity lingered into the 1880s, it was first produced on a large scale in factories run primarily by immigrant English workers. That American parian relied heavily on English models and followed current design trends was evident in 1853, when the parians of both countries appeared virtually side by side at the New York Crystal Palace Exhibition of the Industry of All Nations. The major American parian factories were situated in Bennington and Greenpoint, though others in Cincinnati, New York City, and Baltimore had begun production by the 1870s. In that decade, the Centennial Exposition in Philadelphia, a showplace for the world's achievements in porcelain production, elevated the status of parian to the realm of art.

Parian has a higher proportion of feldspar than the conventional porcelain and is fired at a lower temperature. The increased amount of feldspar causes the finished body to be more highly vitrified, thus possessed of a color verging on ivory and having a marblelike texture that is smoother than that of biscuit, or unglazed, porcelain. At midcentury, parian objects were usually formed by slip-casting—that is, by pouring liquefied clay into a plaster-of-paris mold that absorbed the water from the slip while retaining the fine details of the modeling. Relief ornamentation was either made by hand or in a mold. Most parian was left in its natural, creamy white state, but applied background colors, usually shades of blue, could be used to contrast with the relief motifs. During the 1870s and 1880s, as the parian era flourished and faded, tinted bodies were introduced into the medium. Because the matte surface of the material attracted dirt, which was difficult to remove, much of the parian made here and abroad was protected with what was called a smear glaze. That was achieved by chemicals added to the kiln in much the same way that salt added to a kiln of stoneware creates a glazelike effect on the fired object. The slight sheen of the smear glaze also preserved the parians' crisply molded details, which would have blurred under a viscous finish. (The interiors of vessels intended to hold liquids were, of course, fully glazed.)

In England, several factories claimed credit for developing parian, but the Staffordshire firm operated by William Taylor Copeland and Thomas Garrett was the first to produce it on a commercial scale, about 1842, and went on to become one of the medium's major manufacturers. The factory's first important display, at the Crystal Palace Exhibition in London in 1851, was greeted with much acclaim. The new material was made at several potteries and was marketed under different names: the Copeland firm called it statuary porcelain because of its resemblance to the fine white marble of neoclassical sculpture; Wedgwood named it Carrara, after the Italian quarry patronized by Michelangelo. The word "parian," which quickly became the medium's generic name, was coined by the Minton firm to suggest Paros, the Greek isle that furnished much of the stone used in the classical period.

Less expensive than bronze and more durable than plaster, parian served to bring copies of works of art into the parlors of America's expanding middle class. Copies of classical and contemporary statuary imported from England were distributed throughout the United States. For the first time, works by American artists were also available. Of those, the most popular was undoubtedly Hiram Powers's *Greek Slave* (Fig. 23), which was reproduced in vast numbers. In addition, busts and relief portraits, especially of George Washington and Benjamin Franklin but also of contemporary political figures, including Zachary Taylor and Rutherford B. Hayes, were made by American factories to supply the increasing demands of the domestic market. The subjects of other American parians were borrowed from national sports—the baseball figures made at the Ott and Brewer pottery by Isaac Broome, for example—or from national occupations, such as the blacksmith and the sculptor

Figure 23. *The Greek Slave*, 1848. Minton and Co., Staffordshire, England. H. 14½ in. (36.8 cm.). The Metropolitan Museum of Art, Gift of Mr. and Mrs. Russell E. Burke III, 1983 (1983.492)

executed for the Union Porcelain Works by Karl L. H. Müller. Other forms the factories produced, ranging from ornamental pitchers and vases to more specialized items that included clock cases, cemetery portrait plaques, and shirt buttons, were still imbued with an Englishness that mirrored the heritage of the immigrant potters and the continuing public admiration for imported wares.

Parian was probably first made in America in the mid-1840s, at the Bennington factory run by Christopher Webber Fenton and his brother-in-law Julius Norton during their four-year partnership. Bennington had been a center for the production of utilitarian salt-glazed stoneware since the early part of the century, but Fenton and Norton seized the opportunity to expand their horizons that the developing mechanization of the ceramics industry offered.[1] Fenton, the guiding force, experimented constantly with various ways to create new clay bodies. With the aid of John Harrison, a potter from England's Copeland Works, who arrived in Bennington in late 1843, he was able to begin to manufacture parian about 1846.[2] During the next two years, Norton having abandoned the operation, Fenton used the mark "Fenton's Works; Bennington, Vermont." When he acquired a new partner—a local businessman named Alanson Potter Lyman—Fenton changed the manufactory's name to the United States Pottery Company. By that time, his parian production had risen to an impressive commercial level.

Much of the firm's design work is credited to Daniel Greatbach, a Staffordshire potter who arrived in Bennington after beginning his American career in Jersey City, New Jersey. Consistent with English counterparts of the mid-1840s through the 1850s, relief molding on Bennington pitchers and vases usually consisted of the naturalistically rendered plant forms of the Rococo-revival style. A vessel such as the snowdrop pitcher (cat. no. 38) can resemble an English antecedent so closely as to suggest that it was cast in a mold made from the original piece. The attribution of an unmarked object is all but impossible, though one exception is a pitcher in the form of a waterfall (cat. no. 43), whose originality of concept is as identifiable as it is awkward.

The company's only surviving price list, dated 20 July 1852, does not specify the patterns of its "parian marble" pitchers.[3] They were available in four sizes and were priced accordingly, from four to twelve dollars a dozen. A number of small figural works are listed and can therefore be established as company forms despite the absence of marks. These include animal subjects (greyhound, swan, sheep, or bird's nests) or human figures ("Adoration," "Good Night," Cupid, Indian Queen, and Sailor Boy and Dog).[4] "Adoration" was the most expensive, selling for seventy-five dollars a dozen. The United States Pottery Company, at the peak of its parian production in 1853, the year of New York's Crystal Palace Exhibition, sent a number of parians to the fair, where all its wares made a strong showing. It submitted several patterns of parian pitchers, such as one decorated with climbing roses (cat. no. 39), as well as a few sample objects that, apparently, never went into production. Two conspicuous examples of those were a bust of Christopher Webber Fenton (cat. no. 40) and a figure of a Madonna and Child, both part of the tall monument that was the centerpiece of the firm's display. Another, a parian clock case (Fig. 24), appears in a published engraving of the firm's exhibit. Shortly afterward, the high cost of labor, the high losses by breakage, and the rough competition posed by cheaper imported articles caused the factory to go into severe financial reverses. The domestic industry was marked with the stigma of inferiority, for it was generally held that imported goods, English in particular, were inherently better, whatever their quality. The company was able to raise desperately needed capital in 1855 and in the following year made a laudable showing in Boston at the exhibition held by the Massachusetts Charitable Mechanic Association. Of the Bennington wares, the judges said: "We were much pleased with the Blue Parian Ware, particularly with the Water Jar, which evinces great skill in manufacturing, and is equal, in the judgment of your Committee, to anything of the kind, foreign or domestic."[5] Its successful efforts notwithstanding, the factory was forced to close its doors by May 1858.[6]

Ornamental wares of parian, especially vessels having white relief decoration of foliate motifs—grapes and vines, oak leaves, or climbing roses—against a blue stippled background, enjoyed continuing popularity with middle-class consumers and remained in production for almost three decades. In the late 1850s and early 1860s, William Bloor, pursuing his porcelain career in Trenton and East Liverpool, produced Rococo-revival-style mugs (see cat. no. 45), pitchers, and trinket boxes similar to Bennington examples. The call for wares in that style lasted into the early 1880s, as a vase featuring garlands of grapevines in full relief on a blue stippled ground attests. Though typical of the mid-century vocabulary, the vase bears the name of John Moses

Figure 24. Clock case, ca. 1852–53. United States Pottery Company, Bennington, Vermont, possibly designed by Daniel Greatbach. H. 11½ in. (29.2 cm.). The Bennington Museum, Bennington, Vermont, Bequest of Mrs. E. H. Johnson (66.1212)

Figure 25. Bust of Charles Cartlidge, ca. 1830–47. Modeled by Josiah Jones, probably in England. H. 20 in. (50.8 cm.). Collection of William Cartlidge Vestal, Jr.

& Co. of Trenton, and so must date to between 1878 and 1885 (cat. no. 51).[7] Its retardataire design contrasts with the parians produced in Cincinnati at the pottery of Frederick Dallas, which probably about 1875 began making "candle-sticks, match-boxes, and molasses-jugs."[8] The patterns of pitchers turned out by the factory demonstrate a proficiency in current design, chiefly in the floral motifs of the Aesthetic movement, the iris and the calla lily (cat. no. 47). The restraint of that shallow-relief decoration is in marked contrast to the abundance that characterizes the Rococo-revival-style vessels of other firms. The Dallas company continued in production until 1881, when its founder died.

Though restricting the use of its parian to sculptural works, Charles Cartlidge and Company of Greenpoint, New York, began production in the medium about 1848. (The factory's formula was recorded later in the century: eleven parts china and ball clay to six parts feldspar.)[9] Cartlidge's parian achievements have been largely ignored, probably because so few of them have survived. Josiah Jones, who had married Cartlidge's sister in England and arrived in America in 1847 to help Cartlidge establish his porcelain factory, was responsible for the sculptural works. The son of a Staffordshire potter, Jones had worked as a modeler at various English parian manufactories, producing statuettes, busts, and relief plaques, an invaluable training that he applied to the American venture. The small statuettes of children representing the four seasons that Jones made in Greenpoint are reminiscent of the sentimental figural works produced by the United States Pottery Company in Bennington as well as by many English firms.[10] Like others of his trade, Jones is thought to have brought a supply of English plaster casts and design molds to use in his American career.[11] He also fashioned original works—some of them in the form of relief profiles on parian plaques, from two-color portraits of family members (cat. no. 37) to depictions of political figures. Cartlidge, who admired American icons, decided to have Jones model parian representations of George Washington, Zachary Taylor (cat. no. 35), Chief Justice John Marshall, Daniel Webster, Henry Clay, and Archbishop John Joseph Hughes. These Jones rendered in forms that varied from three-quarter life-size busts to small heads that capped the handles of canes and umbrellas.[12] Jones also executed a bust of Cartlidge in the guise of a Roman senator (Fig. 25). The work, which has descended in the family, portrays Cartlidge as a young man and was likely done in England.[13]

Karl L. H. Müller, an artist from Coblenz, Germany, emigrated to the United States in 1850 and, with his brother Nicholas, did a thriving business catering to the demand for small statuettes in plaster or metal. The Müllers also made clock cases in

Figure 26. Bust of Ulysses S. Grant, 1865–71. Bloor, Ott and Brewer, Trenton, New Jersey. H. 12 in. (30.5 cm.). New Jersey State Museum, The Brewer Collection (CH354.31)

their New York City studio, casting them in relatively inexpensive white metal. In that era, art unions flourished throughout the country. Through their magazines and annual lotteries, they provided subscribing Americans who lived outside of the country's artistic centers with the opportunity to acquire works of art and to know what was going on in the art world. Müller's works were among those the art unions offered. The figures he modeled, from George Washington to baseball players and newsboys, were especially pleasing to the subscribers. When in 1874 the Union Porcelain Works hired Müller to help prepare for its display at the Centennial Exposition, he initially produced figures or relief works resurrected or altered from pieces he had done ten to twenty years earlier. The blacksmith, created first in white metal to a design Müller registered with the United States patent office in 1868, reappeared in porcelain he made and signed at the Greenpoint firm about 1876 (cat. no. 49). He went on to execute other, almost life-size busts in parian, including that of Thomas C. Smith, the porcelain works proprietor, and Edwin Forrest, a contemporary actor.

The Trenton firm run by Joseph Ott and John Hart Brewer began to manufacture parian in the mid-1860s, when they were in partnership with William Bloor, probably induced by Bloor's thor-

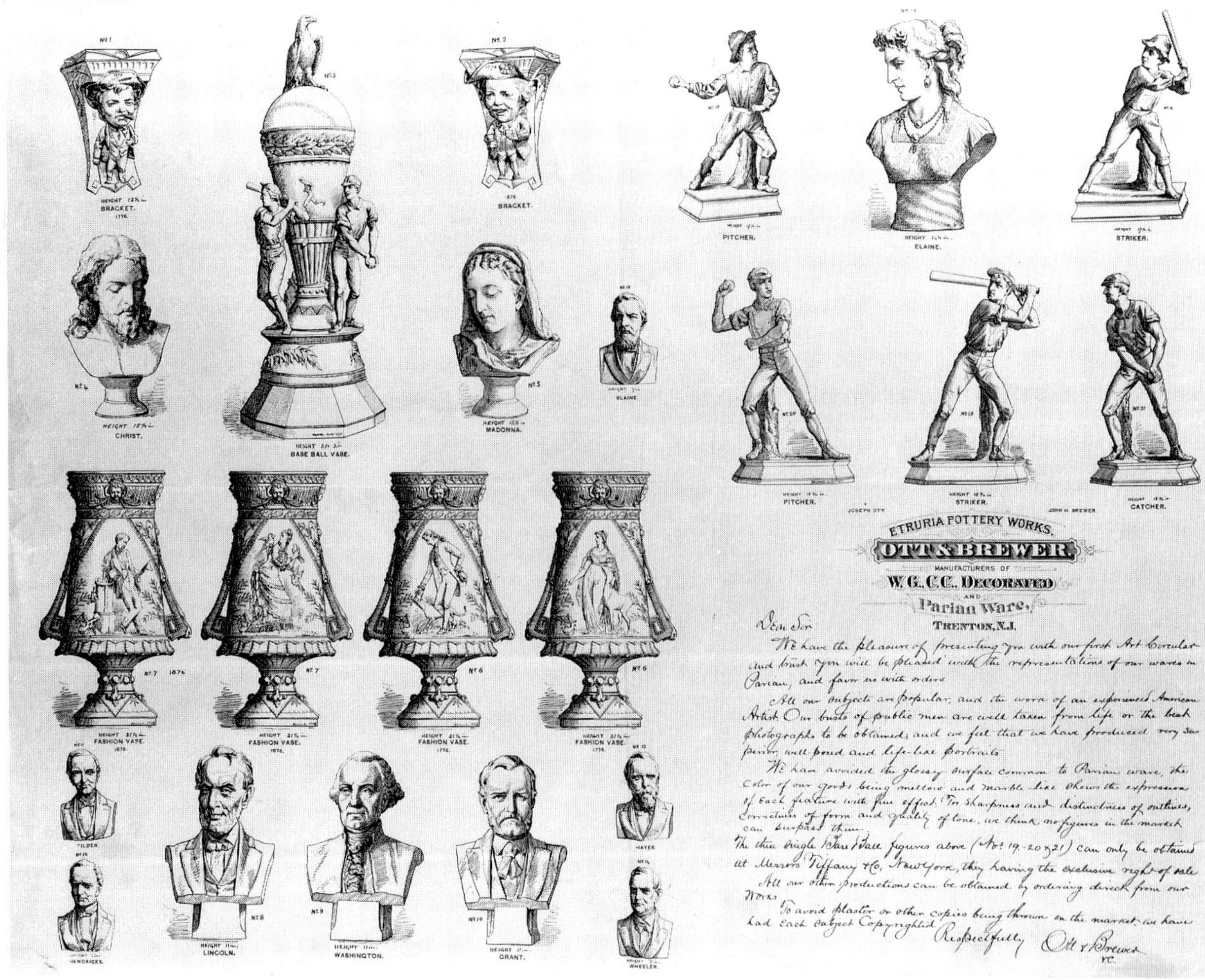

Figure 27. Broadside, undated, Ott & Brewer, Trenton, New Jersey. 16⅞ × 22 in. (42.9 × 55.9 cm.). Collection of David and Barbara Goldberg

ough knowledge and experience in porcelain in all its complexities. Two medium-sized parian busts, those of Ulysses S. Grant (Fig. 26) and Abraham Lincoln, each marked "B.O.& B.," can be attributed to those early years.[14] General Grant, in his uniform as commander of the Union army, is portrayed in a wooden, heavy-handed manner. Another bust of him, made at the factory about 1876, shows him in civilian dress.[15] The second version has a fine detail and sensitivity of handling that are totally absent from the first. The disparity between the two reflects the relative skills of the separate modelers, the first as yet unidentified; the second, Isaac Broome.

Broome, arguably the finest of all American artists in the parian medium,[16] was employed by the firm in 1873. He was also responsible for parian figures described in a company broadside (Fig. 27) as "taken from life or the best photographs to be obtained." The subjects treated encompassed such American luminaries as George Washington, Benjamin Franklin (Fig. 28), Abraham Lincoln, and Rutherford B. Hayes.[17] Broome also designed monumental exhibition pieces that brought glory to the name of Ott and Brewer, among them a pair of baseball vases and a bust of Cleopatra (cat. nos. 54, 56). A finely rendered parian plaque by Broome (Fig. 29), its inscriptions "Liberty" and "1876" indicating that it was intended for the Philadelphia exposition, portrays the American mechanical genius Robert Fulton, whose name appears at the lower right of the plaque.[18] Since the exposition was concerned as much with industry as it was with art, Fulton was an eminently apt symbol of America's contribution to science and industry. During Broome's employment at Ott and Brewer (a scant five years), he turned out an enormous number of excellent works, primarily in the parian medium. An article on American parian dated March 1877 recounted a visit to Broome's studio in the pottery complex, where Broome was assisted by his three daughters, "artists of fine ability themselves."[19] The writer described Broome's work in glowing terms: "He embodies in parian the most exquisite conception imaginable."[20] Broome left

Figure 28. Bust of Benjamin Franklin, 1876. Ott and Brewer, Trenton, New Jersey. H. 10 in. (25.4 cm.). The Metropolitan Museum of Art, Gift of William H. Huntington, 1883 (83.2.252)

the Ott and Brewer firm in 1878 and is not known ever to have resumed his work in parian.

Another firm that successfully worked in the medium, though later and on a smaller scale than Ott and Brewer, was the Chesapeake Pottery of Baltimore, Maryland. Its parian work was first mentioned in December 1882, when a trade journal reported that a new building at the pottery had recently been completed, part of which would be devoted to "parian flower work."[21] A few months later, the same journal described the work as "new parian sprays of flowers mounted on a silk velvet panel," adding that it was "beautiful and cheap."[22]

Figure 29. Plaque of Robert Fulton, 1876. Designed and modeled by Isaac Broome, Ott and Brewer, Trenton, New Jersey. H. 11¼ in. (28.6 cm.), W. 8 in. (20.3 cm.). New Jersey State Museum, The Cybis Collection of American Porcelain (CH68.203)

The material itself was the subject of a later report: "The fine parian body . . . [has] a softness of tone which the delicate material alone can give."[23] The Chesapeake Pottery's talented artist in residence was a sculptor named James Priestman, about whom little is known. He is first mentioned in conjunction with the pottery in June 1883 as having come from Boston.[24] His entry in that year's Baltimore directory lists him as a carver. His preferred form of work seems to have been plaques devoted to designs in relief. Perhaps most noteworthy among them are the allegories of Day and Night (cat. no. 52), after marble reliefs created by Albert (Bertel) Thorvaldsen, Danish master of neoclassical sculpture.[25] Priestman also worked from life, as his most famous work (cat. no. 53), a cow and a bull in extremely high relief, proclaims.

Though the parian medium gradually fell from grace in the public favor, it was later to be utilized, first by the firm of Ott and Brewer, then by other potteries, to produce an American version of the ultrathin, glazed porcelain that had originated in Belleek, Ireland.

Centennial Porcelain (cat. nos. 54–66)

The Centennial Exposition, held in Philadelphia's Fairmount Park in 1876, was perhaps the single most important event in the development of American porcelain, for through the technical and artistic stimulus it provided, a national identity was forged. The objects produced by American factories for exhibition at the national celebration resurrected styles from the past and revitalized them in dynamic and adventurous ways. The ceramics of foreign exhibitors on view in Philadelphia were to influence the manner in which American porcelain would be designed and decorated throughout the remainder of the century.

Plans for the country's hundredth birthday party had begun several years in advance.[1] In 1871, a proposal for an "International Exhibition of Arts, Manufactures, and Products of the Soil and Mine," to honor the anniversary of America's independence, had been approved by Congress.[2] On 5 July 1873, representative foreign countries were formally invited to participate in the exhibition, which was intended to "illustrate the great advances attained, and the successes achieved, in the interest of progress and civilization during the century which will then have closed."[3]

The fair itself was a stupendous event. The vast range of exhibits distributed over a two-hundred-and-sixty-acre area comprised an extraordinary mélange from all over the world of works of art, examples of crafts, specimens of natural resources and agricultural products, as well as ethnographic displays. During the six months from 10 May 1876, when President Ulysses S. Grant officially opened the exposition, until November, when it closed, visitors included nearly ten million Americans enjoying their first panoramic view of the best products the world had to offer.[4]

The ceramics exhibits, numbering some hundred and fifty, were shown in the Main Exhibition Building, situated just inside the principal entrance and one of the fairground's largest structures. They consisted of all manner of earthenware, firebrick, terracotta, utilitarian porcelain, and fine porcelain. The displays, dominated by faience, majolica, and stoneware, but containing at least seventy-five booths of porcelains, varied widely in size and number of objects. Hector Tyndale of Philadelphia, one of the Centennial Exposition judges, writing the official report on the ceramics submitted, found the Japanese exhibit of "first-rate value," adding, "It constitutes the most important contribution to the Ceramic Department which has been brought together by any one country."[5] The Japanese porcelains were particularly remarkable for their perfection of potting technique and for their embellishment. Tyndale called their tours de force, which included large, flat slabs of decorated porcelain and vases eight feet in height, demonstrations "of the utmost dexterity in moulding, in evenness of line, and accuracy of contour of difficult and complicated forms."[6]

The porcelain exhibits from Europe and England were considered deficient in that some factories did not participate at all and those that did submitted wares that to critical eyes were not of great merit.[7] The French National Porcelain Manufactory at Sèvres sent only twenty vases, which were shown not with the ceramics displays but in the fine arts section. Nevertheless, some impressive examples from across the sea were available to the public view: the Königliche Preussische Porzellan-Manufaktur of Berlin, perhaps the sole German porcelain representative, sent several large vases and plaques generally ornamental in character.[8] European entrants that undoubtedly made a lasting impression on American makers were Jules Brianchon, of France, who showed his nacreous-glazed porcelains, and the Royal Copenhagen Porcelain Manufactory of Denmark, which displayed biscuit plaques after marbles by the Danish master Albert (Bertel) Thorvaldsen. Porcelains from England, while deemed technically excellent, were "not remarkable for originality of design."[9] Despite that faint praise, the richly decorated wares sent by the Worcester Royal Porcelain Works, the Minton factory, and the firm of A. and B. Daniell and Son would later prove to have left their mark on American design.

American ceramics manufacturers saw the Centennial Exposition as an opportunity to elevate the general quality of domestic wares and to abandon the mimicry of imported goods that plagued the industry. They realized that it would provide for the first time an international showcase for their wares.[10] To make the most of that opportunity, potters from around the country joined together in January 1875 to form the National Potters Association (later the United States Potters Association) for the purpose of furthering their industry's interests. At that first meeting, which was imbued with an overwhelming spirit of optimism, the primary concern was to encourage new, original designs, created specifically for their countrymen, that would unmistakably proclaim the "stamp of national character."[11] The makers felt that their wares already compared favorably in technique with those from abroad; they believed that consumers had been "using large quantities of American goods sold to them as of English manufacture" for some time.[12] Further, they resolved "that American potters shall make a fine display at the United States Centennial Exhibition, to exhibit to the world at large the extent to which the ceramic art has been carried by American manufacturers."[13] John Moses, president of the association, urged his colleagues on with the plea that they "make great exertions to bring such displays of ware to the Centennial Exhibition as would convince Americans that foreign articles should no longer be regarded as superior to those of American manufacture."[14]

Figure 30. James Carr's New York City Pottery exhibit at the Centennial Exposition, Philadelphia. Stereoscopic photograph, 1876. Library of Congress

Moses's call must have been heeded. When in spring 1876 the exposition gates opened, the American displays—the first great showing of native ceramics at any international or national exhibition—were of surprising magnitude. All the major centers (New York, Trenton, Philadelphia, and East Liverpool) were represented, and all their porcelains illustrated the "first-rate character of the natural materials to be found in the United States, and the laudable desire to utilize and to do justice to such materials on the part of the manufacturers."[15] Most of the displays focused on the improved quality

Figure 31. Bust of Ulysses S. Grant, 1876. Designed and modeled by W. H. Edge, James Carr's New York City Pottery. H. 18$\frac{9}{16}$ in. (47.2 cm.). The Metropolitan Museum of Art, Purchase, Anonymous Gift, 1968 (68.103.3)

noted in the manufacture of hotelwares, highly regarded by the critics for technical, if not artistic, excellence. As one contemporary writer put it: "What is known as the 'white granite' ware, so useful and detestable; thick, that it may resist the hostility of the Milesian maiden, clumsy because of that, without color or decoration of any kind, and cheap: can we expect or demand much?"[16]

Several of the participating firms made an exceptional effort to arrange their booths in an especially novel and exciting fashion and to have their wares express a definite national character. In the months and years prior to the Centennial, to design exhibition pieces that would lend prestige to their firms, James Carr's New York City Pottery, Thomas C. Smith's Union Porcelain Works, and the firm of Ott and Brewer employed the services of professional artists or sculptors. Those proprietors had been instrumental in forming the Potters Association, in which three of them held official posts: Carr as second vice president, Smith as treasurer, and Brewer as secretary. (Smith also served as chairman of the committee that assigned individual exhibitors space in the area allotted to the American ceramics industry.)

Carr hired the sculptor W. H. Edge to design special objects for his New York City Pottery display, which can be seen in a rare photograph (Fig. 30). With all the various kinds and grades of ware mixed up together, the booth has a haphazard, cluttered, and disorganized appearance to twentieth-century eyes. The artistic wares—brightly glazed majolica and the sculptural parians for which the firm was noted (though the judges considered the parian itself only fair)[17]—intermingle with a wide variety of hotelwares, such as the stacks of plates seen in the foreground. Four of the almost life-size, classically conceived parian busts can be identified: those of Christ, George Washington, Andrew Jackson, and Ulysses S. Grant seen from the back. General Grant, portrayed in his uniform, was an appropriate subject not just as a military hero but as president of the United States at the time (Fig. 31). A colored lithograph (Fig. 32) depicting a selection of the New York City Pottery's decorated wares appeared in one of the more lavish publications devoted to the Centennial exhibits, along with a description of Carr's role in the development of American porcelain.[18]

Figure 32. Lithograph illustration of James Carr's Centennial ceramics, published in *Treasures of Art, Industry and Manufactures Represented in the American Exhibition at Philadelphia 1876*, ed. by C. B. Norton (Buffalo, N.Y., 1877), pl. 50

The display of the Union Porcelain Works, of Greenpoint, New York, though not described in great detail in the Centennial press and not awarded any prize, contained many original works of art (cat. nos. 58–66). Several of them were very large in scale—notably a pair of pedestals decorated in relief with episodes from the story of Electra and a pair of large Century vases, each covered with a profusion of historical scenes and novel combinations of patriotic motifs in relief. Those objects must have offered a startling contrast to the white tablewares and hardware trimmings that were the firm's staple production. Another vase, incorporating many of the Century vases' design ideas and probably also exhibited in 1876, was the firm's Kéramos vase. Its name and its decoration, the latter portrayed in narrative format, were inspired by Henry Wadsworth Longfellow's recent poem exalting the ceramic art. The Kéramos vase does not survive, but an engraving of it was published in a period history of ceramics.[19] Possibly its prototype or perhaps another version of it is a vase that has only recently come to light (Fig. 33). The panels on its lower section contain relief vignettes personifying three important periods in the history of ceramic

Figure 33. Vase, ca. 1876. Union Porcelain Works, Greenpoint (Brooklyn), New York. H. 13½ in. (34 cm.). Collection of R. A. Ellison

Figure 34. Parian objects in Ott & Brewer's display at the American Institute Fair, New York City. Photograph, 1877. Collection of Edith Shields Kersey

art: a potter of Egypt, a potter of Greece, and a modern industrial worker.

Trenton, which was represented by as many as twenty factories, made the strongest showing at Philadelphia. Of the Trenton exhibits, that of the firm operated by Joseph Ott and John Hart Brewer was the most spectacular. The creative talent responsible for its success, its parians especially, was Isaac Broome, a sculptor who had been hired in 1873, long before the fair opened. Of Ott and Brewer's "Parian figures, vases, busts, plaques in relief, and toilet-wares," Judge Tyndale wrote that some of them were "commendable for design, especially the plaques, modeled by Broome, which show graceful conceptions of figures."[20] The two most remarkable objects Broome designed and modeled for the fair were a pair of covered vases, on pedestals of creamy white parian (cat. no. 54), in celebration of baseball, America's national sport. The critic for a contemporary periodical, while claiming that most of the American ceramic objects displayed were copies, praised the baseball vases for their originality: "On the other hand, the base-ball vase and plaques of Ott and Brewer are fine models of creative power."[21] Ceramics historian Jennie J. Young, reporting on the firm, discovered there the "first glimmerings of what may be called an art, in the studio of Mr. Isaac Broome."[22]

Presumably less imposing were the porcelains exhibited by other American firms, though Joseph H. Moore, also of Trenton, was mentioned favorably in a Centennial review for his "highly meritorious figures in Parian, and a framed panel (under glass) in which flowers have been modelled with rare fidelity in biscuit porcelain."[23] None of his factory's objects is known to have survived.

An exhibition held in the same year as the Centennial celebration, though of shorter duration, was sponsored by the American Institute in New York City. Many of the potteries sent to it duplicates of their Centennial objects. While it did not receive the publicity or renown accorded the Philadelphia event, industry members found it more advantageous. The following year, the American Institute Fair provided a setting for the wares that had not been sold in Philadelphia or that were uncompleted when the Centennial Exposition closed. There, Ott and Brewer are known to have exhibited Broome's sensational *Cleopatra* (cat. no. 56) among a group of objects that included many parians the firm had also displayed in Philadelphia (Fig. 34).

In spite of the valiant efforts (and in some cases extraordinary originality) on the part of the nation's potters, American objects shown at the Centennial Exposition did not attract the attention that the makers had hoped for, nor did they receive particularly favorable reviews in the newspapers and periodicals of the day. One critic found the American contribution merely "creditable on the whole, but [it] does not compare with the display made by either of the leading European nations, or by China or Japan."[24] A writer for the *Boston Herald*, judging the display of American porcelain "so poor as not to be noticeable artistically," could only wonder at such "rapid progress that there is any display at all."[25] In view of the comparative youth of the domestic industry, there is little question that the American objects, when seen in conjunction with the porcelains produced at European factories, would appear less accomplished. Nonetheless, the American firms deserve credit for their fidelity to the principles espoused by the men who established the National Potters Association: they had not copied the fashionable European wares and they *had* tried to develop an individual American style. One of the few kind reviews of American goods, speaking of the Union Porcelain Works exhibit, declared: "This style of decorating goods is just what we have advocated. Let American manufacturers make their own designs and leave off copying foreign ones!"[26]

Though the Centennial Exposition had afforded American factories their first international audience, it had also exposed their shortcomings. Its effect on the domestic porcelain industry was therefore mixed. While the potters had the satisfaction of knowing that their technique could hold its own with that of their European contemporaries, technical prowess was clearly not enough. The overwhelming critical opinion that American porcelains were basically inartistic discouraged many factories from pursuing a national character in their production, impelling them instead to follow foreign-made counterparts even more closely. In the decades that followed the Centennial, the potteries' technical achievements rose to even greater heights, but their decoration reverted to reiterations of the prevailing styles. Nevertheless, the benefits of the Centennial far outweighed the detriments. The event had served as the goal that potters had striven to reach, surpassing their own limitations and creating the most original porcelains ever made in America in the attempt. At domestic factories specializing in utilitarian wares, it had planted the seeds of more artistic lines that would take root and blossom in the future. Perhaps most important of all, it had been a cogent demonstration to the rest of the planet of America's immense natural resources, wealth, and inventiveness.

Belleek
(cat. nos. 67–82)

Belleek is a form of parian (a porcelain of marble-like texture containing a large proportion of feldspar) and is usually discussed with that medium in any study of porcelain. Because the story of Belleek is one of the greatest successes in the history of American ceramics and because its development can be viewed as a separate phase in the growth of the porcelain industry, it is accorded a section of its own in this catalogue.

Belleek is a light, exquisitely thin, ivory-colored porcelain body originally made from clay indigenous to the British Isles and endowed with a smooth, pearly glaze that was the discovery of the French chemist Jules J. H. Brianchon. The body and the glaze were first combined in the Irish town of Belleek, hence the name. Except for the medium's most famous achievements—its hand-constructed baskets and flowers—Belleek objects, like parians, are formed by slip-casting in molds so porous that they absorb a high degree of moisture, thereby substantially reducing the thickness of the form. The felicitous result is a porcelain exceedingly thin, finely detailed, and light in weight, which, when finished with its characteristic glaze, sometimes virtually colorless, sometimes having a pearly or tinted luster, accounts for Belleek's distinctive appearance.

The origins of Belleek can be traced to the Ivory Porcelain that the Worcester Royal Porcelain Works showed at the London Crystal Palace Exhibition in 1851 and continued to produce well into the 1890s. The development of actual Belleek began in Ireland when John Caldwell Bloomfield discovered deposits of china clay and feldspar on his ancestral estate, in the county of Fermanagh on the Lower Erne River. In 1853, Bloomfield had samples of the clay tested at the Worcester Royal Porcelain Works factory, perhaps through his acquaintance with the architect Robert Williams Armstrong, who was at one time associated with the porcelain works. After successful firings at Worcester, Bloomfield and Armstrong sought financial support from an affluent Dublin merchant named David McBirney with which to establish a manufactory for utilizing the clay. McBirney's response, a considerable investment, led to the opening in 1857 of D. McBirney and Company (later called the Belleek Pottery) in the Irish town, with Armstrong serving as manager and art director. In 1863, after a few years of making earthenware of unknown quantity and quality, Armstrong chose to inaugurate the manufacture of porcelain. To operate successfully in a country that had no porcelain-making tradition, he hired artisans from England's major potting centers, including Worcester and Stoke-on-Trent. Among the Stoke-on-Trent workmen was William Bromley, Sr., who had been a foreman at the William H. Goss factory (and who was later to become a key player in the story of American Belleek).[1] Under Bromley's supervision, the pottery developed a highly refined porcelain clay body from local materials.

The firm experimented constantly to perfect the ultrathin porcelain that is today recognized universally as Belleek. Just when the partnership of Armstrong and McBirney bought the rights to the process known as *décors de couleurs nacrée* (the characteristic Belleek glaze) is unknown, but its patent had been registered in France in 1857. The pearly glaze, achieved by mixing resin, oil of lavender, and salts of bismuth, possesses the iridescence found on the inside of a seashell.

The McBirney company specialized in the production of shapes that were eminently suitable to the porcelain's body and glaze, with marine themes—various species of shells, coral, and sea creatures—predominating. Belleek lent itself to piercing and perforation and the formation of delicate, hand-worked flora and fauna, and also provided an ideal surface for overglaze decoration in polychrome enamels and gold relief. Beginning in the mid-1860s, as the company's reputation became more and more renowned internationally, its Belleek began to enjoy the patronage of members of the British royal family and the nobility.

Americans were admiring Irish Belleek objects as early as 1869. In May of that year, in a lengthy discourse on the pottery's history and wares published in London's *Art Journal*, the unnamed writer mentioned that "trade with America is already large, and is regularly increasing."[2] By the 1870s, Belleek was being sold in the United States through many of the finer china stores, including Tiffany and Company of New York (Fig. 35), and the appreciation shared by a few knowledgeable collectors spread to large numbers of the general public. In 1876, Brianchon's nacreous porcelain was exhibited in Philadelphia at the Centennial Exposition; in 1878, specimens from the Belleek Pottery were accorded immense acclaim at the Exposition Universelle in Paris. That same year, the press remarked on its popularity: "In whatever form it is offered, the extraordinary beauty of the hues reflected or incorporated in it make it most charmingly attractive to the eye. It will certainly become

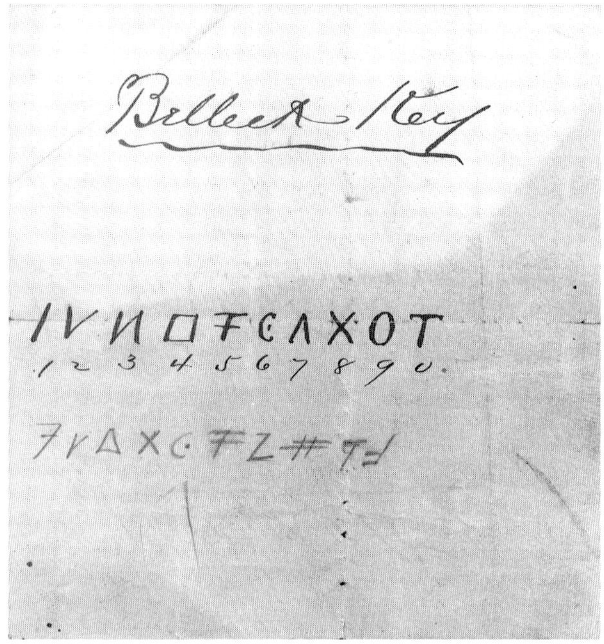

Figure 36. Belleek Key, ca. 1882–1900. Ink and pencil on paper, 4 × 4½ in. (10.2 × 10.5 cm.). New Jersey State Museum, Gift of the Family of the late Frank Trezza (CH85.33.17)

popular . . . it is said to be strong compared to the general run of delicate wares. But it must be seen to be appreciated, being really too pretty to be aptly described."[3] When *The Ceramic Art*, an anthology of world ceramics, was published in 1879, author Jennie J. Young praised the porcelain made in Belleek as "carefully and artistically wrought into ornamental pieces and services," noting that it had been "received with considerable favor both here and in Canada."[4]

During the 1880s, several American potteries took up the challenge of producing an eggshell porcelain that would rival Ireland's Belleek. Since some of the firms were already manufacturing a parian body to use primarily for sculptural designs, they had the means at hand. Despite constant experimentation, however, no American manufacturer succeeded in producing Belleek porcelain until he had hired skilled workmen who had been employed in one capacity or another at the Irish Belleek factory. Just as English artisans had been enticed in the 1860s to McBirney's factory in Belleek—a remote and underdeveloped region—by the prospect of commercial rewards, so in the 1880s craftsmen from Ireland were lured to the city of Trenton (to them just as distant and unknown a place) by the prospect of a more successful life.[5] William Bromley, Sr., was the most important of those experts.[6] Others who would contribute to the endeavor included the junior William Bromley, John Bromley, Thomas Connelly, Joshua Poole, William T. Morris, Francis R. Willmore, Samuel D. Oliphant, and Samuel's sons Richard, Hughes, and Henry.[7] Though the Belleek formula was a closely guarded secret, efforts to discover it continued unabated, for the first pottery to produce an American Belleek would reap the harvest of great artistic prestige and economic gain. Nevertheless, it was not until 1882 that eggshell porcelain was introduced by the firm of Ott and Brewer, and it would be almost five years more before another American pottery, the Willets Manufacturing Company, developed it. One American factory is known to have recorded its Belleek formula in code: a piece of paper, much creased and worn from having been folded and unfolded many times and probably concealed in a foreman's pocket, is headed "Belleek Key." It lists numbers one through zero, each with a corresponding symbol, which would translate into how many units of each ingredient to use in mixing the clay (Fig. 36).[8]

Unlike the porcelains made in earlier decades by such firms as Charles Cartlidge and Company in

Figure 35. Engraved illustration of two Irish Belleek shell dishes, published in Jennie J. Young, *The Ceramic Art: A Compendium of the History and Manufacture of Pottery and Porcelain* (New York: Harper & Brothers, 1879), p. 389

Greenpoint, New York, and the United States Pottery Company in Bennington, Vermont, primarily for a clientele of middle-class tradesmen, American Belleek products were highly prized by the country's consumer elite. Ott and Brewer Belleek was obtainable only at the most fashionable dealers in china and glass, including Tiffany and Company and Black, Starr and Frost in New York, Shreve, Crump and Low and French's in Boston, and Caldwell's in Philadelphia.[9] At each shop, the American products were sold alongside artwares from Ireland, England, France, and Austria. As one reporter noted: "American art in pottery has come into the front rank and need never again have anything to fear from foreign competition."[10]

The Ott and Brewer factory made its Belleek entirely of American materials. The firm had a line of fine ivory-colored porcelain in production during the late 1870s, the period in which it was struggling with experiments that would yield the coveted Belleek formula. By June 1881, according to a period trade journal, probably referring to Ott and Brewer, "an attempt is now being made in this country to produce a grade of fine and delicate porcelain similar to that made at the Belleek Pottery, near Fermanagh, Ireland . . . the parties are in a fair way to succeed; and we hope to be able to chronicle the perfection in this country of this class of goods."[11] By the end of the year, a reporter for the same journal had been shown specimens that prompted him to say that the makers (that time identified as Ott and Brewer) had "succeeded admirably in producing a beautiful body and glaze, which gives all of the fine details of the Belleek goods."[12] With the arrival of William Bromley, Jr., from the Irish Belleek factory, Ott and Brewer went into production in late February or early March of 1882.[13] The following year, the senior William Bromley crossed the Atlantic to work for Ott and Brewer, bringing with him John, another of his sons, and two or three workmen.[14]

In June 1883, the firm announced an extensive range of Belleek: "Among the articles now manufactured are exquisite flower baskets, dainty after-dinner coffees, tete-a-tete services . . . condiment sets, fancy olive shells, and delicate teas and saucers for regular use."[15] Other forms it produced, many of them based on Irish or English prototypes, were potpourri jars (Fig. 37), a hive-shaped honey pot, and a flower stand "made in joints of bamboo" and decorated in rich gold and bronze,[16] this last reflecting the vogue for Japanese designs then at its height.

The new Belleek made its debut in Boston in September 1883 at a fair titled "America Against the World." The company relished the opportunity to display its eggshell-thin objects, designed by both American and foreign artisans, which equaled the Irish counterparts and, in the opinion of some critics, even surpassed them. The event received wide coverage in the press. A reporter for the *Crockery and Glass Journal* lauded the American Belleek for its delicacy of style, its durability, and its cost, much lower than that of the Irish ware. The firm showed its Belleek at all prominent exhibitions of the day—the World's Industrial and Cotton Centennial Exhibition in New Orleans in 1884–85, the Philadelphia Exhibition of Art Industry in 1889, to name just two.

Ott and Brewer, until then known chiefly for its utilitarian hotel china production, gained immeasurable distinction from its new art line. Its Belleek was of undisputed quality, though it was criticized for following too closely after Irish wares, in some cases virtually copying them in form or decoration. One example, a shell dish supported by tiny periwinkle feet (Fig. 38), all but duplicates its Irish prototype (see Fig. 35). By 1889, when the Exhibition of Art Industry (a trade show that featured the products of numerous Trenton potteries) was held at Philadelphia's Memorial Hall, the firm had begun to make more original shapes. A lengthy description of its display, which was awarded a gold medal, read in part: "It is true that their first efforts in this line were duplicates of the few pieces then in the country of the famous Irish Belleek, but a glance at their display at Philadelphia will convince anyone at all acquainted with the art that they have improved and beautified this class of goods to a wonderful extent."[17] Some of the objects, as one pitcher demonstrates (Fig. 39), feature Japanesque shapes and

Figure 37. Covered potpourri jar, ca. 1883–90. Ott and Brewer, Trenton, New Jersey. H. 6¼ in. (15.9 cm.). Private collection

decoration that appear exceedingly contemporary to the modern viewer.

The showing in Philadelphia so impressed the buyer for Tiffany and Company that he ordered the entire Ott and Brewer display to sell in the renowned New York shop, an action remarked on as "more than an ordinary compliment, as it brings with it the substantial appreciation of one of the highest authorities in this country on fine modern porcelains."[18] Even in 1889, when several Trenton factories were offering Belleek lines, Ott and Brewer was still the acknowledged leader in its manufacture.[19] The firm continued to market the fine porcelain until it went into receivership and ceased production in 1893. The quality of its work had remained consistently high for a decade, and it had had almost five unchallenged years as the sole American manufacturer of Belleek porcelain. The pottery, purchased by Charles Howell Cook the following year and reorganized as the Cook Pottery Company,[20] went on making objects in Belleek, some of them replicas of Ott and Brewer shapes and undoubtedly produced from Ott and Brewer molds.

In about 1886, Thomas Connelly, formerly of the Irish factory, began to experiment with the manufacture of Belleek at the Delaware Pottery in Trenton, which had been founded about three years earlier by Samuel D. Oliphant, another Irish worker, and three of his sons.[21] Although Connelly succeeded in producing what was considered some "exquisitely thin trial pieces of the finest grade,"[22] he never made his porcelain in any commercial quantity and he soon discontinued its production.

In March 1887, the Willets Manufacturing Company, also of Trenton, introduced what it called Willets Art Porcelain[e], described in a period trade journal as "a body and glaze of the delicate egg-shell class of porcelain, which is growing in appreciation among a large class of people in this country."[23] Like Ott and Brewer, the Willets factory maintained a steady production of whiteware (a heavy, coarse white ceramic also referred to as graniteware), primarily intended for hotel dinnerware and washstand vessels. In 1884, Walter Scott Lenox, who had previously been head of Ott and Brewer's decorating department, assumed the same post at the Willets works. Perhaps at the suggestion of Lenox, who is credited with having encouraged the firm to produce a finer line of ceramics, Willets began production of what was being called "hard porcelain" by 1886.[24] In the interim, William Bromley, Jr., had been hired away from Ott and Brewer and had brought with him his formula for Belleek. The earliest documented piece of Willets Belleek, now in the Archives of Lenox China, is a pitcher in the shape of a nautilus shell with a putto perched on its ribbon handle. On its base is the inscription "WB/May 4th 1887/WSL." (For a similar version, see cat. no. 72.) Of the many new designs introduced by the Willets factory, notable examples highly derivative of Irish Belleek are delicate woven baskets and oval picture or mirror frames decorated with tiny naturalistic flowers in high relief (cat. nos. 73, 74).

Figure 38. Footed shell dish, ca. 1883–90. Ott and Brewer, Trenton, New Jersey. H. 2 in. (5.1 cm.), W. 4 in. (10.2 cm.). New Jersey State Museum, The Cybis Collection of American Porcelain (CH71.356)

In 1888, with an economic blight affecting the country, the pottery industry suffered severe reverses. In an effort to retrench, the Willets firm suspended production of its Belleek and, at the end of the year, reorganized the factory. Probably as a result, Lenox resigned. Having learned the ropes in all branches of the business at both Ott and Brewer and Willets, he may have been harboring the idea of starting his own porcelain works for some time. The efforts at both Trenton firms had been instrumental in the successful production of American Belleek porcelain and had fostered in the domestic consumer the desire for a native product. Lenox continued that tradition in Trenton from 1889, when, with his partner, Jonathan Coxon, Sr. (a former superintendent at Ott and Brewer), he founded the Ceramic Art Company for the purpose of producing a "fine grade of porcelain in the Belleek and Sevres styles."[25]

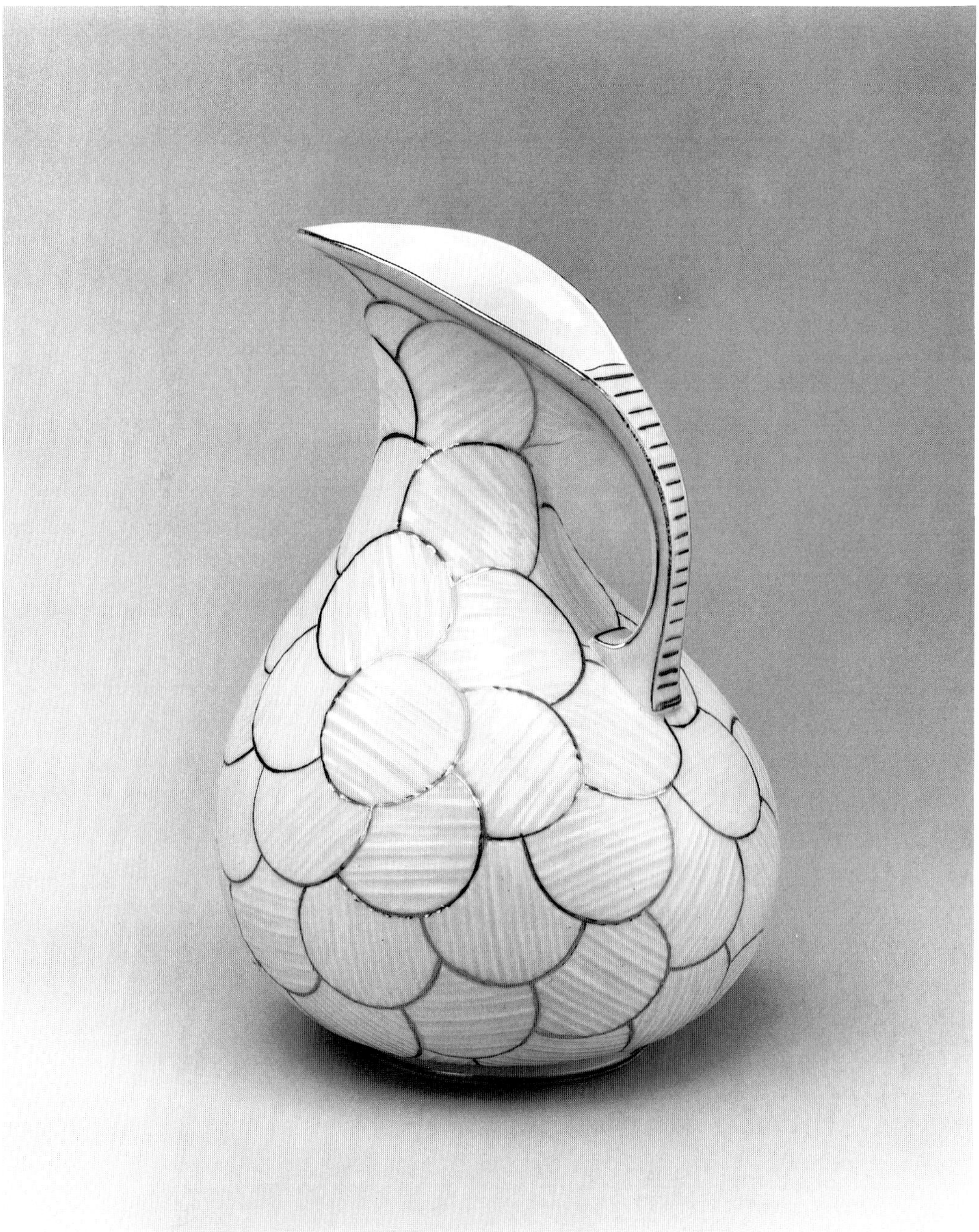

Figure 39. Pitcher, ca. 1883–90. Ott and Brewer, Trenton, New Jersey. H. 6 7/16 in. (16.4 cm.). Collection of Florence I. Balasny-Barnes

The primary difference between the other manufacturers of fine eggshell porcelain, who all made and sold large quantities of white graniteware and cream-colored hotelware, and the new Ceramic Art Company was that Lenox and Coxon set out with the sole intent of producing an art line. They kept their factory to a modest size, designed to employ only fifty persons, including molders, modelers, designers, and decorators.[26] The effect was that of an artist's atelier, especially when compared with the company's larger, more industrial neighbors. One visitor described the plant as "more like the studio of an artist than the real, live working pottery that it is."[27]

The company prided itself on the delicate texture of its clay body, the originality of its forms, and the artistic character of its rich decoration. It had an impressive roster of artists, of English or European descent for the most part, though in its first months of existence, Lenox, aware of the immense popularity of oriental objects that had swept the country in the wake of the Aesthetic movement, was shrewd enough to employ a Japanese.[28] With the successful production of a fine paste and a clear, colorless glaze of superior quality well under way, the firm turned its attention to decoration, made irresistible to professionals and amateurs alike by the immensely inviting Belleek surface. The Ceramic Art Company was among the first American porcelain factories to have its artists sign the objects they had painted. The company carried its emphasis on painted decoration even to its own mark, one version consisting of its conjoined initials and a palette and brushes, which appeared on many objects the factory turned out.

In the early 1890s, with the advent of eggshell-thin porcelain production in several other American factories, the Ceramic Art Company and the Willets firm, which had resumed its Belleek manufacture, met with tough competition. Though in business for only about four years, the American Art China Company, established by the partnership of John C. Rittenhouse and George Evans in Trenton in 1891, was producing excellent Belleek wares. The firm's few surviving products are superb examples of an exceedingly thin-walled body, much of it with hand-painted decoration of an unusually delicate nature (cat. no. 81).[29]

The Columbian Art Pottery was founded in 1892 in Trenton. It was named for the World's Columbian Exposition, held in Chicago the following year, where it exhibited objects it had produced in anticipation of that event. The excellence of its pieces can be attributed to the experience and expertise of its two proprietors, William T. Morris and Francis R. Willmore, both English and both former workers at the Worcester Royal Porcelain Works. (Morris had also been employed at Ireland's Belleek factory.) In America, they had been hired by Ott and Brewer in the 1880s, when the firm was Trenton's leading manufacturer of Belleek. The Columbian Art Pottery made a line of souvenir items that included transfer-decorated mugs and a Liberty Bell made of the smooth Belleek body. It also produced tea sets, some duplicating Irish counterparts, others in the exuberant Rococo-revival style (Fig. 40). A small number of surviving vases, pitchers, and tea vessels demonstrate the firm's facility in using its ultra-smooth Belleek surface for skillfully painted figural and landscape decoration in the fashion found on late-nineteenth-century European porcelain (cat. no. 82).

Trenton's greatest rival as a center of Belleek manufacture was East Liverpool, Ohio. Situated on the banks of the Ohio River, which provided necessary transportation routes, the city was rich in clay and coal, materials essential to the manufacture of pottery. From its earliest days, in the 1840s, its ceramics industry was based on English factory practices and manned by English workers. The factory founded in 1854 by Isaac Watts Knowles, which was to become incorporated as Knowles, Taylor and Knowles in 1870, when John N. Taylor and Homer S. Knowles bought into the company, was the first pottery in the American Midwest to develop a Belleek porcelain and to market it successfully.[30] After enjoying a thriving trade in yellow earthenware throughout the 1860s and 1870s, it fired its first kiln of whiteware in 1872. The whiteware soon became a staple product that rivaled the

Figure 40. Tea set, 1893–1900. Columbian Art Pottery (Morris and Willmore), Trenton, New Jersey. H. teapot, 7 in. (17.8 cm.), sugar bowl, 4½ in. (11.4 cm.), cream pitcher, 4 in. (10.2 cm.). New Jersey State Museum (CH70.110.1–3)

hotel china being produced in the East. In 1888, probably motivated by the publicity that Ott and Brewer and Willets were garnering for their Belleek, Knowles, Taylor and Knowles constructed a new plant for the production of porcelain. The medium had not been made in East Liverpool since about 1862, during the brief life of William Bloor's factory, and knowledge of the process was not readily available. Sometime in late 1888 or early 1889, Joshua Poole, a former manager of the Irish Belleek Pottery, joined the firm and supervised the production of its first eggshell porcelain, which was announced in January 1889.[31] The specimens, exceedingly thin and creamy in color, were largely based on Irish examples, some of them even replicating the nacreous glaze. The firm was destined to produce very little Belleek, for only nine months after it had seen its kiln's first draw, the factory burned to the ground.

Though the plant was rebuilt in the spring of 1890, Knowles, Taylor and Knowles did not resume manufacture of its creamy Belleek, but instead began to make a completely different kind of porcelain that was to compete with the Belleek of Trenton firms. The new line, which the firm named Lotus Ware, matched in quality the exceptional bone-china wares then being produced in England and Europe. The decoration, in white clay relief, sometimes incorporating elaborate, often profuse quantities of flowers, leaves, and filigree, all worked and applied by hand, bestowed on the objects a highly distinctive appearance. The factory also introduced different colored bodies, such as olive or celadon green, which contributed to the exotic effect. To enhance the appeal of its ornamental wares, the firm gave them names that conjured up visions of ancient worlds: Arcanian, Cremonian, Etruscan, Parmian, Thebian, and Umbrian.[32] Because the highly ornamental nature of the line required much handwork, Lotus Ware proved too costly to be economically feasible, and its production was discontinued about 1897.

Although the glorious heyday of American Belleek was over, the production of the actual porcelain body was maintained in one form or another, at one center or another, until after the Second World War.[33] Even today, it lives on as the basis of the fine porcelain the Lenox firm continues to make.

The Post-Centennial Decades (cat. nos. 83–100)

The production of artistic wares begun by American porcelain factories at the time of the Centennial Exposition became a virtual requirement for the manufacturers' success. After 1876, when great exhibitions began to grow in number, companies had more frequent opportunities to display their artistic lines, not only internationally, as in Paris at the Exposition Universelle of 1878, but also domestically (perhaps even more important to the American porcelain industry), at the American Exhibition of the Products, Arts and Manufactures of Foreign Nations of 1883 in Boston, the World's Industrial and Cotton Centennial Exhibition of 1884–85 in New Orleans, the World's Columbian Exposition of 1893 in Chicago, and the Louisiana Purchase Exposition of 1904 in Saint Louis. Those fairs introduced American-made products to a wide audience and also gave visitors the opportunity to become acquainted with the best European workmanship, an influence that would pervade the rest of the century. In the same era, Trenton led American factories in the production of fine porcelain artwares and tablewares, which, with the growing prosperity of the middle class, were finding a wide market. The industry was also making inroads in the upper-class trade, a progress reflecting the growing fashion for formal dining. In the last quarter of the century, many Americans had become affluent enough to afford luxury and service previously beyond their means. Dining, now a social art, developed its own set of rituals, etiquette, and equipage, calling for special kinds of tablewares and dictating the manner in which they were used, mostly in emulation of habitudes already observed across the Atlantic.

Porcelain factories at home and abroad had begun by mid-century to meet the demand for tablewares that widened in range as the century progressed: extensive dinner services with specially designed sets for separate courses, such as fish and dessert; tea sets; after-dinner coffee sets; individual breakfast sets; and a wide variety of serving pieces.[1] Increasingly popular was the use of the ornately decorated service plates that ensured that guests' places at table would never be bare. These, one of the specialties of the Ceramic Art Company, were to become renowned in the days of its successor firm, Lenox, Incorporated. Some forms were developed to accommodate newly cultivated tastes. Porcelain oyster plates, accompanied by appropriate silver or plated forks and serving pieces, belong in that category (Fig. 41). They presented the delicacy that was frequently the first of a formal dinner's many courses, as the engraved, individual menu cards that were a custom of the time record.

Instead of pursuing the individuality and American character that had been the hallmark of many Centennial exhibits, potteries fell back on their old adherence to imported styles, still preferred by most Americans. The eggshell-thin medium copied from Irish Belleek was one indication of that tendency; other evidence is found in the domestic factories' mimicking of elaborately decorated porcelains from England, France, Austria, and Germany. The period's emphasis on the artistic integrity of every household object, from the plates from which one ate to the cups from which one drank, was the bequest of the Aesthetic movement of the 1870s and 1880s. Except for one company, artwares were a supplemental production at factories, where they were made in limited quantities, at greater expense, and sold at much higher prices. Their value was the prestige they added to the firms' names, but when a company's economic stability was threatened, the art line was the first to be dropped.[2]

From the mid-1890s through the first two decades of the twentieth century, the relatively small pottery founded in Trenton in 1889 by Walter Scott Lenox and Jonathan Coxon, Sr., became the leader in the area of fine commercial art porcelains.[3] The production of their Ceramic Art Company was at first restricted to artwares, which the firm made in an ivory-colored Belleek body. About 1902, it went on to develop a white bone-china body for its dinnerware. The intended market was the social elite, and the firm sold its products only through illustrious shops, Tiffany and Company of New York and Bailey, Banks and Biddle of Philadelphia among them. In the introduction to the Ceramic Art Company's first catalogue, in 1891, the proprietors stated that their "aim and ambition was to create a class of artistic ceramics that would merit the distinction of high esteem, in that they might

Figure 41. Oyster plate, 1881. Union Porcelain Works, Greenpoint (Brooklyn), New York. L. 8½ in. (21.6 cm.), W. 6½ in. (16.5 cm.). "Pat. Jan. 4–1881" and "Tiffany & Co/New York" appear among the marks on the bottom. The Metropolitan Museum of Art, Purchase, Anonymous Gift, 1968 (68.99.2)

Figure 42. Decorating shop at the Ceramic Art Company, from the company catalogue of 1897, p. 20. Archives of Lenox China

be treasured, not only for their beauty and present worth, but for their prospective value to posterity as legitimate works of art."[4] Designed for their wealthy clients were the handsomely decorated service plates that the firm specialized in in the early 1900s, their retail prices rising from two hundred dollars a dozen for examples adorned with a simple monogram and gold border to five hundred dollars a dozen and upward for more lavishly painted versions.[5]

Painted decoration was the primary ornament, often used to such an extent that a form's white porcelain body was completely obscured. Vases and plates were covered with floral, figural, scenic, or other designs, often complemented with elaborate gilding. The period's stylistic eclecticism was a reflection of the differing backgrounds of the decorators employed by the factories. As the Ceramic Art Company proclaimed in its catalogue of 1891: "The organization of our corps of professional decorators is broadly cosmopolitan in its character, including, as it does, highly trained ceramic artists from England, France, Germany, and Japan, and the best available native talent."[6] Presumably, the decorators (Fig. 42) were paid by the piece, a method of compensation practiced in English factories. Because the artists who painted them signed many of the works made by Lenox's company, their nationalities can be determined, as can the sources of the imported styles.

Porcelains produced in England at Minton, Worcester, or Derby, which borrowed their decoration from Near and Far Eastern shapes, motifs, and compositions, were consciously imitated by American potteries (Fig. 43). Jeweled effects, particularly prized abroad, were produced at several domestic factories. Occasionally, the effect derived from an actual object, as the jeweled gold chain on a teacup and saucer made by the Union Porcelain Works shows (Fig. 44). The style for naturalistically painted figures and flowers executed so successfully in Great Britain was also popular in America. The strong allegiance to England still visible in domestic porcelain of the period can be attributed to the large number of English workers and decorators who thrived in American factories beginning in the 1850s. The best-known English decorators working for the Ceramic Art Company were Wil-

Figure 43. William Tams, Greenwood Pottery Company, Trenton, New Jersey. Design drawing for a Japanesque cup, ca. 1883–86. Pencil on paper, 6⅛ × 6½ in. (15.6 × 16.5 cm.). New Jersey State Museum, Gift of Mrs. Arthur K. Twitchell in memory of her grandfather William Henry Tams and her father, James Elmore Moffett Tams (CH79.1.52i)

Figure 44. Cup and saucer, 1876–85. Union Porcelain Works, Greenpoint (Brooklyn), New York. H. cup, 1 15/16 in. (4.9 cm.); Diam. saucer, 4 3/4 in. (12.1 cm.). Private collection

liam H. Morley (cat. nos. 93, 98) and his brother George. The interest in oriental designs dating to the mid-1870s prevailed through subsequent decades. Apparently, two Japanese artists—Fouji and M. Tekauchi—were employed at the company during the early 1890s.

In the late 1890s and early 1900s, a new breed of highly skilled potters and decorators emigrated from Europe's porcelain factories. Under Lenox's supervision, the years from about 1897 until 1905 were a scintillating period for porcelain decoration at his firm. The works its decorators produced and ornamented vied in technical excellence with those of their transatlantic colleagues, though the lack of originality reflected the American preference for the same type of conservative compositions that had been popular since the early 1800s. Of the European decorators identified as having worked at that time for Lenox, the best known are Bruno Geyer from Austria, Hans Nosek from Czechoslovakia, and Antonin Heidrich and Sigmund Wirkner from Germany.[8] In addition to painting for Lenox, probably on a free-lance basis, some of them may also have decorated imported blanks (plain porcelain forms) and sold them on their own. In keeping with their European heritage, they specialized in figural work, copying academic oil paintings onto porcelains whose entire surfaces were then covered with opaque enamels. A porcelain plaque, brilliantly decorated with a scene of Venus and Tannhäuser (Fig. 45), was painted on a German blank by Wirkner.[9] It is documented to him by a surviving bill, which reads: "Trenton N.J. October 10th 1899/Mr. Walter Henry Heidweller/to Sigmund Wirkner/Picture on China, 'Tannhauser' $100—/Received Payment/Sigmund Wirkner."[10] The flawless execution of the plaque is a testament to the artistry of the men employed at Trenton in those days. Wirkner's

Figure 45. Sigmund Wirkner. Venus and Tannhäuser plaque, 1899. Decorated in Trenton, New Jersey, on blank made by the Imperial Porcelain Manufactory, Berlin, Germany. H. 11¼ in. (28.6 cm.), W. 13⅜ in. (34 cm.). Collection of Arthur V. Colletti

choice of subject matter afforded him an incomparable opportunity to exhibit his ability to render in an exemplary manner various fabrics, surfaces, and textures.[11]

The period following the Centennial witnessed the nationwide phenomenon of the amateur china decorator, most of them women, whose ranks increased by the thousands in the next decades. China painting, as it was called, enabled the women to express their artistic ideas in their own homes or in small workshops. In quality, their work varied widely, though numerous handbooks and trade-magazine articles provided instruction. The social aspect of the pastime centered around classes sponsored by the decorative-arts societies then springing up in towns and cities throughout the United States.[12] Domestic porcelain factories, notably the Willets Manufacturing Company and the Ceramic Art Company, competed with Continental firms to sell porcelain blanks to those dedicated amateurs. In 1890, advertisements Willets published in a popular period trade journal promoted the virtues of its porcelain blanks: "The Willets White Art Porcelaine for amateur decorations has an established reputation for beauty and elegance."[13] In 1891, the Ceramic Art Company also claimed that its china-painters' wares were highly meritorious: "The unique character of the forms designed by our modelers provides the widest possible scope for original work on the part of the amateur, and yet presents surfaces of low relief in such a manner that the gilding of the amateur may be made to greatly enhance the value of the finished result."[14] The trade in china-painting materials remained brisk well into the twentieth century.

A new fashion for earthenwares and porcelains with painted decoration in monochrome blue, in evocation of the Dutch delft of earlier centuries, came into vogue about the mid-1890s. Imitations were being imported and in America copies were being made in mediums as diverse as coarse earthenware and fine porcelain. The Cook Pottery in Trenton and the Ceramic Art Company were among the several domestic factories that produced versions of delftware in porcelain to meet the growing demand.[15]

Dominating signed porcelains from the end of the old century into the early decades of the new were special-order pieces and artwares made in specific historical styles. At Lenox's firm, beginning with the development of its bone china about 1902, tablewares made of the new body became a major part of the factory's production. The creamy Belleek was maintained as an art line, but about 1910, Lenox began to use it for dinnerware as well. Responsibility for decoration shifted from the professional china painter to the designer, with artisans performing the specialized tasks of executing raised paste work, and enameling and gilding. The altered method meant that instead of producing a number of unique objects the firm could now fabricate a design in multiple quantities. Some of the Lenox shapes and their overglaze painted and gilded decoration reflected the Art-Nouveau style then sweep-

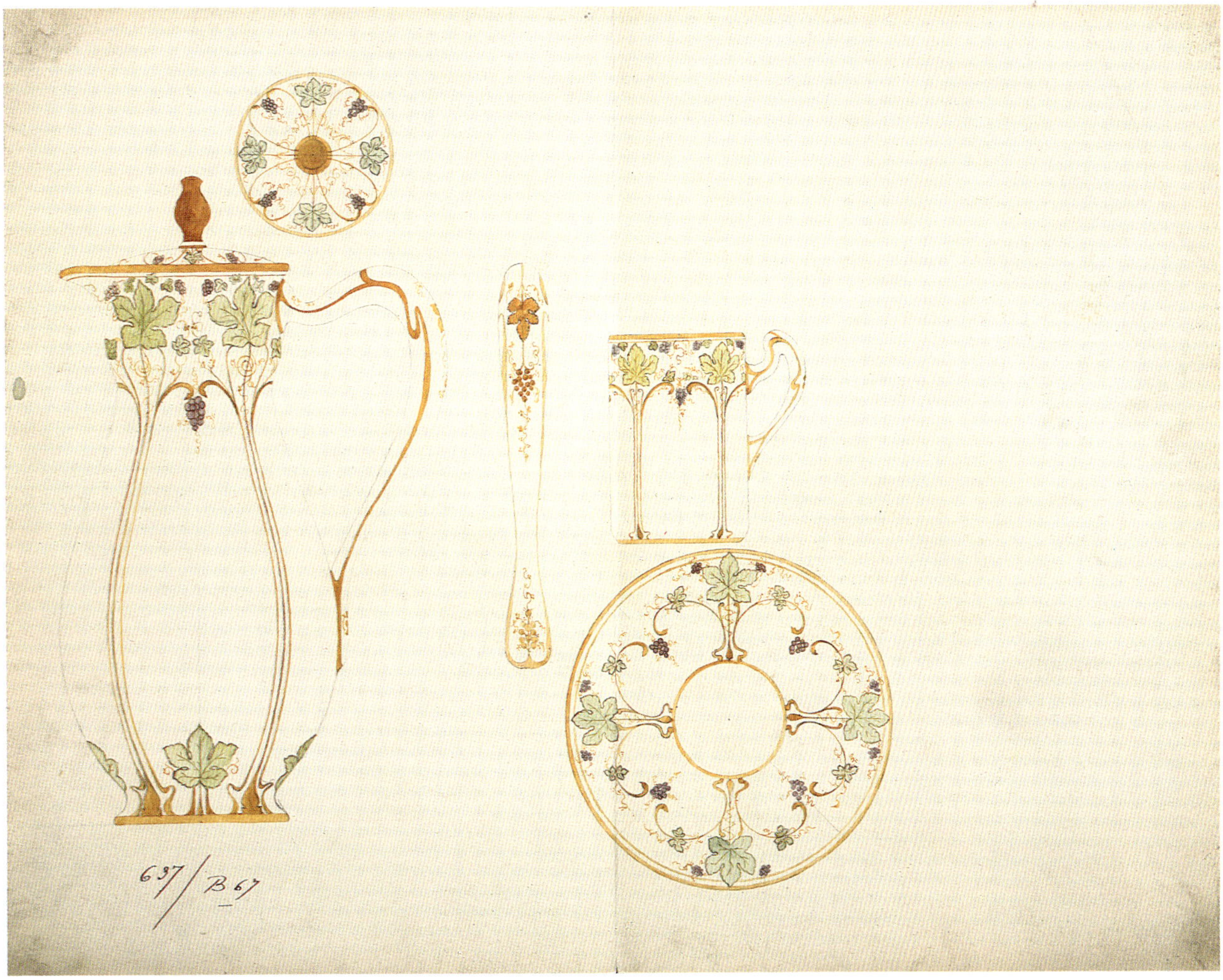

Figure 46. Probably Frank G. Holmes, Ceramic Art Company. Design drawing for a chocolate pot and cup and saucer, 1905. Watercolor, pencil, and ink on paper, 14 × 18½ in. (35.6 × 47 cm.). Archives of Lenox China

ing Europe (see cat. no. 97); others adapted earlier styles to use in elegant borders. Nearly every influence, from baroque extravagance, to rococo delicacy, to neoclassic restraint, to oriental exoticism, was represented.

Early in the century, Walter Scott Lenox began to lose his eyesight. In 1905, he surrendered his supervision of design to Frank G. Holmes, though he continued as the nominal head of the firm until his death, in 1920. Holmes, who had studied at the Rhode Island School of Design in Providence and at the New York School of Art, started his professional career as a silver designer.[16] It was undoubtedly he who embraced the graceful Art-Nouveau style, for it first appeared on Lenox dinnerware about 1905. A rich and stylized assemblage of green leaves, purple grapes, and gold vines in the Art-Nouveau mode can be seen in the original design drawing of an attenuated chocolate pot and an accompanying cup and saucer (Fig. 46).[17] During his long tenure at the firm, Holmes created an overwhelming number of patterns, some still in production today. He designed the first American-made state dinner service, comprising seventeen hundred pieces, ordered for the White House in 1918 by President and Mrs. Woodrow Wilson.[18]

The hiring of professional artists, which had been instigated at American potteries in preparation for the Centennial Exposition, continued to the end of the century. Those artists were highly trained in their craft, primarily in English and European porcelain manufactories, and they performed in a traditional manner. Perhaps for that reason and perhaps because they worked in a refined medium, none of them ventured into the class of ceramics known as art pottery, a major component of the emerging Arts and Crafts movement.

Art Porcelain (cat. nos. 101–21)

The art pottery movement, closely allied to the Arts and Crafts movement and spanning the years from about 1875 to about 1920, paralleled the development of artwares in commercial porcelain factories after the Centennial Exposition. Although art pottery was sometimes produced at relatively large factories, it was always made with aesthetic intent and with respect for the handcrafted object. On it, painted decoration predominated in the early years of the movement; later, potters took up other methods, including new and often experimental glazes. Earthenware was the primary medium, largely because it was easier to handle and to fire. Porcelain-making had always been confined to the industrialized factories, where the intricacies of mixing the formula and attaining the extremely high temperature firing the body required could be accommodated. Beginning in the 1890s, however, a few highly ambitious artist-potters, notably Kate B. Sears, M. Louise McLaughlin, and Adelaide Alsop Robineau, began to turn their attention to the making of high-fired porcelain, in defiance of its myriad pitfalls. Although each of the three was from a different part of the country, they had a common background in the china-painting or wood-carving movements that in the 1870s had begun to be legitimate craft activities for women.[1] It may have been those early pursuits that drew the three women to the medium. The primary distinction between their work and that of commercial manufactories was in their preferred mode of decoration. Whereas elaborate and highly skilled painted varieties dominated the products of potteries such as Trenton's Ceramic Art Company and Willets Manufacturing Company, the women chose to focus on carving, cutting away the porcelain's brittle surface to leave a design in relief.

Kate Sears, active from about 1891 through 1893, was a transitional figure. An artist who worked in a large porcelain factory, albeit in a most individual manner, she laid the groundwork for the artist who worked alone, in a small, independent studio. She

Figure 47. M. Louise McLaughlin. Vase, probably 1902. H. 7 11/16 in. (19.6 cm.). Collection of R. A. Ellison

was the first American to attempt the painstaking work of carving porcelain for decorative effect (cat. nos. 101–3), a procedure extremely difficult, time-consuming, and risky. The objects she executed at the Ceramic Art Company show little awareness of European stylistic trends, but are designed and realized as innocent scenes of childlike appeal. That she prided herself on her artistry is manifested in her habit of inscribing her signature, sometimes accompanied by a date, on the majority of her pieces. Little else is known about Kate Sears. Apparently, she did not pursue her career as an artist in porcelain beyond 1893, for nothing dated after that year has come to light. Her oeuvre is of immense value, apart from its charm; it may have inspired others to explore further the vein she had tapped. Though nothing proves that either McLaughlin or Robineau, who succeeded her as carvers of porcelains, had been influenced by Sears's work, it is not unreasonable to think that they may have known of it. In 1893, one of Sears's pieces was exhibited at the World's Columbian Exposition in Chicago, an event neither of the other women was likely to have ignored.

Toward the end of the century, the stylistic change from figural to nonfigural depictions on porcelain was typical of the revolution in all phases of design. Experiments in glazing on porcelain, probably inspired by the earthenware glazes introduced at the same time, resulted in extraordinary flambé and crystalline finishes. McLaughlin and Robineau were fully conversant with the contemporary ceramic movements in Europe (an influence that can be seen in their work), though each maintained an abiding reverence for the unique and timeless beauty of Chinese porcelains. The contributions the two made in bringing porcelain fabrication into the realm of the art-potter's small studio were of immeasurable value.

M. Louise McLaughlin, of Cincinnati, Ohio, had a thorough training in china painting, wood carving, and underglaze slip decoration on earthenware.[2] Porcelain, a medium she began to master in 1898 in her small backyard studio, was just one of the many daring avenues she traveled during her multifaceted career. Her china-painting experience may have sparked her interest in working in porcelain, which she felt had a "peculiar beauty and translucence."[3] Again, perhaps she was drawn to the medium because it had not been explored by any individual before her. As she recorded in 1898: "Now unable to resist entering what appeared to be an unoccupied field, I determined to attempt the making of porcelain."[4] In 1938, looking back on her career, she wrote, "The delicacy and fineness of the ware with the possibilities of rich coloring as well as the difficulties of the manufacture make porcelain the goal of the highest ambition of the potter."[5] Her attaining the goal of fabricating porcelain in the face of numerous constraints, including the total absence of published instructions, is nothing short of miraculous. She said the formula she used had come from a "printed description of the method used at Sevres."[6] Inevitably, she had many failures, but her determination never faltered: "Having started, I would not give up, having a kind of dogged persistence which does not recognize defeat."[7] In the beginning, she worked with an experienced potter, but she soon found herself in disagreement with his methods and she fired him that winter. Afterward, most of her pieces were cast by her friend and helper Margaret Hickey.

McLaughlin named her porcelain Losanti, after a former name for Cincinnati. Her carved vases do not reveal the mastery of technique and the meticulous finish that are characteristic of Sears's work. Instead, they appear to have been hastily executed, almost as if McLaughlin were working as quickly as possible to see her ideas realized. The flowers and scrolls that dominate her designs derive in part from Danish porcelains she admired, which were made by the Bing and Grøndahl factory. Her curvilinear patterns may also have been influenced by the Art-Nouveau style, which was then taking hold in Europe. She was related by marriage to Edward Colonna, a major proponent of the style, and he may also have contributed to her interest in it.[8] Glazes were equal to carving in McLaughlin's approach. She began in 1898 to maintain a manuscript book in which she faithfully recorded her formulas for clay bodies, her own glazes (numbering upwards of sixty), the shapes she used, as well as each item she made and each firing she did.[9] Her vases are generally oriental in shape (Fig. 47); her glazes, mainly soft, milky colors, variations on the celadon and peachbloom of Chinese origin. She also followed the oriental mode in making her porcelains—that is, treating the body and glaze to a single firing.

McLaughlin was fortunate to possess private means ample enough to allow unlimited experimentation in her costly and unremunerative pursuit. Even in 1901 and 1902—her most successful years—during which she made almost seven hundred vases, she brought to completion only little over half and sold even fewer. In 1901, her income from her porcelains was $126.00, representing from 431 attempts 15 sales; in 1902, she realized $127.82 from 262 attempts.[10] The sums were ludicrous; they could not have provided subsistence for a month. Ultimately, about 1904, McLaughlin's high costs and her lack of a profitable commercial line to supplement her purely ornamental pieces ended her porcelain venture.

Even if Adelaide Alsop Robineau, of Syracuse, New York, was unaware of Kate Sears's carved porcelains, she had to be fully familiar with McLaughlin's work. Having begun her ceramics career as a china painter, Robineau must have consulted McLaughlin's publications on that subject.[11] In 1900, when she exhibited her painted decoration on imported blanks at the Exposition Universelle in Paris, McLaughlin was showing her carved and glazed porcelains at the same fair. (McLaughlin's works were among the few that redeemed the American entries in the judges' eyes, for they considered it a detriment that the majority were painted on foreign wares.) Robineau started to model ceramics as early as 1901; within only about two years she had begun to make her own porcelain. She was no doubt aided by the publication, begun in 1903, of her husband's translation of the formulas and methods of Taxile Doat, the celebrated

Figure 48. Adelaide Alsop Robineau. Vase, ca. 1905. H. 4 9/16 in. (11.6 cm.). Collection of Martin Eidelberg

Sèvres potter. Robineau, like McLaughlin, did not have to support herself with her porcelain work (nor would she have been able to); she and her husband earned a decent income, largely derived from the profitable *Keramic Studio*, a periodical they published.

Robineau's porcelains show relatively little stylistic progression over the quarter century or more that she worked in the field. Her career can be divided into three periods. The first—beginning about early 1903, when she started her experiments in the medium—was an exciting seven-year span in which she developed her own repertoire of matte and crystalline glazes. In a letter her husband, Samuel E. Robineau, wrote in February 1904 to Edwin AtLee Barber, champion of American ceramics, he said, "She is getting extremely interesting and artistic results and is beginning to emerge from the experimental stage." He added, "Her work is almost exclusively mat glazes on porcelain."[12] In 1905, Robineau started carving, incising, and excising porcelain in the intricate designs that would forever distinguish her work. At the same time, she began her attempts in the perilous, eggshell-thin medium. It was during those years that she completed her lantern (cat. no. 110) and her Viking and Crab vases, three of her most famous and complicated works. She usually provided her forms with a rigid structure consisting of bands of decoration dominated by geometric plant or insect motifs (Fig. 48). Her preoccupation with designs inspired by oriental, Egyptian, American Indian, and South American art began in the same period, many of them revitalized from her china-painting patterns. Throughout her life, she continued to rework and to expand upon the ideas she had formed in the early years of the century.

The second phase of Robineau's career began in 1910, when she and her husband moved to University City in Saint Louis, Missouri, to join Taxile Doat (Fig. 49). Doat was to direct a porcelain-making and educational establishment formed by Edward G. Lewis, the visionary founder of the parent organization, the American Woman's League. The scheme started out with the highest ideals, as

Figure 49. Taxile Doat, working at University City, Missouri. Photograph, ca. 1910. University City Public Library Archives

Figure 50. Adelaide Alsop Robineau with her Scarab vase. Photograph, 1911. University City Public Library Archives

Figure 51. Adelaide Alsop Robineau. Scarab vase, 1910. H. 16⅝ in. (42.2 cm.). Everson Museum of Art, Museum Purchase (30.4.78)

Doat described it to Barber: "[For] establishing a ceramic school there destined to equal or surpass those of Sevres, Berlin, and Copenhagen."[13] As soon as Doat and Robineau arrived at University City, both of them began work on elaborate concepts—Doat on his University City vase, one of the first large pieces made there, presently unlocated and possibly not surviving; Robineau on her Scarab vase, also called "The Apotheosis of the Toiler" (Fig. 50). The vase, a masterpiece in the medium, is intricately excised from base to cover with a repeated stylized design of scarabs, the Egyptian symbol of immortality (Fig. 51). The carving alone is said to have taken a thousand hours (Robineau's reticulated lantern required three hundred). The artist was in part rewarded for her excruciatingly painstaking work when the vase was awarded a prize at the Turin International Exhibition of 1910. (It has been less universally praised on stylistic and aesthetic grounds.)[14]

Edward Lewis's dream survived for about a year. By the spring of 1911, the pottery and educational facility were beginning to be mired in financial difficulties; some of the workers were laid off. That June, the Robineaus left for Syracuse. Doat, however, stayed on, and the factory was reorganized. During its four years in operation, it produced an impressive number of porcelains, the most artistic of which date to the first year. Throughout its existence, most of its output was profoundly influenced by the work of director Doat, but the pieces Robineau created at University City are expressions of her response to the artistic climate it provided her.

The last phase in Robineau's career began in mid-1911, when she returned to her Syracuse studio and resumed her work, and ended in 1929 with her death. During that last period, she pursued perfection in both her carving and her glazes, the latter including one thin and bronzelike she developed and used on several of her carved vases (cat. no. 117). Her continuing work with crystalline glazes is evident in her numerous test pots—tiny molded vases on which she would try out her new finishes. She offered some of them for sale, with or without

Figure 52. Adelaide Alsop Robineau. Vase, 1923. H. 3⅜ in. (8.6 cm.). The Metropolitan Museum of Art, Purchase, Edward C. Moore, Jr. Gift, 1923 (23.52)

carved porcelain stands and covers (Fig. 52). At the end of that final period and nearly at the end of her life, she mastered the eggshell-thin porcelains that had tested her ability and fueled her ambition from her earliest years as an artist-potter (cat. no. 121).

By the time of her death, Robineau and all who had gone before her had elevated American porcelain to the level it merited. She is still unchallenged as America's preeminent woman potter (perhaps the foremost among both sexes) of the twentieth century, the first artist-potter to be given a retrospective exhibition at The Metropolitan Museum of Art. She and her colleagues in the field paved the way for the development of the studio movement in porcelain that began again during the 1960s and continues to flourish today.

NOTES

The Eighteenth Century (pp. 6–11)

1. Hood 1968, p. 170, quoting A. Candler, ed., *Colonial Records of Georgia*. Hood's article is the definitive work on Duché and his experiments in porcelain.
2. Hood 1968, pp. 169–70.
3. Ibid., p. 170, quoting *Colonial Records*, entry of 1739.
4. Ibid., p. 171, entry of May 1741.
5. Ibid., entry of June 1741.
6. A small porcelain bowl attributed to Duché has been published in R. M. Gilmer, "Andrew Duché and His China, 1738–1743," *Apollo* 45 (May 1947), pp. 128–30. Hood (1968, p. 183, n. 30) convincingly argues that the bowl is more likely to be Chinese.
7. In the absence of surviving wares, existing documentation must be relied on. A comment Stephens made at about the same time, however, cannot be overlooked (though his reference to "earthenware" suggests not porcelain but a refined version of the coarser medium): "How far it [Duché's ware] may deserve the Name of Porcelane . . . must be left to proper Judges, for its present Appearance differs very little (if any Thing) from some of our finest Earthenware made in England." Hood 1968, p. 172, quoting *Colonial Records*.
8. Quoted in Hood 1968, pp. 173–80.
9. See *Bow Porcelain, 1744–1776*, exh. cat. (London: The Trustees of the British Museum, 1959), p. 8.
10. Quoted in Hood 1968, p. 174.
11. Ibid., p. 177.
12. Hood 1968, p. 179; p. 183, n. 32. When the Cherokee clay was mentioned to Josiah Wedgwood in 1766, he too experimented with American materials, though he abandoned the idea of using them. See A. Finer and G. Savage, *The Selected Letters of Josiah Wedgwood* (London: Corey, Adams and Mackay, 1965), pp. 270–73.
13. Quoted in Clement 1947b, p. 57.
14. Ibid.
15. Dow 1927, p. 88.
16. Prime 1929, p. 128; Dow 1927, p. 90.
17. Franklin, in London, to Deborah Franklin, in America, 19 February 1758, in Leonard W. Labaree, ed., *The Papers of Benjamin Franklin*, vols. 1–14 (New Haven and London: Yale University Press, 1959–70), 7, p. 381.
18. Franklin, in London, to Humphrey Marshall, in Chester County, Pennsylvania, 9 July 1769, in William B. Willcox, ed., *The Papers of Benjamin Franklin*, vols. 15–26 (New Haven and London: Yale University Press, 1972–87), 16, pp. 173–74.
19. Franklin to Marshall, 18 March 1770, in Willcox, *Papers*, 17, pp. 109–10. Franklin was probably referring to Pierre-Joseph Macquer, a chemist in charge of ceramic research at the Royal Porcelain Manufactory at Sèvres from 1759 to 1783.
20. Brown 1989, quoting Benjamin Rush to Thomas Bradford, 15 April 1768, in L. H. Butterfield, ed., *Letters of Benjamin Rush* (Princeton, N.J.: Princeton University Press, 1951), p. 54.
21. Brown 1989, quoting Rush to Bradford, 3 June 1768, in Butterfield, *Letters*, pp. 60–61.
22. Prime 1929, pp. 114–16, quoting *Pennsylvania Chronicle*, 1 January 1770. For a definitive study on Bonnin and Morris, see Hood 1972.
23. Prime 1929, p. 116, quoting *South Carolina Gazette*, 15 March 1770. Bonnin and Morris undoubtedly advertised in South Carolina to lure workers away from John Bartlam's pottery, in operation there at that time. See Hood 1972, pp. 12–13, 21, 71–72; p. 72, n. 20.
24. Prime 1929, p. 116, quoting *Staatsbote*, 30 October 1770.
25. Hood 1972, p. 12, quoting "A Memoir of Thomas Gilpin," *Pennsylvania Magazine of History and Biography* 49 (1925), pp. 309–10.
26. Prime 1929, p. 117, quoting *Pennsylvania Journal*, 10 January 1771.
27. Hood 1972, p. 44, quoting "A Memoir of Thomas Gilpin."
28. See Hood 1972, p. 55, for reproductions of Cadwalader and Wharton bills of January and May 1771.
29. Franklin, in London, to Deborah Franklin, in America, 28 January 1772, in Willcox, *Papers*, 19, p. 43.
30. Prime 1929, p. 117, quoting *Pennsylvania Journal*, 10 January 1771; p. 119, quoting *Pennsylvania Packet*, 13 January 1772.
31. Ibid., p. 119, quoting *Pennsylvania Gazette*, 2 January 1772.
32. Hood 1972, p. 38, fig. 53.
33. Ibid., p. 55.
34. Prime 1929, p. 120, quoting *Pennsylvania Chronicle*, 14 November 1772.
35. Ibid., p. 122, quoting *Pennsylvania Chronicle*, 3 May 1773.
36. Ibid., quoting *Pennsylvania Chronicle*, 19 October 1774.
37. Hood 1972, p. 21.
38. Johann David Schoepf, *Travels in the Confederation [1783–1784]*, ed. and trans. by Alfred J. Morrison (Philadelphia: William J. Campbell, 1911), p. 119.
39. Prime 1929, p. 124, quoting *New-Jersey Gazette*, 12 September 1785.
40. Ibid.
41. I am grateful to Arlene Palmer Schwind, a scholar in the field of American ceramics and glass, for generously sharing this information with me.

The Early Nineteenth Century (pp. 11–21)

1. Bishop 1868, 2, p. 166.
2. Letter from John Murray, in Monkton, to Abijah Bigelow, in Washington City, 30 January 1812. Downs Manuscript and Microfilm Collection, The Henry Francis du Pont Winterthur Museum, Winterthur, Del.
3. Ibid.
4. Lawrence B. Romaine, "American Porcelain Clay," *Early American Industries Association Chronicle* 2 (April 1839), p. 68, quoting *New England Gazetteer*.
5. *Supplement to Niles Weekly Register* 9 (September 1815–March 1816), p. 185. I am grateful to Arlene Palmer Schwind for this reference.
6. For biographical material on Mead, I have relied on Clement 1947b, pp. 65–66, and Stradling 1987, which Mr. Stradling kindly allowed me to read.
7. Stradling 1987, [p. 6].
8. *Niles Weekly Register*, 27 February 1819, p. 24. I thank Arlene Palmer Schwind for this reference.
9. Ibid.
10. Stradling 1987, [p. 8], quoting *New York Commercial Advertiser*, 7 October 1819.

11. In 1820, Mead petitioned the New York Common Council to discuss the "practicability of employing the paupers in the Alms House and criminals in the Penitentiary in the manufacture of porcelain." Quoted in Clement 1947b, p. 66.
12. *New York Commercial Advertiser*, December 1824.
13. [Brick seller's] Account Book, dated 1824–1827. Downs Manuscript and Microfilm Collection, Winterthur Museum.
14. Stradling 1987, [p. 9].
15. For an analysis of the saucer and for the information on Chanou's activities in France, I am indebted to Antoine d'Albis, of the National Porcelain Manufactory at Sèvres.
16. For an account of the fire, see Stradling 1987, [p. 12], quoting *New York American*, 28 July 1827. The listing in New York City directories of 1827 and 1828 of a Joseph Toyer, who had possibly worked at the firm and whose occupation was given as "china-maker," at 65 Lewis Street (the street on which the factory had stood), is the sole suggestion that porcelain was still being manufactured on the site.
17. Stradling 1987, [p. 11]; Joan Leibowitz, *Yellow Ware: The Transitional Ceramic* (Exton, Pa.: Schiffer Publishing, 1985), p. 28.
18. Though his name is not on the list of original backers, Mead may have participated in establishing the factory. See Clement 1947b, p. 66, quoting Mead's obituary in *Brother Jonathan*, 25 February 1843, which refers to Mead's having manufactured porcelain in Jersey City.
19. Stradling 1987, [p. 10], quoting *New York Commercial Advertiser*, 24 August 1826.
20. Clement 1947b, p. 68, quoting *Journal of the Franklin Institute*, 1826.
21. Stradling 1987, [p. 11], quoting *New York Commercial Advertiser*, 24 August 1826.
22. Myers 1980, p. 100, citing Franklin Institute Report, Third Exhibition (1826).
23. Day Book of William Ellis Tucker, Vol. 1, 1821–1827, p. 31. Library, Philadelphia Museum of Art, Rare Books Collection.
24. Clement 1947b, p. 70, citing George W. Carpenter, "Mineralogy of Chester County, Pa., Delaware and Maryland," *American Journal of Science and Arts* 14 (July 1828).
25. Curtis 1972, pp. 32–34.
26. Ibid., p. 109, quoting letter from Benjamin Tucker to Hooper, 1830.
27. In a letter of 5 February 1827 to Benjamin Ferris, in Wilmington, Delaware, Benjamin Tucker mentioned a "kiln of fine Porcelain ware" just being drawn by his son, and added that he hoped for like success in the glazing. Tucker Archives, American Department, Philadelphia Museum of Art.
28. Benjamin Tucker to Isaac C. and Hannah Jones, 16 February 1827. Tucker Archives, American Department, Philadelphia Museum of Art.
29. Myers 1980, p. 25, quoting *Philadelphia Poulson's American Daily Advertiser*, 19 February 1827.
30. Benjamin Tucker to Marcus C. Stephens, 27 June 1827. Tucker Archives, American Department, Philadelphia Museum of Art.
31. Tucker to Stephens, letter of 18 July 1827.
32. Myers 1980, p. 101, quoting Franklin Institute Report, Fourth Exhibition (1827).
33. Ibid., quoting Franklin Institute Report, Sixth Exhibition (1830).
34. In the attribution of unmarked Tucker porcelain, a characteristic often cited is a halo effect around the gilding, visible under a shortwave ultraviolet light. The effect is probably caused by the presence of lead in the gilding process, a process discontinued in France by about 1800.
35. Tucker pattern books, Library, Philadelphia Museum of Art, Rare Books Collection.
36. An advertisement for a sale of "American china," sponsored by the New England Society for the Promotion of the Manufacture and the Mechanic Arts, which appeared in the *Boston Gazette* of 8 March 1827, enumerated among an impressive variety of forms "Busts of Washington, Lafayette . . . etc." The china maker was not named, but Tucker is a distinct possibility.
37. Barber 1893, pp. 131–32, quoting President Jackson's letter of 3 April 1830 to Tucker. Jackson was the subject on more than one Tucker factory porcelain vase: an article on the factory printed in 1833 in the *United States Gazette* referred to an artist "engaged upon a large and beautiful vase, upon which he was copying a full length likeness of General Jackson." The same article appeared in the *West Chester Republican and Democrat* of 6 July 1833 and the *Maine Farmer and Journal of the Arts* of 10 August 1833. I am grateful to Arlene Palmer Schwind for the *Maine Farmer* reference.
38. Benjamin Tucker to William Ellis Tucker, 29 April 1828. Tucker Archives, American Department, Philadelphia Museum of Art.
39. Curtis 1972, p. 25, quoting letter from Benjamin Tucker to William Ellis Tucker, 20 May 1831.
40. Clement 1947b, p. 83, quoting letter from William Ellis Tucker to John F. Anderson, 20 December 1830.

The Mid-Nineteenth Century (pp. 21–28)

1. Silliman and Goodrich 1854, p. 110.
2. Barber 1895, "Historical Sketch," p. 21.
3. *Official Catalogue, New York Exhibition of the Industry of All Nations 1853* (New York: George P. Putnam and Company, 1853), p. 223.
4. See Richardson 1960.
5. Barber 1895, "Historical Sketch," pp. 7–9.
6. Ibid., p. 15.
7. Cartlidge soon discontinued his porcelain button production when much cheaper bone buttons entered the market.
8. Barber 1895, "Historical Sketch," p. 18.
9. Ibid., pp. 22–23.
10. Ibid., pp. 24–26.
11. In 1856, when the Cartlidge firm closed down, Jones departed to Kaolin, South Carolina, to work at the newly founded Southern Porcelain Works. Presumably, he manufactured porcelain pitchers there, utilizing his Greenpoint cornstalk molds. The porcelain output of the Southern Porcelain Works is the subject of much confusion. Barber (1893, pp. 188–89) illustrates "a white porcelain corn pitcher" owned in 1893 by a Mrs. Edward Willis of Charlesfon, to whom it was given in 1861 while she was visiting the factory. The company's incorporation papers suggest that the partners' original intent ("to excavate, sell, and manufacture porcelain clay, in the district of Edgefield") was to refine the local clay for sale to various factories rather than to use it for their own production. See Act of Incorporation, South Carolina Department of Archives and History, Columbia, South Carolina.
12. In England, Lockett's father, George, was a color-maker and manager for the Alcock pottery in Burslem; Smith had worked for the Davenport company in Longport; Tatler, whose father was also a flower painter, had apprenticed at Minton's. No further information on Washington has yet come to light.
13. Barber 1895, "Historical Sketch," p. 21.
14. Collard 1984, p. 196, quoting *Montreal Gazette*, 14 April 1851.
15. Ibid.
16. *Official Catalogue, New York Exhibition of the Industry of All Nations 1853*, p. 223.
17. Smith's Brooklyn Directory, 1855–56.

18. *Union Porcelain Co.'s Price List of House Trimmings* (New York: Francis & Loutrel, 1861), Library of Congress.
19. The firm spawned several other enterprises. In 1860, when Millington and Astbury went off on their own, it was renamed William Young and Sons; when William died, in 1871, it became William Young's Sons. In 1879, the family sold it to the Willets brothers, founders of the Willets Manufacturing Company. Millington and Astbury built their own factory with one additional partner, Theophilus Poulson of Philadelphia, and they too produced commercial whiteware. Their best-known work, a pitcher depicting a Civil War event in relief, commonly called the "Ellsworth pitcher" and often marked by the firm, was generally of a heavy white earthenware, yet some examples of the form have a slight translucence that approaches that of porcelain.
20. Goldberg 1983, p. 20, quoting an unidentified Trenton newspaper.
21. Ibid.
22. Myers 1980, p. 103, citing Franklin Institute Report, Twenty-first Exhibition (1851).
23. Beech is better known for his factory-molded fine earthenwares, decorated with colored Rockingham glazes, and for an innovative decorative ware that he patented and produced, which required what he called "Japanning on Earthenware," sometimes inlaid with "pearls, gems, &c." See Myers 1980, pp. 33–34.
24. Ibid., pp. 34–35.
25. Barber 1893 (rev. ed.), p. 557.
26. Myers 1980, p. 103, quoting Franklin Institute Report, Twenty-third Exhibition (1853).
27. Ibid., quoting Franklin Institute Report, Twenty-fourth Exhibition (1854).
28. Ibid., pp. 69–70.
29. Barber 1893, p. 183.
30. Ibid.
31. Myers 1980, p. 103, quoting Franklin Institute Report, Twenty-fourth Exhibition (1854).
32. Ibid.
33. Wendell Garrett, "Clues and footnotes," *The Magazine Antiques* 106 (August 1974), p. 290, quoting *Philadelphia Public Ledger*, 18 December 1857.
34. Barber 1893, p. 185.
35. Letter from William C. Gates, former curator, East Liverpool Museum of Ceramics, to J. Garrison Stradling, 26 November 1982, quoting *Wellsville Patriot*, 14 August 1860. I am grateful to Mr. Gates for allowing me to refer to his letter and to Mr. Stradling for acquainting me with it.
36. Gates and Ormerod 1982, p. 16.
37. The price list is in the collections of the East Liverpool Museum of Ceramics.

Parian (pp. 29–37)

1. For further information on the Bennington ceramics industry, see Watkins 1950, pp. 141–52.
2. Though legend has it that the first parian made in Bennington was in the form of a small baby intended as a gift to Mrs. Julius Norton on the birth of her first child, in November 1843, it is highly unlikely that parian manufacture had begun there at that early date. Watkins 1950, p. 212.
3. Reproduced in Barrett 1957, p. 10.
4. Ibid.
5. *The Eighth Exhibition of the Mass. Charitable Mechanic Association* (Boston: Press of Geo. C. Rand & Avery, 1856), p. 80.
6. See Watkins 1950, p. 217.
7. Trenton producers of parian included Joseph H. Moore and Isaac Davis, who have been recorded as exhibiting the medium at the 1876 Centennial Exposition, Moore's display including "Specimens of biscuit and Parian, with fine flowers in high relief"; Davis's, "some specimens of Parian and biscuit." See Tyndale 1880, pp. 99–100.
8. "Cincinnati Enterprise," *The Crockery Journal* 1 (27 February 1875), p. 7.
9. Barber 1895, "Historical Sketch," p. 37.
10. Ibid., p. 41, where "Autumn" is illustrated.
11. Ibid., p. 44.
12. Ibid., p. 50.
13. Ibid., p. 57.
14. The bust of Lincoln is at the New Jersey State Museum, Brewer Collection (acc. no. CH354.33). Unfortunately, because the names of three Bloor and Ott partners all begin with *B*, the busts cannot be attributed confidently to the period of Bloor, Ott and Booth; Bloor, Ott and Burroughs; or Bloor, Ott and Brewer, though the last, which dated from 1865 to 1871, is the most likely.
15. For illustration, see James R. Mitchell, "Ott & Brewer: Etruria in America," *Winterthur Portfolio* 7 (1972), p. 220, fig. 7.
16. Broome also contributed substantially to the technical side of parian production through his invention of an "Improved porcelain or parian kiln," said to give "an equal distribution and perfect regulation of the heat." See Young 1879, p. 79.
17. Ott and Brewer, undated art circular, collection of David and Barbara Goldberg; Ott and Brewer, undated price list, collection of the New Jersey State Museum (acc. no. CH85.33.6).
18. Broome may have used the plaque to work out his design before utilizing it on an elaborate parian vase, known today only through a period engraving. See Elliott 1879, p. 341.
19. "American Parian," *Crockery and Glass Journal* 5 (22 March 1877), p. 15.
20. Ibid.
21. "Baltimore Reports," *Crockery and Glass Journal* 16 (28 December 1882), p. 341.
22. Ibid. 17 (15 February 1883), p. 30.
23. Ibid. (21 June 1883), p. 10.
24. Ibid.
25. Ibid., where stated that Priestman's "medallion heads" of Summer and Winter are soon to be introduced on the market, in June 1883.

Centennial Porcelain (pp. 37–43)

1. In 1869, the Franklin Institute of Philadelphia made a formal proposal that an international exhibition be held in the city's Fairmount Park as an appropriate recognition of the nation's Centennial.
2. Quoted in Jane Shadel Spillman, *Glass from World's Fairs, 1851–1904* (Corning, N.Y.: The Corning Museum of Glass, 1986), p. 29.
3. From the official communication sent to foreign ministers in the nation's capital by the secretary of state, quoted in Anne C. Golovin, "Foreign Nations," in Post 1976, p. 177.
4. The attendance figure is especially notable in that the entire population of the United States numbered only forty million.
5. Tyndale 1880, p. 7.
6. Ibid., pp. 8–9.
7. Ibid., p. 6.

8. See Young 1879, p. 342.
9. Elliott 1878, p. 317.
10. For a thorough discussion and checklist of American ceramic manufacturers at the Centennial, see Stradling 1976, pp. 146–58.
11. "American Pottery," *The Crockery Journal* 1 (23 January 1875), p. 4.
12. Ibid.
13. "The National Potters' Association," *The Crockery Journal* 1 (23 January 1875), p. 4.
14. Ibid.
15. Tyndale 1880, p. 11.
16. Elliott 1878, pp. 340–41.
17. Tyndale 1880, p. 98.
18. Norton 1877, pl. 50.
19. For an illustration, see Young 1879, p. 477.
20. Tyndale 1880, p. 100.
21. "Ceramics at Philadelphia.—XI." *The American Architect and Building News* 1 (21 October 1876), p. 342.
22. Young 1879, pp. 464–65.
23. "Ceramics at Philadelphia," p. 342.
24. McCabe 1876, p. 354.
25. Quoted in Susan Myers, "Ceramics," in Post 1976, p. 111.
26. Ibid.

Belleek (pp. 43–52)

1. Goss also had ties to America: he knew noted ceramics historian Edwin AtLee Barber well enough to present him with at least six items from his factory, among them a "large 3-handled Loving Cup," described as "thin 'Belleek' China Made by Mr. William Henry Goss, of Stoke-on-Trent, England," and a small two-handled loving cup and a large beer mug of Belleek especially decorated for Barber with the enameled insignia of the Society of the Sons of the Revolution. See *Illustrated Catalogue of China, Pottery, Porcelains, and Glass [Collected by] the Late Edwin AtLee Barber*, estate sale, Samuel T. Freeman & Co., Philadelphia, 10 and 11 December 1917, pp. 80–81.
2. "The Belleek Pottery," *Art-Journal* (London) 8 (1 May 1869), p. 152.
3. Wendell Garrett, "Clues and footnotes," *The Magazine Antiques* 103 (June 1973), p. 1189, quoting *Demorest's Monthly Magazine*, 1878, p. 93.
4. Young 1879, p. 388.
5. The reorganization of the Belleek company in 1884 (the year in which McBirney and Armstrong both died) may also account for the migration of Irish workers to America. See S. McCrum, *The Belleek Pottery* (Belfast: Ulster Museum, n.d.), p. 18.
6. At Bromley's death, he was called "one of the leading workmen in the manufacture of Belleek ware." *Crockery and Glass Journal* 22 (15 October 1885), p. 26.
7. Brewer 1934, pp. 96–108.
8. The piece of paper is preserved in the Archives of the New Jersey State Museum (acc. no. CH85.33.17).
9. "The Potteries: Trenton," *Crockery and Glass Journal* 18 (20 December 1883), p. 14.
10. "Rivaling English Ware: What Ott and Brewer Have Done," *Trenton Times*, 15 October 1883, p. 1.
11. ["An attempt is now being made,"] *Crockery and Glass Journal* 13 (16 June 1881), p. 18.
12. "The Potteries: Trenton," *Crockery and Glass Journal* 14 (22 December 1881), p. 60.
13. Ibid. 15 (2 March 1882), p. 14. Although Ott and Brewer did not announce having successfully produced a Belleek-like porcelain until 1882, the medium had reportedly been patented by an unnamed firm in the United States by 1880, at which time only Ott and Brewer would have been qualified. See Blake 1880, p. 171.
14. Barber 1893, p. 215.
15. "The Potteries," *Crockery and Glass Journal* 17 (7 June 1883), p. 10.
16. Ibid. 19 (17 January 1884), p. 16.
17. "Trenton Potteries at the Philadelphia Exhibition," *Crockery and Glass Journal* 30 (31 October 1889), p. 21, reprinted from *Trenton True American*.
18. Ibid.
19. L. W. Miller, "The Exhibition of Art Industry at Philadelphia," *Art Amateur* 21 (November 1889), p. 134.
20. Cook began his career in the pottery industry in 1876 as an office worker at Ott and Brewer. He left in 1881 to organize with William S. Hancock the Crescent Pottery, which was sold to the Trenton Potteries Company. See "Prominent Trenton Potters," *Crockery and Glass Journal* (17 December 1903), p. 141.
21. For an account of Thomas Connelly's association with the Delaware Pottery, see Anna D. Reilly, "American Belleek," *Spinning Wheel* 8 (June 1952), p. 8. I am grateful to David J. Goldberg for providing me with information on the Oliphant family and the Delaware Pottery.
22. Barber 1893, p. 229.
23. "The Potteries: Trenton," *Crockery and Glass Journal* 25 (3 March 1887), p. 24.
24. See "Backgrounds: Trenton and Walter Scott Lenox," Denker 1988, [pp. 28–29].
25. "Trenton," *Crockery and Glass Journal* 29 (30 May 1889), p. 27.
26. See "The Ceramic Art Company, Founding and Early Years 1889–1896," Denker 1988, [p. 4].
27. "Trenton," *Crockery and Glass Journal* 36 (11 August 1892), unpaged.
28. Hiring Japanese artists to decorate pottery and porcelain was not unique to Lenox's firm. Two years earlier, in 1887, Kataro Shirayamadani had begun work at the Rookwood Pottery in Cincinnati, Ohio, where he remained until his death in 1948. He is credited with some of the firm's best decorated work.
29. Of the relatively small number of known American Art China Company wares, those that are marked have either the founders' initials or the conjoined first letters of the factory name and the words "Belleek China." See Gaston 1984a, p. 14.
30. For an extensive historical background on Knowles, Taylor & Knowles, see Gates and Ormerod 1982, pp. 115–16; Cox 1942, pp. 152–57.
31. Cox 1942, p. 155, quoting *East Liverpool Tribune*, 14 December 1889. The announcement appeared in "East Liverpool, O.," *Crockery and Glass Journal* 29 (10 January 1889), p. 24.
32. From one of two extant pages of Knowles, Taylor & Knowles Lotus Ware catalogue, collections of the Museum of Ceramics at East Liverpool, Ohio.
33. The 1920s saw a revival of Belleek manufacture in America, largely to compete with the Lenox firm's profitable success. The Morgan Belleek China Company was in operation in Canton, Ohio, from 1924 to 1929; the Coxon Belleek Pottery, in Wooster, Ohio, from 1926 to 1930; Perlee, Incorporated, in Trenton, N.J., made a Belleek-type porcelain from 1922 until about 1930. See Gaston 1984, pp. 45, 75, 96.

Notes

The Post-Centennial Decades (pp. 52–58)

1. For a thorough discussion of dining customs and accoutrements in Victorian America, see Williams 1985.
2. For example, the Greenwood Pottery discontinued its art-porcelain line by the early 1890s, though it continued production of its white granite hotelware until 1933, when the factory is presumed to have closed. See "James Tams Has Had an Interesting Career," article from an unidentified newspaper [1910?], clipping files, New Jersey State Museum.
3. When the Ceramic Art Company was incorporated on 16 May 1889, two additional partners, William S. Hancock and Joseph Rice, had invested in the firm.
4. *The Ceramic Art Co.* 1891.
5. See "The Ceramic Art Company, Lenox's Presidency, 1896–1905," Denker 1988, [p. 26].
6. *The Ceramic Art Co.* 1891.
7. See Ellis 1985, pp. 76–81.
8. Nosek is said to have emigrated to America in 1903 and worked for Lenox and Willets from then to about 1907; Heidrich, to have been employed by the firm during the 1890s; Wirkner, from about 1900. See Robinson and Feeny 1980, p. 43.
9. Wirkner's name appears only in the Trenton city directory of 1899, where his occupation is listed as "decorator." I am grateful to Ellen Paul Denker for providing me with this information. Wirkner's other signed works seem primarily to have figural subjects, including a vase with a portrait after David Teniers. See Robinson and Feeny 1980, p. 45.
10. In the collection of the owner of the plaque.
11. The Tannhäuser scene is copied from a painting of 1873 by the German artist Otto Knille, in the collections of the Staatliche Museen in Berlin, where it has been housed since it was executed. The canvas was exhibited at the Berlin Nationalgalerie in 1898 (the year before the plaque was painted); it also appeared as an illustration in an American periodical of unrecorded date put out by the Haskell Publishing Company. Director of Archives Robert Tuggle, Metropolitan Opera Association, found a lithograph of the painting on tissue paper for me. The subject is also known on a Viennese porcelain charger, grayer and bluer in color and generally less skillfully painted than Wirkner's example. See sales catalogue, *19th Century Furniture, Decorations and Works of Art*, Sotheby's (New York), sale no. 5610, 19 September 1987, lot no. 42.
12. Frelinghuysen 1986, pp. 220–28; Brandimarte 1988.
13. Advertisement, Willets Manufacturing Company, *Crockery and Glass Journal* 31 (31 July 1890), p. 10.
14. *The Ceramic Art Co.* 1891.
15. See "Delft Ware, Old and New," *Crockery and Glass Journal* 43 (7 May 1896), unpaged.
16. "Trenton China Designer and His Work Attract Wide-spread Attention at Exhibition in the Metropolitan Museum of Art," undated [1923?], unidentified newspaper clipping in company scrapbook. Lenox Archives, Lawrenceville, N.J.
17. For an illustration of the actual porcelain chocolate pot and the cup and saucer, see Clara Ruge, "American Ceramics—A Brief Review of Progress," *The International Studio* 28 (1906), p. 24.
18. See Klapthor 1975, pp. 146–53.

Art Porcelain (pp. 58–64)

1. For a discussion of the parallel movements in china painting and wood carving, see Frelinghuysen 1986, pp. 220–28. For a summary of the china-painting movement in America, see Brandimarte 1988.
2. McLaughlin also painted designs in underglaze blue on porcelain. An example made by the Union Porcelain Works in Greenpoint, New York, is in the collection of the Cincinnati Art Museum. See *The Ladies, God Bless 'Em: The Women's Art Movement in Cincinnati in the Nineteenth Century*, exh. cat., introduction by Carol Macht (Cincinnati, Ohio: Cincinnati Art Museum, 1976), p. 37. See also McLaughlin 1938, pp. 217–25; Ellen Paul Denker and Bert Randall Denker, "Mary Louise McLaughlin," in Kaplan 1987, pp. 249–50.
3. M. Louise McLaughlin, *Pottery Decoration under the Glaze* (Cincinnati, Ohio: Robert Clarke & Co., 1880), p. 15.
4. M. Louise McLaughlin, Losanti Record Book, 1898–1903, unpaginated section, Cincinnati Art Museum Library, Gift of Mr. and Mrs. James Todd.
5. McLaughlin 1938, p. 220.
6. Losanti Record Book, unpaginated section. McLaughlin's experiments predate the published accounts of Taxile Doat.
7. Quoted in Monachesi 1902, p. 11.
8. Martin Eidelberg published the Colonna–McLaughlin family relationship in "Art Pottery," Robert Judson Clark, ed., *The Arts and Crafts Movement in America 1876–1916*, exh. cat. (Princeton, N.J., and Chicago: The Art Museum, Princeton University and the Art Institute of Chicago, distributed by Princeton University Press, 1972), p. 164. See also Martin Eidelberg, *E. Colonna* (Dayton, Ohio: Dayton Art Institute, 1983), p. 61. (McLaughlin's views on the Art-Nouveau style are quoted in *American Porcelain* at cat. no. 108.)
9. Losanti Record Book.
10. Ibid., pp. 180, 263.
11. M. Louise McLaughlin, *China Painting: A Practical Manual for the Use of Amateurs in the Decoration of Hard Porcelain* (Cincinnati, Ohio: Robert Clarke & Co., 1877); *Pottery Decoration under the Glaze* (Cincinnati, Ohio: Robert Clarke & Co., 1880); *Suggestions to China Painters* (Cincinnati, Ohio, 1884).
12. Robineau to Barber, letter of 6 February 1904, quoted in Clancy 1982, p. 31.
13. Doat to Barber, letter of 14 July 1909, quoted in Clancy 1982, p. 46.
14. Frederick Hurten Rhead apparently disliked the vase. See Frederick Hurten Rhead, "The University City Venture," ed. by Paul Evans, Weiss 1981, p. 215, n. 18.

The Catalogue

1
Fruit basket, 1770–72

American China Manufactory (Bonnin and Morris), Philadelphia
Soft-paste porcelain; H. 2⅛ in. (5.4 cm.)
Marks (on bottom, painted in underglaze blue): P
Mr. and Mrs. George M. Kaufman

PIERCED FRUIT BASKETS and shell pickle stands (see cat. no. 3) were among the most elaborate objects produced at the porcelain works founded in 1770 by Gousse Bonnin and George Anthony Morris. The only successful makers of American porcelain during the colonial period, they achieved truly remarkable results. In view of the complexity of the porcelain venture, it is astonishing that their accomplishments could include such difficult pieces as this object in the earliest days of their firm's short existence.

In common with the manufactory's few known surviving examples, the open basket copies the fashionable English blue-and-white wares that had found a ready market in the prosperous city of Philadelphia by the time the Bonnin and Morris factory began production. The basket's straight sides are composed of bands of interlaced circles and horizontal struts embellished on the exterior with applied stylized floral rosettes highlighted in blue. The small flowers and the sides match in shape and character unglazed, unfired fragments excavated from the factory site in 1968. The Englishness of the form, which has direct prototypes in Worcester porcelain of the same period, is discernible in the underglaze blue decoration on the interior and, on the rim, in the scroll border similar to ornament often found on Lowestoft porcelain.

Nonetheless, the piece is linked with the Philadelphia manufactory not only by the presence on the bottom of the underglaze *P* but also because its floral-and-scroll border relates it to four other known Bonnin and Morris fruit baskets, two of them having a history of ownership in Philadelphia. Of these, one now at the Winterthur Museum descended in the family of John Morris, George Anthony Morris's uncle (Fig. 5, p. 10). The other, the first piece of Bonnin and Morris work to have come to light, is a largely intact basket now at the Philadelphia Museum of Art.[1] Originally presented to the Franklin Institute in 1841 by Dr. James Mease of Philadelphia, it was accompanied by a letter identifying it as part of a dinner set made for Mease's father, reputedly one of the factory's first backers, with an investment of five hundred pounds.[2]

The subject of this entry is unique in the group in featuring a landscape scene rather than the butterfly and flowers that appear with slight variations on the other known examples (transfer-printed on the one at Winterthur). The painted motifs, among the group's most complicated, demonstrate in their clarity and detail the assurance of the hand that executed them. The scene combines Western-style buildings and landscape in an oriental format, differing from the pseudo-Chinese vignettes that appear on the manufactory's other known forms. The typical chinoiserie formula consists of a large foreground at the lower right divided by a body of water from a smaller promontory projecting into the space from the upper left, but the individual motifs are drawn from the English or the Dutch countryside or, more likely, from such a view depicted in a print. An incongruous element is a Chinese fishing boat in the water.

Among the owners of America's first porcelain were some wealthy Philadelphia families. A surviving bill to John Cadwalader from Archibald McElroy, the agent Bonnin and Morris chose to retail their goods, documents an order taken in 1770 and paid for in January 1771, only weeks after the first kiln of porcelain was drawn.[3] The sizable list of objects includes "Foure fruit Baskets @ 10s.," which probably resembled this one, though no mention is made of

the medium. A bill to Thomas Wharton of Philadelphia from McElroy, however, does specify "American china"; the prices of the items, a fruit basket among them, are identical to those charged to Cadwalader.[4] The baskets Cadwalader purchased were undoubtedly what was referred to as "4 blue & white country china fruit baskets" in the inventory taken of the household furnishings of the wealthy young Philadelphian and his wife on 23 January 1771.[5]

1. Of the remaining two baskets, one is at the Detroit Institute of Arts (acc. no. 70.836); the other, at the Museum of Fine Arts, Boston (acc. no. 1977.621).
2. Edwin AtLee Barber, "The Oldest American China," *The Clay-worker* 24 (November 1895), p. 440.
3. Hood 1972, p. 55, quoting in full the bill in the Cadwalader Collection, Historical Society of Pennsylvania.
4. Ibid., quoting *Pennsylvania Magazine* 33 (1909).
5. Nicholas B. Wainwright, *Colonial Grandeur in Philadelphia: The House and Furniture of General John Cadwalader* (Philadelphia: Historical Society of Pennsylvania, 1964), p. 55. I am grateful to Arlene Palmer Schwind for bringing this reference to my attention.

2
Covered basket, 1770–72

American China Manufactory (Bonnin and Morris), Philadelphia
Soft-paste porcelain; H. 4 in. (10.2 cm.)
Marks (on bottom and inside cover, painted in underglaze blue): P
The Colonial Williamsburg Foundation, Gift of
Mr. and Mrs. Lewis Rumford II (G1969-41)

On 25 May 1772, having produced porcelain for a year and a half, the American China Manufactory advertised "an assortment of Blue and White Ware, both useful and ornamental."[1] This openwork basket undoubtedly fell into the latter category. An uncovered example in the collection of the Yale University Art Gallery has also come to light, but the pierced cover with its delicate flower finial makes this object a unique survival. It is almost cylindrical in shape, its upper part cut out in a design of interlacing circles similar to that on the sides of the factory's open fruit baskets (see cat. no. 1), though here the fleurettes applied to the circles are smaller.

The intended function of the form, which is not known in eighteenth-century English porcelain, is open to speculation. Graham Hood, in his seminal study of the Bonnin and Morris factory and its wares, has suggested a potpourri dish.[2] Because of its similarity to the open fruit baskets and pickle stands made by the Philadelphia factory, however, it seems more likely meant for use during a meal, perhaps for the presentation of fruit or warm chestnuts with the dessert course. A study of the various pattern books of English creamware dating to the late eighteenth and early nineteenth centuries, though they contain no identical form, helps to confirm this hypothesis. The earliest creamware pattern book, published by Wedgwood in 1774, shows at least two dessert dishes, one of which, called a "pierced chestnut or orange basket," has a pierced bowl and a pierced lid.[3] A pattern book first published by the Leeds Pottery in 1783 pictures a "Pierced Cover'd Fruit Basket and Stand" and a "Chestnut Basket and Stand," the latter a partly pierced dish having a fully pierced cover.[4] Although dating several years later, the form that perhaps most closely resembles the subject of this entry is a vessel described in the Spode pattern book of 1820 as a "pierced, round basket with pierced cover" and listed under the category "violet pots and baskets."[5]

The Colonial Williamsburg basket has a history of ownership in Philadelphia. Acquired by Catherine Deshler about the time of her wedding to Robert Roberts in 1775, it was number 173 in a list of the family china compiled in the 1880s, where it was referred to as "Box open worked, blue & white."[6] The basket descended directly in the Roberts and Canby families.[7]

1. Prime 1929, p. 120, quoting an advertisement in the *Pennsylvania Chronicle*, 25 May 1772.
2. Hood 1972, p. 33.
3. Barnard 1924, pls. 6, 9.
4. Towner 1963, pp. 65, 104.
5. Whiter 1970, pp. 102–3.
6. Recorded by Elizabeth Rumford, a fourth-generation descendant of the original owner. Information provided by John C. Austin, curator of ceramics and glass and senior curator, Colonial Williamsburg Foundation, letter to author, 17 May 1988.
7. Hood 1972, p. 33.

3
Pickle stand, 1770–72

American China Manufactory (Bonnin and Morris), Philadelphia
Soft-paste porcelain; H. 5½ in. (14 cm.)
Unmarked
Division of Ceramics and Glass, National Museum of American History, Smithsonian Institution, Washington, D.C. Gift of the Barra Foundation (cat. no. 70.597)

Pickle stand, 1770–72

American China Manufactory (Bonnin and Morris), Philadelphia
Soft-paste porcelain; H. 5⅛ in. (13 cm.)
Marks (on bottom, painted in underglaze blue): P
Mr. and Mrs. George M. Kaufman

PERHAPS the most ambitious in concept of all the known forms surviving from the American China Manufactory is what was called the shell pickle stand at the time it was made. Sometimes known as pickle shells (a reference to their shape), the name by which some imported ones were advertised in 1776,[1] or as sweetmeat stands, they were intended to hold various comfits, such as sugared fruits or nuts, during the dessert course of a meal.[2]

According to two known bills for Bonnin and Morris's porcelain (John Cadwalader's, paid in January 1771, and Thomas Wharton's, dated 10 May of the same year), the pickle stand, at fifteen shillings, was the most expensive item sold by the company.[3] That was five shillings more than the next most expensive items—fruit baskets (see cat. no. 1), for instance.

Each of these blue-and-white pickle stands is composed of four porcelain shells: three joined together and standing on small, conical feet; the fourth, crowning a shaft covered with coral and tiny, delicately formed shells of several varieties, including scallop and clam, all fused together as if a natural marine encrustation. They compare with the Rococo-revival-style sweetmeat stands produced in England at the Plymouth and Bow factories. Accounting for that influence is the great quantity of porcelain being imported into America in those days, along with fine English pottery, providing the standard for tableware in the more prosperous colonial homes. To be able to compete with that flood of wares from abroad, Bonnin and Morris encouraged English potters to come to Philadelphia and took pride in the work their new factory produced. In January 1771, an announcement by the firm was published in several British newspapers: "By a late letter from Philadelphia we are informed, that a large china manufactory is established there, and that better china cups and saucers are made there than at Bow or Stratford."[4]

Apparently, pickle stands were available from the American China Manufactory either fully decorated or plain, as demonstrated by these two examples. Though each has an air of elegance, the three larger shells on the first exhibit finely painted floral decoration in underglaze blue, which relates to that found on Bonnin and Morris baskets (see cat. no. 1), and details of the mollusks are highlighted in blue. The second, probably to provide the consumer with a less costly choice, is adorned only with a simple border of blue painted along the edges of the shells. One other known example, at the Brooklyn Museum, is also decorated with blue flowers, though the painting is somewhat coarser than that on the first of these sweetmeat stands.

1. Quoted in Belden 1983, p. 130.
2. Ibid., pp. 91–134, where a detailed study of the making and serving of such treats is presented.
3. Hood 1972, p. 55.
4. Brown 1989, p. 8, quoting *London Gazetteer and New Daily Advertiser*, 10 January 1771.

4
Vase, ca. 1816

Dr. Henry Mead, New York City
Porcelain; H. $13\frac{3}{16}$ in. (33.5 cm.)
Unmarked
Philadelphia Museum of Art (43-67-7)

THIS TWO-HANDLED VASE is the only surviving porcelain that can be assigned with any certainty to the factory of Dr. Henry Mead. The attribution rests on a paper label affixed to the base when the vase was owned by the Franklin Institute, a concern founded in Philadelphia in 1824 for "the promotion and encouragement of manufactures and the mechanic and useful arts."[1] The label, now missing, read: "Finished in New York 1816."[2] Dr. Mead's enterprise was the only American porcelain factory in existence in 1816. Though no record of the acquisition of the vase exists, it probably entered the collection in the institute's early years. Despite its importance as a historical document, the object has a somewhat obscure history. Dr. Mead may have presented it to the Philadelphia organization as a specimen of the excellent porcelain he was manufacturing in America of American materials. The institute was always interested in the products of new American factories and made a practice of holding annual competitions to foster "examples of American ingenuity and industry." In 1892, the noted ceramics historian Edwin AtLee Barber, then honorary curator of ceramics at the Pennsylvania Museum (now the Philadelphia Museum of Art), negotiated the loan of the vase to the museum, into whose permanent collections it entered in 1942, by exchange from the Franklin Institute.

Made over forty years after the previous successful manufacture of porcelain in the United States, the Mead Vase, as it is now referred to, is an extraordinary accomplishment. The body of the clay is fine and of good color and the glaze is extremely thin and smooth. The classical ovoid form, its two caryatid handles embellished with crisply molded decorative details, is straight out of the design vocabulary of the French Empire style in vogue during the first decades of the nineteenth century. The form, known in Continental porcelain, was also made in England by the Davenport and Herculaneum-Liverpool factories.[3] The Tucker factory in Philadelphia produced similarly shaped vases, but at a slightly later time (see cat. no. 13).

Typically, such a vase would have been covered with gilding and polychrome painted ornament. This one, however, is completely devoid of overglaze decoration, though the factory apparently knew the art of enameling. In 1819, a widely circulated Baltimore newspaper reported that samples of Mead porcelain had been presented for inspection to the New-York Historical Society and that "their forms, their composition, their enamelling and everything gave universal satisfaction."[4] The effect of the Mead Vase derives from its simplicity. It may well have been left undecorated so as not to obscure the body and glaze, of which the factory would have been justifiably proud, a well-founded supposition if the object was indeed intended for presentation to the Franklin Institute.

1. Myers 1980, p. 99.
2. The quoted legend on the label is that recorded by Arthur W. Clement in Clement 1947b, p. 66. According to accession files in the American Department at the Philadelphia Museum of Art, however, the label read "No. Vases 16 Finished New York 1816."
3. See Godden 1983, pls. 228, 230; Godden 1974, pl. 310.
4. *Niles Weekly Register* 16 (27 February 1819), p. 24. I am grateful to Arlene Palmer Schwind for providing me with this reference.

5
Tea set, 1824–27

Decasse and Chanou, New York City
Porcelain; H. teapot, $6\frac{1}{2}$ in. (16.5 cm.), sugar bowl, $5\frac{5}{16}$ in. (13.5 cm.), cream pitcher, $4\frac{1}{4}$ in. (10.8 cm.), cup, $2\frac{5}{16}$ in. (5.9 cm.); Diam. saucer, 5 in. (12.7 cm.), plate, $8\frac{5}{16}$ in. (21.1 cm.), plate, $7\frac{3}{8}$ in. (18.7 cm.)
Marks (on bottom, within circle): DECASSE & CHANOU./ eagle/New York. (stamped in red, except for teapot and large plate); EC No 3/x (incised, on large plate)
Mr. and Mrs. George M. Kaufman

THE DELICATELY GILDED Decasse and Chanou tea service is a major and hitherto unpublished document of American porcelain. If it had not come to light, the partnership of the two men would probably have remained completely unknown, for their factory is not mentioned in any previous history of American ceramics. The service is the only known group of objects bearing the mark (ill.) of Louis Decasse and Nicolas Louis Edouard Chanou, whose New York City porcelain firm, located on the premises formerly occupied by Dr. Henry Mead (see cat. no. 4), produced wares of superb quality for three brief years.[1] This set and a small, undecorated saucer in the Musée National de Céramique at Sèvres, France (Fig. 6, p. 12), are the only porcelain objects that can be said to have been made at the factory. The paste of the tea set is good, the forms even and thin, and the gilding rich in color and delicate in design. Those qualities were probably the contribution of Chanou, whose father, Jean-Baptiste Chanou, was master of pastes and high-temperature kilns at Sèvres from 1793 to 1825. Moreover, the large cake plate is incised with the legend *EC No 3*, initials probably referring to the son.

The inspiration for these tea vessels belies the partners' French ancestry. The forms, rectangular and squat rather than classic, cylindrical, and restrained in the manner characteristic of the French Empire style, relate to standard English porcelains of the period—the kind that would have found a ready market in America. The profile of the teacup, for example—straight, tapering sides on a turned, molded foot and an angular handle whose high back edge curves forward as if to look into the cup—typifies what in English porcelain of the early nineteenth century is known as the London shape, the term used in a Spode factory pattern book dating to about 1820.[2] Numerous English potteries manufactured that teacup form with minor variations and sold it in quantity in both domestic and overseas markets. Its popularity, at its height in the 1820s, continued at least into the 1830s. At that time, a similar cup was illustrated in a Minton pattern book, where it was called the Cottage pattern, which suggests that the shape had by then been accorded a humbler status.[3]

A departure from English precedents is seen in the decoration. Instead of the usual colored enamel, that

5. Detail (mark)

on the Decasse and Chanou tea set is restricted to gold, in an elaborate combination of vertical lines and a finely painted leafy border. The typically English stamped mark, not of a kind found on French porcelain of the period or on subsequent American porcelains of only slightly later date, is composed of the surnames of the partners and the factory's location. Here, however, the two elements are separated by an American eagle, perhaps a symbol of the proprietors' pride in having made in America a superb porcelain from American materials.[4]

1. I credit and thank J. Garrison Stradling for discovering this tea set, for tracking down the elusive Decasse and Chanou, and for generously sharing the results of his pursuit with me.
2. See Godden 1983, p. 221.
3. Ibid., pp. 220–36, where the London pattern is discussed.
4. The firm is documented as having produced its porcelain of American materials by a paper label that accompanied the small saucer to the museum at Sèvres. Sent in May 1826 to Alexandre Brogniart, the Sèvres technical director, the note said that the saucer had been made in New York in 1825 of *matière du pays*. I thank Ellen Paul Denker for bringing this information to my attention and I am grateful to Antoine d'Albis and Antoinette Hallé for elaborating on it.

6
Bowl, ca. 1825–28

Jersey Porcelain and Earthenware Company, Jersey City, New Jersey
Porcelain; H. 2 in. (5.1 cm.); Diam. 4½ in. (11.4 cm.)
Marks (on bottom, on paper label): Jersey City / The oldest / factory
The Art Museum, Princeton University, Trumbull-Prime Collection (37-147)

THIS MODEST BOWL may be the only survival from the Jersey Porcelain and Earthenware Company, whose existence was no longer than that of Decasse and Chanou, its rival across the Hudson River (see cat. no. 5). The first mention of what was probably this object appeared in 1879, when the author Jennie J. Young, writing of the Jersey City firm, recorded: "We have a specimen of this porcelain, made in 1826—a

small bowl, with excellent body and glaze, and decorated with a gold band round the outside of the rim."[1] Presumably, the bowl then became part of the extensive Trumbull-Prime collection, which had been formed by Mary Trumbull Prime, wife of William Cowper Prime, a trustee of The Metropolitan Museum of Art from 1873 until 1891. As ceramics historian Edwin AtLee Barber noted in 1893: "In the Trumbull-Prime collection is a small porcelain bowl, with heavy gold band, which was made at this [Jersey City] pottery, of good body and excellent glaze."[2] Much of the Trumbull-Prime collection was given to the newly founded Art Museum at Princeton University in 1890. The present locus of the bowl at Princeton, its appearance, and its old paper label would seem to establish that it is indeed the one described by both Young and Barber.

The quality and rich gold border confirm the company's claim that its porcelain was made in the French style. From a newspaper account of 1826 it is evident that the firm was producing a wide range of forms, available with a great variety of decoration, "from plain cups and saucers to the richly painted and gilded ware of many descriptions, including elegant chimney ornaments."[3] Its objects were judged superior to those being produced by the recently built furnaces of William Ellis Tucker in Philadelphia: when both firms exhibited at the Franklin Institute in 1826, the Jersey company was awarded a silver medal for the "best china from American materials."[4]

The Princeton bowl is accompanied by a shallow domed cover of unknown origin, which does not match the shape of the bowl or the color and quality of its paste. Its crudely painted grisaille decoration consists of a pair of doves on one side and a quiver and arrows within some clouds on the other.

1. Young 1879, p. 455.
2. Barber 1893, pp. 118–19.
3. Stradling 1987, [p. 7], quoting *New York Commercial Advertiser*, 24 August 1826.
4. Barber 1893, p. 118.

7
Sugar bowl, 1828

Tucker and Hulme, Philadelphia
Porcelain; H. 5⁵⁄₁₆ in. (13.5 cm.)
Marks (on bottom, painted in red): Tucker & Hulme / MANUFACTORERS / Philadelphia 1828
Inscribed (on one side): PHOENIX HOSE C°
The State Museum of Pennsylvania / Pennsylvania Historical and Museum Commission (65.134.5)

DEPICTED ON one side of the bowl is a detailed, black-and-gold painting of a fire-pump wagon and its apparatus, the wagon ornamented with a star, a phoenix, and the Latin motto SURGO LUCIDIUS ("I arise in radiance"). The other side is embellished with a larger star and phoenix and the words "Phoenix Hose Co." (ill.). The accoutrements and the emblem refer to a private fire-fighting company in Philadelphia.[1] The bowl is apparently one piece of what was once a large tea set ordered by the fire fighters from the factory of William Ellis Tucker for Mrs. John Briggs, wife of a Phoenix company founder, "in consideration of the many obligations of various sorts the company was under" to her.[2] In the Phoenix Hose Company's minute book, an entry in April 1827 included mention of a "tea sett of American porcelain to the value of $50.00 to be manufactured by W. E. Tucker, and ornamented with sketches of the Hose House—apparatus—badge, and other subjects associated with the Phoenix Hose Company."[3] The fledgling porcelain factory may have had technical difficulties with the commission, for it was not until August of the following year that the minutes recorded the set to be completed. At the time, it was said to have "the distinction of being the first complete sett of china manufactured in this country."[4] Unfortunately, the bowl, its two handles broken, is the set's only known surviving piece.

Whether Mrs. Briggs's was indeed the first set of porcelain the William Tucker factory made is not documented, but it does date to within the company's first two years of business. The bowl's squat, oblong shape relates to English porcelain and earthenware tea sets of the early nineteenth century. Both the gold decoration at the top rim and on the cover—today often called the Spider pattern—and the shape are illustrated in the Tucker Pattern Books.[5] The two-volume set (one book polychrome, one monochrome, both hand-drawn by William Ellis Tucker's brother Thomas) is now in the collections of the Philadelphia Museum of Art. In the first book, at the illustration of the first pattern, a vase, is the inscribed legend: "Patterns of China, Made at the China Factory S. W. corner of Schuylkill 6th and chestnut sts from the Year 1832 until the Year 1838—at which time I discontinued the making of China. [Signed] Thomas Tucker." The inscription is repeated in the second book at the first pattern, a pitcher.

1. The fire company was formed by Robert Aertson, John Briggs, Sr., Benjamin Carmen, Henry B. Carrell, Ashbell G. Jaudon, Charles Macalister, Jr., Dr. McEuen, John McPhail, Dodsworth Peacock, H. B. Reese, and Edward Yerke. It was situated in the Niagara Fire Company's House on Zane Street, near Seventh, in Philadelphia. See Woodhouse 1933, p. 134.
2. Ibid.
3. Ibid.
4. Ibid.
5. Tucker Pattern Book 1, no. 22; Tucker Pattern Book 2, no. 33, Library, Philadelphia Museum of Art, Rare Books Collection.

7. Reverse side

8

Tureen, 1828–37

William Ellis Tucker, Tucker and Hulme, Tucker and Hemphill, or
Joseph Hemphill, Philadelphia
Porcelain; H. 9⅜ in. (23.9 cm.)
Marks (on bottom): PHILAD (painted in red); N (incised)
Wyck Association, Philadelphia

THIS COVERED TUREEN is an impressive component in a dinner set of approximately a hundred pieces housed at Wyck, the home of Reuben Haines, where original furnishings that descended in nine generations of one family are preserved.[1] Considering the wealth of documentary material at Wyck, it is surprising that no bill for this service survives, though Haines is known to have maintained an interest in domestic and local manufactories. As he recorded in his expense book on 27 May 1828, "[I] took Eliz. Bowne & Sarah Grenelle to Water works, Tucker's Factory at Woodside."[2] The following year, his expense book included a listing of the purchase of "Tucker's ware 2 pitchers 2.28."[3]

The dinner set relates to known Tucker porcelain both in the style of its decoration and in many of its forms. The tureen's spherical finial, for example, resembles that on a covered dish of the same period (see cat. no. 9). Further, five pieces, including the tureen, bear the abbreviated name PHILAD, a mark that appears on several documented objects of Tucker production. Each piece in the set, displaying a different hand-painted scene in grisaille, all possibly derived from English landscape prints, has the appearance of transfer-printed English porcelains of comparable date. The scenes are similar both in composition and feeling: one or two structures, some great houses and others modest cottages, situated on the bank of a body of water whose opposite bank, in the foreground, curves up at either side to complete the circular or oval vignette. That loose outline is sometimes accentuated by one or two flanking trees, which curve skyward toward the middle. Although all in one color, the painted scenes have a fresh and assured look. Similar charcoal-colored scenes appear on Tucker porcelain made during the factory's entire twelve-year existence.

Sets of tableware must have been a staple product of the Philadelphia pottery. On its only known business card, now at the Philadelphia Museum of Art, the firm offered a "superior assortment of China, comprising DINNER SETS . . . either plain or ornamented."[4] In 1831, an editorial urging Americans to patronize domestic wares advised "families of fortune [to] order sets with their names on each piece."[5] Two years later, a reporter writing of the Tucker company's products observed: "We saw a large and complete set of china made to order for a lady in Lancaster . . . and a proportionate number of other vessels, all to be made of the shape and with the degree of patterns furnished by the purchasers."[6]

Included in the dinner service at Wyck are a number of unusual forms of varying sizes—platters, oval and circular covered serving dishes, plates, shell dishes, *pots-de-crèmes*, and one fruit basket. In the absence of documentation, most Tucker products are difficult to date. While this service is no exception, there is evidence to link it with the later years of the factory, from 1832 to 1838, a period associated with the PHILAD mark. Whereas earlier signatures incorporated the Tucker name, the practice was no longer followed after William Ellis Tucker's death, in 1832. The only known piece bearing both the Philadelphia mark and the year is dated 1834.

1. See Sandra MacKenzie Lloyd, "Wyck," *The Magazine Antiques* 124 (August 1983), pp. 276–83.
2. Letter to author, 15 April 1988, from Sandra MacKenzie Lloyd, quoting Haines Family Expense Book, 1828, Wyck Association.
3. Ibid., quoting expense book of 1829.
4. Accession files, American Department, Philadelphia Museum of Art. Apparently, the firm did not otherwise advertise its wares. In Phillip H. Curtis's survey of three Philadelphia newspapers of the period, no advertisement for the Tucker factory was found. See Curtis 1972, p. 62.
5. Ibid., p. 67, quoting *West Chester Village Record*, 19 January 1831.
6. Ibid., p. 61, quoting *West Chester Republican and Democrat*, 9 July 1833.

9
Covered dish, 1831–38

Tucker and Hemphill, or Joseph Hemphill, Philadelphia
Porcelain; H. 7⅛ in. (18.1 cm.)
Unmarked
The Metropolitan Museum of Art, Purchase,
Mr. and Mrs. George M. Kaufman Gift, 1982 (1982.34ab)

THE STRIKINGLY MODERN appearance of this covered serving dish, with its straight sides and angular handles, is enhanced by the starkness of the unornamented white porcelain. Nonetheless, the dish matches exactly item no. 53 in a Tucker pattern book (ill.), where the factory price of $2.50 is listed.[1]

The dish descended in the family of Judge Joseph Hemphill, of Philadelphia, whose investment of seven thousand dollars in the Tucker firm in 1831 enabled the factory to weather the financial crisis in which it was foundering. On the death of William Ellis Tucker, in 1832, Hemphill became the sole owner of the firm.[2] A covered dish identical in form but with gold banding and the gold initials *SHW* is in a private collection, part of a large service made for Samuel H. Williams of Philadelphia.[3]

1. Tucker Pattern Book 2, Library, Philadelphia Museum of Art, Rare Book Collection.
2. Curtis 1972, pp. 24–25.
3. Letter to author, 19 January 1988, from Mrs. Norlyne K. Atwood, who has inherited part of the Williams service.

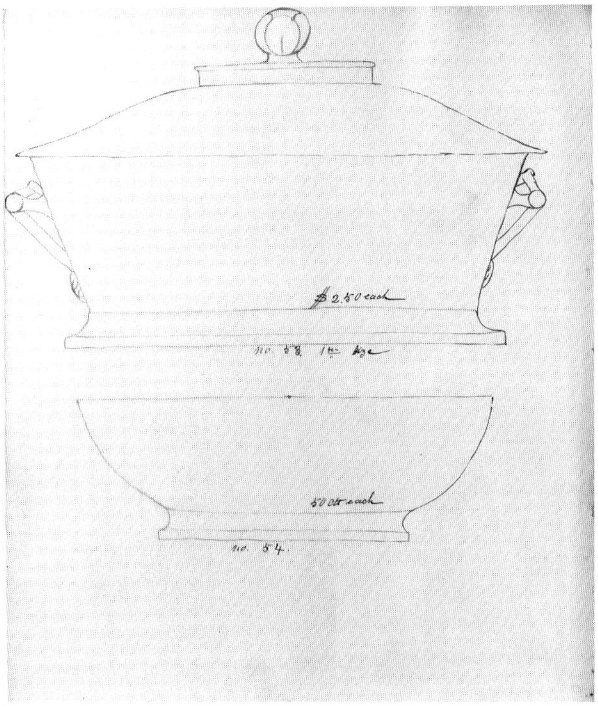

Tucker Pattern Book 2, nos. 53, 54. Library, Philadelphia Museum of Art, Rare Book Collection

10
Pitcher, 1828

Tucker and Hulme, Philadelphia
Porcelain; H. 9½ in. (24.1 cm.)
Marks (on bottom): Tucker & Hulme / China / Manufacturers / Philadelphia / 1828 (painted in red); X (incised)
Division of Ceramics and Glass, National Museum of American History, Smithsonian Institution, Washington, D.C. (cat. no. 76.15)

THIS PITCHER, a classic Tucker form, was no. 7 in a Tucker pattern book, where it was identified by a penciled inscription as Vase shape, selling for "$1.00 each."[1] Loosely based on the classical shapes then in great demand, it appears to be unique to Tucker. (Though nothing identical has turned up from any English factory, a pitcher related in general profile and in the molded leafy decoration under the spout was made by the H. and R. Daniel pottery of Stoke-on-Trent about 1825.)[2] Because no other Tucker form has survived in such quantity, it must have been one of the firm's most popular offerings. The known dated examples—the majority, including this one, marked 1828; others, as late as 1834—prove that the form was made and sold during the entire existence of the factory founded by William Ellis Tucker.

The pitcher was sold either unadorned or in a wide range of decoration drawn from the design vocabulary of the day—from simple gold bands and initials, to elaborate gilding, to overglaze, polychrome-painted fruits and flowers, landscape views, or portraits of famous men—many to special order and undoubtedly varied in price accordingly. The widely disparate quality of the painted decoration suggests that the factory employed several decorators at any one time.

The subject of this entry has pleasing ornamentation of gold stylized flowers and scrolls. On one side is a bouquet of exquisitely painted flowers in polychrome enamels; on the other, a peach, grapes, and forget-me-nots arranged in the manner of a nineteenth-century still life. A pitcher having a similar floral bouquet on one side and fruit and a basket of flowers on the other is in the collections of the New Jersey State Museum.[3] So many of the details are common to both pitchers that they may have been conceived as a pair: each has the same inscription on the base, identical decoration in gold, and painted work of consistent high quality.

1. Tucker Pattern Book 2, Library, Philadelphia Museum of Art, Rare Book Collection.
2. See Godden 1983, p. 287, fig. 428.
3. Acc. no. CH72.76.

11
Pitcher, 1828

Tucker and Hulme, Philadelphia
Porcelain; H. 4¼ in. (10.8 cm.)
Marks (on bottom, painted in red): Tucker & Hulme/Ph[ilad]elphia. /1828
Inscribed: J, F. (under spout); AFFECTION (on handle)
Private collection

ALTHOUGH DIMINUTIVE, this pitcher is exemplary for the delicacy of its painted decoration. The proportions of the compositional elements are somewhat distorted, yet the romantic scene on one side—a classical funerary urn on a pedestal surrounded by branches, leafage, and oversize flowers, with an English-style country house in the background—has a softness and subtlety not often found in Tucker porcelain. The other side features an exotic bird of colorful plumage within an idealized landscape (ill.), a typical design in English porcelain of the period. Numerous pitchers of this shape are known, many monogrammed and some dated, as is this one, which is further distinguished by its "Affection" inscription, a documentation that many of these small objects were given as tokens of friendship. The custom relates to another of the same period, when several British factories made small mugs inscribed with dedications such as "a present for Mary."

11. Reverse side

Because the pitcher is marked only with the initials *J.F.*, the identity of the intended recipient is unknown. Another pair of similar shape also have handles with the painted "Affection" inscription and the date 1828.[1] At least eight other known pitchers of the same form but in varying sizes carry the Tucker and Hulme mark and the same year. Not every one of the many made was inscribed with a date, but 1828 was the year that appeared on all that were.

Like the vase-shaped example (see cat. no. 10), this particular pitcher is not known in English porcelain. According to its illustration in a Tucker pattern book, it was called the Walker shape.[2] The reference is to Andrew Craig Walker, "one of the best hands employed in moulding the finer pitchers" at the Tucker factory.[3] The pitcher was made in four sizes, but the only specific volume listed was that of the next to the smallest—a one-pint jug. The price decreased with the size: the two larger sold for a dollar each; the two smaller, for thirty-seven and a half cents.[4]

1. See "Rarities in Tucker porcelain in the collection of Philip H. Hammerslough," *The Magazine Antiques* 74 (September 1958), p. 241.
2. Tucker Pattern Book 2, no. 9, Library, Philadelphia Museum of Art, Rare Book Collection.
3. Barber 1893, p. 152.
4. Tucker Pattern Book 2, no. 9, Library, Philadelphia Museum of Art, Rare Book Collection.

12
Pitcher, 1827–38

William Ellis Tucker, Tucker and Hulme, Tucker and Hemphill, or
Joseph Hemphill, Philadelphia
Porcelain; H. 8⅞ in. (22.5 cm.)
Unmarked
Philadelphia Museum of Art, Gift of John T. Morris (14-1)

THE RELIEF MOLDING that encircles this large pitcher is unusual in the Tucker factory repertoire. The design, a representation in relief of a fox hunt at the kill, was a common one on Staffordshire wares in the early decades of the nineteenth century. It may have been what Benjamin Tucker, William's father, referred to in a letter of 12 June 1827 as a "horse pattern."[1] A variation on the scene is found in a number of smaller, vase shaped Tucker pitchers undoubtedly based on counterparts made in the Staffordshire area of England.

1. Benjamin Tucker to Marcus C. Stephens, Tucker Archives, American Department, Philadelphia Museum of Art.

13
Vase, 1828–38

Possibly painted by Thomas Tucker
William Ellis Tucker, Tucker and Hulme, Tucker and Hemphill, or
Joseph Hemphill, Philadelphia
Porcelain; H. 14¼ in. (36.2 cm.)
Unmarked
Philadelphia Museum of Art, Gift of Eliza Amanda Tucker,
in memory of Thomas Tucker (31-55-1)

PAINTED VIGNETTES of local or imaginary landscapes are not uncommon on porcelain vases and pitchers made at the Tucker factory. This example is unusual, however, in that it depicts a Philadelphia site that was especially meaningful to the Tucker firm—the factory itself, in its earliest years of operation. The square, two-chimneyed stone structure is abutted by two smaller ones: that on the left having a flat roof; that on the right having a steep roof and a cloud of black smoke issuing from a bottle kiln. At the side of the main building is a post-and-rail fence and a wall on which sit three plain white pitchers, presumably drying before being fired. The pitchers and the kiln, signs of a working factory, are a marked contrast to the pastoral ambience of the scene. No workmen are visible. The only figures present are a young boy in the foreground playing with a hoop and a stick and, closer to the factory, a running dog.

The building is the old Philadelphia waterworks, leased by William Ellis Tucker for his porcelain factory in 1826 and in use until 1831, when Tucker was able to buy a tract of land and move his operation into larger quarters. It is not known if the view was painted from life, as would be plausible, or perhaps after a print in Watson's *Annals of Philadelphia*, first published in 1830, which includes a remarkably similar scene. Thomas Tucker, who entered his family firm in 1827 and was given more responsibility the next year, was soon elevated to the post of chief decorator. His artistry, as revealed by the draftsmanship in his pattern books and the idyllic and personal representation of the scene on this vase, suggests that he was indeed the author of the design.

The classic form of the vase, with its crowned and winged caryatid handles, has origins in the Paris porcelains of the early nineteenth century. The shape, a popular one in English porcelain of about 1810–25, was also used by Dr. Henry Mead of New York (see cat. no. 4). Here, the modeling of the handles lacks crispness: the caryatids' facial features and feathered wings appear soft and indistinct. The factory may have encountered technical difficulties in executing the design. A strut from the vase to the wings serves as additional support—a feature not found on English or French counterparts—and the corners of the plinth are not on a level plane, a distortion that occurred during the firing.

Thomas Tucker became plant superintendent in 1832 after the death of his brother William. This vase descended in his family, first to his wife, then to Ella Gertrude Tucker, and, finally, to Eliza Amanda Tucker, who gave it to the Philadelphia Museum of Art in Thomas's memory.

14
Pair of vases, 1833–38

Tucker and Hemphill or Joseph Hemphill, Philadelphia
Porcelain, applied gilt-bronze handles; H. 22 in. (55.9 cm.)
Unmarked
Philadelphia Museum of Art, Purchased: The Baugh-Barber Fund,
the Thomas Skelton Harrison Fund, the Elizabeth Wandell Smith Fund,
Funds given in memory of Sophie E. Pennebaker,
and funds contributed by the Barra Foundation, Mrs. Henry W. Breyer,
Mr. and Mrs. M. Todd Cooke, the Dietrich American Foundation,
Mr. and Mrs. Anthony N. B. Garvan, the Philadelphia Savings Fund Society,
and Andrew M. Rouse (1984-160-1, 2)

THESE VASES, probably the most spectacular and important pieces in the entire known Tucker oeuvre, are remarkable for their large size, their splendid painted views of two Philadelphia landmarks—the new waterworks and the dam and bridge at Fairmount Park—their elaborate gold decoration, and their applied gilt-bronze handles. Their preeminence suggests that they were made for one of the Franklin Institute's annual exhibitions, in which the Tucker factory participated regularly.

Unfortunately, the names of many of the artists who decorated Tucker forms are unrecorded. Thomas, one of William Ellis Tucker's brothers and head of the firm's decorating department, who is known to have painted both floral and landscape vignettes, has been proposed as the painter of this pair.[1] A careful examination of the vases, however, shows that they were the work of two different hands. Despite an overall identical composition, one reveals a lighter palette, more subtle detailing, and finer painting. The gold decoration also exhibits significant differences in style: on the neck and the shoulder of each vase are Gothic arches, the lower set enclosing a lyre and a sunburst, but on one the pattern is a stylized vine; on the other, a geometric motif.

A reporter, writing on his visit to the factory in 1833, commented: "Artists were drawing landscapes, Philadelphia scenery, the water works, neighboring farms, &c. and it was observed to us that any picture would be almost immediately copied on the pitchers, vases, &c. which a purchaser might order."[2] In 1822, almost as soon as they were completed, the dam and

Figure 1. *Fairmount Waterworks*, 1833. Lithograph by George Lehman, 7⅛ × 10¹³⁄₁₆ in. (18 × 27.5 cm.). Published by C. G. Childs & G. Lehman, Philadelphia. The Historical Society of Pennsylvania

Figure 2. *Fair Mount Water Works*, 1828. After a drawing by Thomas Doughty. Engraving by J. Cone, 3⅛ × 4⅜ in. (7.9 × 11.1 cm.). Published by C. G. Childs. The Historical Society of Pennsylvania

bridge on the Schuylkill River, the waterworks along the east bank, and the surrounding land made into Fairmount Park became popular subjects for painters and printmakers alike.[3] Their appeal was no less for decorators of porcelain. The view of the waterworks found on this pair of vases is identical to that on a Tucker vase of krater shape at the William Penn Memorial Museum, in Harrisburg, Pennsylvania.[4] On the pair, the painted scenes were copied from two different print sources: the waterworks from a lithograph (Fig. 1) by George Lehman, published by C. G. Childs and Lehman in 1833; the dam and bridge from an engraving (Fig. 2), published by Childs in 1828, by J. Cone after a painting by Thomas Doughty.[5]

The classical form, the ornamental gilding, and the convention of a painted landscape scene embodied in this pair of vases are characteristics of the French porcelain that achieved much favor in this country before mid-century. The great demand for such vases is implicit in the number of imported examples adorned with portraits of American patriotic figures or with depictions of American landmarks. The gilt-bronze handles in the shape of winged griffins, which lend added ornateness, are found on one other Tucker pair (see cat. no. 15). No identifying marks have been found on them, but because their form is similar to a marked mold in the collection of the Philadelphia Museum of Art,[6] they have been attributed to Cornelius and Company of Philadelphia and are probably the work of Cornelius designer John Henry Frederick Sachse.

1. Curtis 1972, pp. 59–60.
2. Ibid., p. 61, quoting *West Chester Republican & Democrat*, 9 July 1833.
3. Prints of the Philadelphia waterworks in the Historical Society of Pennsylvania, for example, include those by Thomas Birch (1824), Thomas Doughty (1828), Charles Burton (1831), George Lehman (1829, 1830), John Caspar Wild (1838), and John T. Bowen (1838).
4. See de Jonge 1974, p. 52.
5. I am grateful to Sandra MacKenzie Lloyd, a colleague in the field of American decorative arts, for tracking down these print sources, which are in the Historical Society of Pennsylvania.
6. Accession files, American Department, Philadelphia Museum of Art.

15
Vase (pair), 1832–38

Tucker and Hemphill or Joseph Hemphill, Philadelphia
Porcelain, applied gilt-bronze handles; H. 20⅝ in. (52.4 cm.)
Unmarked
Philadelphia Museum of Art, Gift of Mrs. Alfred J. Brannen (44-14-1) (1);
Purchased, Joseph E. Temple Fund (16-185) (2)

Identical in shape to counterparts depicting views of the Philadelphia waterworks and the dam on the Schuylkill River (see cat. no. 14), these vases boast elaborate floral and gold ornament in the design vocabulary of the day. The type of dense floral ornament and allover gold decoration they display is usually associated with the period from 1832 to 1838, when Thomas Tucker was in charge of the factory. The full clusters of roses, dahlias, pansies, and other flowers, while characteristic of the standard adornment on Tucker pitchers and vases, are here given a more specifically French flavor by the addition of light peach-colored bands and tight gold laurel garlands encircling each vase.

The applied gilt-bronze handles in the shape of winged griffins, also in the French manner and identical to those on the previous pair, contribute to the impression of opulence. Bronze mounts, a sumptuous addition to objets d'art, were popular in France from the eighteenth century. Porcelain was a suitable medium for that embellishment, and when the handles themselves were porcelain, such as those in the form of winged and crowned caryatids on the Tucker factory vase (see cat. no. 13), they were usually gilded to give the appearance of precious metal.

These two vases, although undoubtedly intended as a pair, have different Philadelphia histories. One was purchased by the Philadelphia Museum in 1916

from Miss Ella G. Tucker, a family descendant; the other was given to the museum by the grandniece of Lewis Davis of Philadelphia, the original owner.[1] Thus were the pair reunited.

1. Philadelphia city directories list several Lewis Davises from 1829. One was a storekeeper at 28th and 8th streets, 1829–1833; another, a confectioner at 45th and 2nd, 1833–1837; another, referred to as Captain, was at 13 New Street, 1835/36–1839. See accession files for 44-14-1, American Department, Philadelphia Museum of Art.

16
Vase, 1832–38

Tucker and Hemphill or Joseph Hemphill, Philadelphia
Porcelain; H. 9¾ in. (24.8 cm.)
Marks (at lower right of portrait): C.
Private collection

THIS KRATER-SHAPED VASE is graced with the likeness of Major General Anthony Wayne, of Philadelphia, a hero of the American Revolution. Known as Mad Anthony because of his impetuous nature and choleric disposition, he was nevertheless an able officer who distinguished himself on the field of battle. The representation of the bewigged and uniformed Wayne was painted either from the portrait by Charles Willson Peale of about 1784 (which Peale exhibited in the Gallery of Great Men in his private museum in Philadelphia) or possibly from an engraving after the Peale portrait.

The vase may have been a companion piece to one illustrated with a view of Saint David's Church, near Radnor, Pennsylvania, famous for being Wayne's house of worship and also situated close to a monument commemorating his service to his country.[1] Another related piece is a vase-shaped pitcher marked "Manufactured by Jos. Hemphill, Philad.," made for Colonel Isaac Wayne, Anthony's son.[2] Now at the William Penn Historical Museum, it was considered as early as 1893 to be one of a pair.

An unusual feature of the vase is the mark *C.* at the lower right corner of the portrait reserve. It is undoubtedly the initial of the artist. The names of most of the painters who worked at the Tucker factory are unknown, and few Tucker objects are signed. Ceramics historian Edwin AtLee Barber, who by talking with the pottery's last surviving workman gleaned what little information on his fellow employees is now known, mentions two decorators. One was William Chamberlain, possibly the *C.* who painted this vase.

1. Barber 1895, "Historical Designs," p. 106.
2. Barber 1893, pp. 136–37.

17
Three scent bottles, 1828–38

William Ellis Tucker, Tucker and Hulme, Tucker and Hemphill, or Joseph Hemphill, Philadelphia
Porcelain; H. 1⅞ in. (4.8 cm.) (1), 1¾ in. (4.5 cm.) (2), 1⅞ in. (4.8 cm.) (3)
Unmarked
Inscribed (on front): Mary Earp/1835 (1)
Philadelphia Museum of Art, Gift of Miss Anne Tucker Earp (51-17-1, 2) (1 and 2); Gift of W. Hampton Carson (29-126-13) (3)

Among the smallest objects known from the Tucker porcelain factory, these three scent bottles are also among the most charming. The bottles, designed to hold perfume, may also have been put to ornamental use as a dressing-table accessory or, perhaps, worn on a ribbon around the neck. Though their shapes—two a shield and one a heart—are not recorded in the Tucker pattern books, a plaster shield-shaped mold incised *T. T.* (presumably for Thomas Tucker), preserved from the Tucker factory and formerly housed at the Franklin Institute, is now in the collections of the Philadelphia Museum of Art.[1] The scent-bottle form is said to have been made also by the short-lived Smith, Fife and Company of Philadelphia (see cat. no. 19), which produced pitchers identical in form to Tucker's.[2]

The heart-shaped vial is painted with a view of the Philadelphia waterworks and the Schuylkill River bridge. One of the shield-shaped flasks displays polychrome floral decoration typical of the Tucker factory but at the same time suitable for a feminine object: on one side, a basket of flowers; on the other, flowers and fruit. The polychrome decoration on the other shield-shaped vial is atypical in Tucker factory work: on the front, an open book resting on top of a closed Bible; on the back, musical instruments and flowers. The inscription on the bottle—"Mary Earp, 1835"—is for the young woman who married Thomas Tucker

Mary Earp

in June of 1838, but not before she had received more inscribed Tucker porcelain than anyone else in the firm's history. Her pieces, many of them dated, were all made in the factory's last three years of existence, implying that during a lengthy courtship Thomas persuaded her to accept his hand in marriage partly through the demonstrations of affection he lavished on her—primarily, objects of porcelain he made and decorated himself. For example, there are two pairs of scent bottles, between seven and ten inches in size and of differing shapes, marked "Mary [or M.] Earp" and dated 1837. Of the three vials under discussion, the smallest, dated 1835, is the earliest article inscribed with her name. A large tea and coffee service at the Metropolitan Museum[3] may be the last porcelain gift Mary received before her marriage (Fig. 9, p. 15). Decorated with simple gold banding and crossed laurel branches beneath the monogram *MET*, it may have been Thomas's wedding present to his bride. It has been suggested that because Mary was displeased by the extended hours her new husband had to keep as plant superintendent, the marriage may have spelled the end of the porcelain works.[4]

1. Acc. no. 43-67-4, 5. See also Barber 1893, p. 148.
2. Barber 1904, p. 22.
3. Acc. no. 63.88.1–25.
4. Horace H. F. Jayne, "A Note on Thomas Tucker," *Philadelphia Museum of Art Bulletin* 54 (Spring 1957), p. 58. Mr. Jayne's theory, however appealing, is not supported by any documentary evidence.

18
Plaque, 1830

William Ellis Tucker, Philadelphia
Probably decorated by Thomas B. Harned
Porcelain; Diam. 4 1/16 in. (10.3 cm.)
Marks (on back, painted in red): Manufactured by / W E Tucker. / Philadelphia. / June 10th 1830 / II / Thos H
Private collection

THE PLAQUE is an unusual form; its function, purely decorative. This is the only known example from the Tucker porcelain factory. Its subject is a puce-colored urn containing a profusion of flowers against a landscape also adorned with an abundance of blossoms. Surrounding the design is a molded rim decorated with a meandering vine of stylized leaves and petals painted in gold, which serves as a frame.

The plaque can be hung on a wall by means of a small indentation on its back, which fits over a nail. Also on the back are the name W. E. Tucker and the date, written in precise script, as well as the abbreviation *Thos H*, probably for Thomas B. Harned, one of the few identified workmen known to have been associated with the Tucker factory.[1] Harned's name, along with that of modeler Andrew Craig Walker, is signed as a witness on the copy of an agreement dated 15 June 1835 between the Joseph Hemphill Porcelain Company and Thomas Tucker, relating to Tucker's disclosure of the "secret of china."[2]

1. Barber 1893, p. 152.
2. *Tucker China 1825–1838*, exh. cat., Philadelphia Museum of Art, 1957, cat. no. 586.

19
Pitcher, 1830

Smith, Fife and Company, Philadelphia
Porcelain; H. 7½ in. (19.1 cm.)
Marks (on bottom, painted in red): Smith. Fife & C° / Manufacturers / Phil[a]
Inscribed (on front): TM[c]A
The Brooklyn Museum, Dick S. Ramsay Fund (42.413.2)

THIS PITCHER, one of a pair at Brooklyn, is inscribed in somewhat awkward script with the name of the Smith and Fife firm. It is identical in shape to those identified in a Tucker pattern book as Grecian, which were made by the Tucker factory from about 1826 until 1838.[1] It also features gold and polychrome enamel decoration in a floral style popular during the 1820s and 1830s and made by Tucker as well as by numerous English factories. The initials of Thomas McAdam, the original owner, appear on each of the Brooklyn pitchers. McAdam conducted a well-known classical school in Philadelphia and is listed as a teacher in the city directories for 1835 and 1836.[2] The pitchers passed down to his son, and were then bought by Samuel W. Woodhouse, Jr., an early collector, before entering the collections of the Brooklyn Museum.[3]

The McAdam family always referred to the pair as the "Franklin Institute Pitchers."[4] That undoubtedly related to the exhibition the Franklin Institute held each year in Philadelphia, though the only recorded appearance of porcelain made by Smith, Fife and Company was at the institute's sixth exhibition, which opened in the Masonic Hall on 4 September 1830. The more than hundred and fifty pieces of porcelain submitted by William Ellis Tucker were noted by the Committee on Premiums and Exhibitions for their "considerable variety of forms, designs, and styles [which] elicited much admiration."[5] But the committee could not "omit also paying a merited compliment to Messrs. Smith, Fife & Co. of this city, for two beautiful porcelain pitchers, exhibited by them, and the committee had only to regret that their display was not more extensive."[6]

This marked pitcher is adorned with a bouquet of mixed flowers, the polychrome painting of high quality. There is additional decoration in gold: a thick band delineating the waist, a delicate vine surrounding the neck, and highlights on the molded spout's raised design. Also attributed to the Smith, Fife firm is a pair of unmarked pitchers similar to this one not only in shape and gilding but also in the character of painted decoration. The pair is now in the collections of the Philadelphia Museum of Art.[7] The only other object of known Smith and Fife manufacture is a pitcher (Fig. 14, p. 20) at the Winterthur Museum. Of the same form as this, but with simpler floral decoration in a more limited palette, it is marked by the same firm.

1. Tucker Pattern Book 2, no. 8, Library, Philadelphia Museum of Art, Rare Book Collection.
2. See accession files, American Department, Philadelphia Museum of Art.
3. Woodhouse 1933, p. 135.
4. Ibid.
5. Quoted in Myers 1980, p. 101.
6. Ibid.
7. Acc. no. 93-299a.

20
Pitcher, 1854–56

Charles Cartlidge and Company, Greenpoint (Brooklyn), New York
Porcelain; H. 13⅛ in. (33.3 cm.)
Unmarked
Inscribed (on sides and front): Presented by the / M & M. Union / To the Governor. / Of the state of / New York.
Private collection

THE DECORATION on this pitcher identifies it unquestionably as one of the "large water pitchers with relief figures of eagles and patriotic devices in colors" listed in a memorandum book found among the effects of Charles Cartlidge after his death.[1] Here, an American eagle supports a spout beneath which appears a broad shield in colors of red, blue, and gold. Most of the remaining surface is covered with oak leaves and acorns in relief, highlighted in gold. Though the pitcher's form is heavy, squat, and inelegant, its size, motifs, and lavish gold accents are expressions of an exuberant concept.

"To the Governor" is inscribed in Gothic lettering in the band across the shield; "Of the state of New York" and "Presented by the M & M. Union" are written in script within the reserves on either side. The M. and M. Union was the Manufacturing and Mercantile Union. The organization, about which little is known, was probably founded both to promote New York manufacturing and to protect it from foreign domination. The union was listed in the New York City directories first at 360 Broadway, beginning in 1854/55, and later, until 1860/61, at 304 Broadway. Those dates, spanning only a brief period, allow for an unusually specific dating. The object could not have been made before 1854, when the organization presumably was formed, or after 1856, when the Cartlidge factory closed its doors.

The pitcher is one of a pair. Its mate, similar in size and decoration, is now in the Brooklyn Museum.[2] It differs in the inscription on the shield, which is in script and reads, "To the Assembly." The legend in the reserves is the same, except it is in Gothic lettering. The occasion on which the pitchers were presented is unknown, but what undoubtedly prompted the gift was the hope that the governor and the members of the State Assembly would look with favor on the city's manufacturing and mercantile interests.[3]

Cartlidge pitchers of varying volume but with similar decoration are known. Others in this size—the largest and rarest made by the firm—are inscribed across the shield: one, with "Capt. Briggs" in Gothic script; one, at the Henry Ford Museum, Dearborn, Michigan, with "Washington" in block lettering; and another, having a history of descent in the Cartlidge family, with "C. Cartlidge" in Gothic script.[4]

1. Quoted in Barber 1893 (rev. ed.), p. 446.
2. Illustrated in *19th-Century America: Furniture and Other Decorative Arts*, exh. cat. (New York: The Metropolitan Museum of Art, 1970), no. 140.
3. The terms of the state's two governors of that period—Horatio Seymour (1853–55) and Myron Holley Clarke (1855–57)—are too close to allow for identification of the pitcher's recipient.
4. For an illustration of the Briggs pitcher, see catalogue, Sotheby-Parke-Bernet sale no. 4316, 27 November–1 December 1979, lot 221. The Ford museum pitcher (acc. no. 69.79) is further inscribed on one side: "First in war / First in peace / and first in the hearts / of his countrymen." On the other side is the legend: "Nature made him / childless, / that a / nation might call / him father."

To the Governor.
Of the

CLAREMONT

21
Pitcher, 1853–56

Charles Cartlidge and Company, Greenpoint (Brooklyn), New York
Porcelain; H. 10¾ in. (27.3 cm.)
Unmarked
Inscribed (on front): E. Jones./CLAREMONT./
American Porcela[in]
Museum of the City of New York, Gift of Miss Dorothy Rogers and
Mrs. Edward H. Anson (49.44.4)

Pitchers with relief embellishment in the form of stalks and ears of corn were the most common type produced by the Cartlidge firm and other Brooklyn porcelain factories (see cat. no. 25) in the mid-nineteenth century. The majority have some kind of decoration, either simple—a name or initials in gold—or more elaborate, as here. On the front of the pitcher is an American shield having broad, slightly shaded red-orange vertical bands alternating with white stripes created by the uncolored body, over which is a blue band incorporating many tiny white stars. On the shield are the words "Claremont" and, in script along one of the white stripes, "American Porcelain," the last two letters worn off (Fig. 1). The "E. Jones" that appears at the top of the pitcher is for Edmund Jones, lessee and proprietor of the Claremont, a resort hotel popular with pleasure-loving New Yorkers of the era.

Figure 1. Detail (inscription)

Jones's name first appears in connection with the resort in the city directory of 1853/54.[1] Originally a private house, the Claremont was built in the early years of the century on the Bloomingdale Road (Riverside Drive) at what is now 124th Street, where it would have commanded a spectacular view of the Hudson River. A painting by an unidentified artist depicts it at the height of its fame (Fig. 2). Flying from one of the building's wings is a banner emblazoned with the name E. Jones. One of Jones's contemporaries, writing his memoirs in 1871, commented nostalgically: "What old or middle-aged resident does not with pleasure recall the good cheer dispensed by Edmund Jones, first at the Second Ward Hotel, in Nassau Street between Fulton and John, and subsequently, until his death, at the celebrated Claremont, on the Bloomingdale Road."[2]

This porcelain object made by Charles Cartlidge and Company may well be the vessel from which Edmund Jones dispensed good cheer at the Claremont. (The pitcher descended in his family to his great-granddaughters, who donated it to the Museum of the City of New York.) Cartlidge may have given it to Jones in an attempt to advertise his firm's products. The "American Porcelain" inscription would have been easily visible to anyone standing at the Claremont bar, on which the pitcher probably rested, or to someone whose beverage, perhaps ale, was poured from the vessel. That hypothesis is strengthened by

Figure 2. Unidentified artist. *The Claremont*, undated. Oil on canvas, 25½ × 34 in. (64.8 × 86.4 cm.). The Metropolitan Museum of Art. The Edward W. C. Arnold Collection of New York Prints, Maps, and Pictures, Bequest of Edward W. C. Arnold, 1954 (54.90.169)

the small number of other Cartlidge examples of the same molded corn pattern inscribed with persons' names and the words "American Porcelain."

A search in New York City directories for the names that appear on some of these pitchers reveals that several belonged to proprietors of saloons or porterhouses. For example, one, now in a private collection, decorated on the front with the name E. P. Fox, was undoubtedly owned by Ephraim (or Edward) P. Fox, of what was listed as "Arbor," Porterhouse, or Saloon, at 332 Broadway in New York from 1849/50 until 1855/56.[3] On his, the words "American Porcelain" are found on the interior of the spout. A counterpart at the National Museum of American History, though lacking that inscription, does display the names of John Higham and the Union Hotel. Higham's place of business was given as a porterhouse in New York City from 1848/49 until 1854/55.[4]

On these pitchers, when the "American Porcelain" inscription is present, it is always modestly placed, either on the interior of the spout or along one stripe of the shield.[5] The discreet legend was possibly a Cartlidge promotion strategy.

1. For this and for further information on the Claremont, see Natalie Spassky, *American Paintings in The Metropolitan Museum of Art, Volume II*, ed. by Kathleen Luhrs (New York: The Metropolitan Museum of Art, 1985), pp. 26–27.
2. Ibid., p. 27, quoting Abram C. Dayton, *Last Days of Knickerbocker Life in New York* (1882), pp. 266–67.
3. New York City directories. I am grateful to Kay Freeman, whose research yielded this information.
4. Ibid.
5. Another example having the words "American Porcelain" inside the spout was originally one of a pair at the Henry Ford Museum, Dearborn, Michigan (acc. no. 57.63.9A). It features a shield on the front over the name Continental John Mosher and, on the bottom, the words "Presented by Alderman Jas. Steers" in block lettering. Mosher and Steers are listed in the directories not as hotel proprietors but as ship carpenters and shipbuilders.

22
Pitcher, 1848–56

Charles Cartlidge and Company, Greenpoint (Brooklyn), New York
Porcelain; H. 3 3/16 in. (8.1 cm.)
Unmarked
Inscribed: L. F. Wilde (on front); Presented by E. Herbert
(on bottom, painted in red)
The Metropolitan Museum of Art, Gift of Florence I. Balasny-Barnes,
in memory of her parents, Elizabeth C. and Joseph Balasny, 1986 (1986.443.1)

JUST OVER three inches high, this pitcher is of the smallest size manufactured by the firm of Charles Cartlidge. A nineteenth-century manuscript on the life of Cartlidge, still in the possession of his descendants, lists among the numerous wares made by the establishment "Pitchers of all sizes from a toy up to two gallons."[1] Whereas the largest size made by the factory is represented by the example presented by the M. and M. Union to the governor of New York (see cat. no. 20), this is undoubtedly one of what the firm called toy pitchers. Though minuscule, it features the relief-molded decoration of corn ears and stalks found on other objects of Cartlidge manufacture (see cat. no. 21).

A search of both Brooklyn and New York City directories reveals no listing for L. F. Wilde, though E. Herbert is probably Edward Herbert, whose place of business was an unnamed hotel in Brooklyn's Eastern District, not far from Cartlidge's Freeman Street factory.

1. Robert Pollok, "Biographical Data re Charles Cartlidge," undated, unpaginated manuscript, private collection.

23
Paperweight, ca. 1853

Charles Cartlidge and Company, Greenpoint (Brooklyn), New York
Porcelain; H. 1¾ in. (4.5 cm.), L. 3¹³⁄₁₆ in. (9.7 cm.),
W. 2½ in. (6.4 cm.)
Unmarked
Inscribed (on bottom, in ink): [W]ashing[ton] Irving
Historic Hudson Valley (#SS. 62.227)

FOR MANY YEARS, paperweights like this, in the form of a spaniel seated on a cushion, were thought to have been the product of the United States Pottery Company in Bennington, Vermont.[1] That supposition has since been disproved. A memorandum book, found among Charles Cartlidge's effects after his death, included a listing of some of the objects produced at his porcelain factory, among them "paper-weights in the forms of eagles and spaniels."[2] Specific information that Cartlidge offered such objects for sale is contained in the same memorandum book: "Spaniel paper weights, white, $3.38 a dozen."[3] Conclusive documentation to the Greenpoint, New York, factory is to be found in a letter from Washington Irving concerning the subject of this entry.

About 1853, a young poet named William Watson Waldron eagerly sought the approval and friendship of Irving, then an established author. In an effort to ingratiate himself with Irving, Waldron presented him with several gifts, including a watercolor that today hangs at Sunnyside, Irving's home at Irvington-on-Hudson. The paperweight, another present from Waldron, was also at Sunnyside. In Waldron's biography of Irving, written sometime around 1863, he quotes from a charming and witty note from the author, dated Sunnyside, 10 June 1853, which is evidence that the gift was the work of Cartlidge:

> My Dear Sir:
> Accept my thanks for the beautiful little dog which you have had the kindness to send me, as a specimen of the porcelain manufacture of Mr. Charles Cartlidge. It does great credit to his factory. You say it is intended to guard bank notes; if it can keep mine from vanishing it will prove a more effectual guard than any I have as yet set over them.
> Yours very truly,
> Washington Irving.[4]

The majority of spaniel paperweights are completely white, but this is an example of some that are decorated in black to suggest the dog's coloring and to delineate its facial features, as well as in gold, here the border around the cushion.

1. Barret 1958, pls. 391, 408.
2. Barber 1893 (rev. ed.), p. 446.
3. Barber 1895, "Historical Sketch," p. 23.
4. William W. Waldron, *Washington Irving and His Contemporaries in Thirty Life Sketches* (New York: W. H. Kelley & Co., 1863), p. 246.

24
Doorplate, 1848–50

Charles Cartlidge and Company, Greenpoint (Brooklyn), New York
Decorated by Elijah Tatler
Porcelain; H. 1¾ in. (4.5 cm.), W. 3⅛ in. (7.9 cm.)
Unmarked
Inscribed (on back, in pencil): New York Harbor/Painted by/Tatler
Mary M. Rowan

THE BREAD-AND-BUTTER business at the factory of Charles Cartlidge was what was called "Porcelain Trimmings, for Houses, Locks and Furniture."[1] The trimmings included doorplates, which, hanging from a nail by means of a molded notch on the back, gave the address or the name of the householder or, as here, served as a house decoration. Most of them were plain; others were available with names or designs in gold; still others featured polychrome embellishment consisting of flowers or birds painted by the factory's decorators, most notable among whom were Elijah Tatler and Frank Lockett. This doorplate, though common in function and diminutive in size, stands apart from the standard production because of its finely painted view of New York City taken from Brooklyn. In the foreground of the scene is the sandy shore on the Brooklyn side; beyond is considerable waterfront activity, including two schooners under full sail, a steam-powered riverboat, and two rowboats, against a background consisting of the spires of city buildings. Castle Garden, a former fort, still standing, is at the far left. This may well represent the view as seen from a window in the Cartlidge establishment, which, according to a contemporary manuscript, was on land that "connected with some shallow water lots in the East River opposite new york."[2] Before he founded his own factory, Cartlidge worked for a time as an American agent for the Ridgway firm, producers of Staffordshire pottery. The scene of the doorplate does not relate to any view appearing on the large quantities of blue-transfer-printed earthenware he imported during that period, nor has any print source yet come to light.

Edwin AtLee Barber, author of an important monograph on the Cartlidge firm, considered the delicately decorated doorplate to be "the finest painting of Mr. Tatler's which has survived."[3] He continued: "In this little gem . . . the lines are fine and distinct and the color tones are quiet and harmonious. This piece alone would be sufficient to establish Mr. Tatler's reputation among the foremost ceramic artists of his time."[4]

Elijah Tatler, son of a skilled flower painter at the Minton factory in England, may have started his training there. He worked as a painter for the Copeland factory in Stoke-on-Trent before emigrating to America in 1848. He was employed at the Cartlidge firm for a period of between two and three years, part of which he spent as head of the decorating department. He went back to England in 1850 and stayed until after the Civil War, when he returned to the United States and eventually set up an independent decorating practice in Trenton.[5] He may have been responsible for much of the decorated porcelain sold by the Cartlidge firm, but this object is the only surviving piece of porcelain attributed to him.

The doorplate descended in the family of Charles Cartlidge to its present owner, Cartlidge's great-great-granddaughter.

1. Smith's Brooklyn Directory, 1856/57.
2. Robert Pollok, "Biographical Data re Charles Cartlidge," undated, unpaginated manuscript, private collection.
3. Barber 1895, "Historical Sketch," pp. 31–32.
4. Ibid.
5. After the Civil War, Tatler was employed as a decorator at the Trenton firm of Taylor and Davis. He established his own decorating business in 1876, shortly before his death. William H. Tatler succeeded his father as president of what was then called the W. H. Tatler Decorating Company. See Barber 1893 (rev. ed.), pp. 450–51. Several years later, William joined partner Frederick Swan, sometimes spelled Swann, in a similar venture that located first in New York City and by 1880 in Trenton. That spring, when W. R. Whitehead bought into the firm, its name was changed from Swan and Tatler to Swan, Tatler, & Co. See "Decorated China Ware," *Trenton Times*, 1 November 1883. Tatler was also associated with several other Trenton firms. See Anne M. Tatler, "The Search for Tatler-decorated China," *The Antique Trader*, 14 October 1987, pp. 68–70. (Mrs. Tatler's husband is a direct descendant of Elijah Tatler's.)

25
Pitcher, 1844–60

William Boch and Brothers, or American Porcelain Manufacturing Company of Anthony and Francis Victor Boch, Greenpoint (Brooklyn), New York
Porcelain; H. 7 3/16 in. (18.3 cm.)
Unmarked
Inscribed (on front): Presented/by/A. & F. V. Boch/to/D. K. Thorne.
The Newark Museum, Purchase 1972,
Anonymous Endowment Fund (72.161A)

For a time, two firms belonging to the Boch brothers were operating in Greenpoint concurrently with the porcelain factory begun by Charles Cartlidge. One, William Boch and Brothers, at Fifth, later Eckford, Street, between L and Calyer streets, in the Greenpoint section of Brooklyn, was established in 1844 by the partnership of William, Anthony, and Francis Victor Boch, and was in production for about seventeen years; the other, named the American Porcelain Manufacturing Company, was founded in Greenpoint in 1858 by Anthony and Francis Victor Boch on Eagle Street, near Franklin, and apparently lasted for about two years.[1]

In both form and decoration of relief-molded ears and stalks of corn, the subject of this entry is identical to many produced by the Charles Cartlidge factory (see cat. nos. 21, 22), proving that the pitcher was not exclusive to Cartlidge but was produced at more than one other Greenpoint firm.

Another example of similar shape and decoration is possibly attributable to one of the Boch brothers plants. Decorated in gold and blue, it is inscribed with the name F. K. M. Kropp, who is said to have been a worker at a Boch factory.[2] After 1857, when the firm of William Boch and Brothers was reorganized into the Union Porcelain Company, with headquarters at 82 John Street in New York City, it continued to make such objects: in 1861, its catalogue offered "Corn Pattern Pitchers . . . 4 quarts . . . $24.00 [per dozen]," undoubtedly of this kind.[3]

The majority of pitchers made and inscribed with traceable names were produced by Greenpoint porcelain manufacturers primarily for local tradesmen from the Eastern District of Brooklyn or the New

York City area. Though the occasion at which the presentation of this pitcher was made is no longer known, D. K. Thorne has been identified through city directories, where he is listed from 1848 until 1868/69 as a carriagemaker at addresses recorded as 235, 236, and 237 First Street and 90 Broadway, in the Williamsburgh section of Brooklyn.[4]

1. There is a separate listing in the Brooklyn directory of 1858/59 for A. and F. V. Boch and in that of 1859/60 for Anthony and F. Boch as porcelain manufacturers at Eagle Street near Franklin. See also Ketchum 1987, pp. 73–75.
2. Information on F. K. M. Kropp provided by one of Kropp's descendants. The Kropp pitcher is at The Brooklyn Museum (acc. no. 84.127).
3. *Price List of House Trimmings, consisting of Porcelain Door Knobs, Escutcheons, Bell Pulls, etc., both White and Decorated. Also Silver Plated Butts, Knobs, &c. Plumbers' ware. Hollow Ware, for Hotel and Family Use. Porcelain Wheel Castors* (New York: Union Porcelain Co., 1861), p. 162. The only extant copy is in the Library of Congress. I am grateful to Regina Blaszczyk at the National Museum of American History, the Smithsonian Institution, for her help in obtaining this information.
4. Williamsburgh directory, 1848/49–1868/69.

26
Pitcher, 1844–57

William Boch and Brothers, Greenpoint (Brooklyn), New York
Porcelain; H. 9⅝ in. (24.5 cm.)
Marks (impressed, on bottom): W. B & BR'S./GREEN POINT. L. I.
The Metropolitan Museum of Art, Purchase,
Anonymous Gift, 1968 (68.112)

THIS ALL-WHITE PITCHER is enlivened on both sides with relief-molded references to Bacchus. The wine god is portrayed in the guise of a nude child seated amid grape vines and displaying his attributes of a staff and a goblet of wine. These motifs suggest that the pitcher was intended for the dispensing of alcoholic beverages. The asymmetrical composition of the design and the profusion of ornament—a scrolled medallion embellishing the front and leafage in relief decorating the foot and the handle—derive directly from the vocabulary of the Rococo-revival style then at the height of its reign in America.

While the clay body is purest white and translucent when seen through transmitted light, it is of inferior quality—thick and heavy, speckled with black, and with a surface so pitted as to resemble the skin of an orange. It can be compared not with the imported porcelains destined for the houses of the privileged but instead with the relief-molded objects turned out by the Cartlidge company for service in the saloons and hotels of New York.

After 1857, when the Boch firm was reorganized into the Union Porcelain Company, with offices at 82 John Street in New York City, this relief-molded shape remained in production. Identical pitchers are marked: MANUFACTURED & DECORATED/BY THE/UNION PORCELAIN CO./82 JOHN ST N.Y.[1]

1. One example so marked is at the Henry Ford Museum, Dearborn, Michigan (acc. no. 57.63.7); see also Fig. 21, p. 26.

27
Mug, 1844–57

William Boch and Brothers, Greenpoint (Brooklyn), New York
Porcelain; H. 4 11/16 in. (11.9 cm.)
Marks (impressed, on bottom): W. B. & BR'S. GREEN POINT. L. I.
Private collection

THE RELIEF-MOLDED theme of the mug's decoration is the same as that of a Boch company pitcher (see cat. no. 26), but the goblet-brandishing god is portrayed now as a bearded old man. The mug further differs from the pitcher in the position of Bacchus, seated not in a grape arbor but within a shell cartouche suspended by two winged putti, and in the wheat stalks and leaves that provide additional relief-molded decoration around the rim. The figures are so ill-defined in the soft modeling of the piece that if it were not for the gilded details, the scene would be unreadable.

In an advertisement, William Boch and Brothers proclaimed that it maintained a steady production of "all kinds of house, lock, & furniture trimmings."[1] In the same context, it promoted its production of "porcelain pitchers, mugs, vases, and other fancy wares."[2] To date, the pitchers and mugs that are marked with the factory name are virtually the only objects that can be ascribed with any certainty to the Boch Brothers firm.

1. Smith's Brooklyn Directory (Eastern District), 1855–56, facing p. 81.
2. Ibid.

28
Pitcher, 1853–57

William Young and Company, Trenton, New Jersey
Porcelain; H. 7½ in. (19.1 cm.)
Unmarked
Inscribed (on front): W$^{\underline{m}}$ Young / Sen$^{\underline{r}}$.
New Jersey State Museum, Gift of Mr. and Mrs. William Young Bellerjeau
(CH86.44.21)

Consistent with the majority of porcelain pitchers produced in mid-nineteenth-century America, this example is inscribed in front with the maker's name. William Young, along with many of his contemporaries, got his practical experience in his native England, where he served as head of the transfer-printing department at the John Ridgway pottery before emigrating to America in 1848.[1] It may have been through his

connection with Ridgway that Young became acquainted with Charles Cartlidge, who started his porcelain works that same year in Greenpoint, New York, and soon employed Young as his factory manager. In 1853, at the urging of Charles Hattersley, who had also been in Greenpoint and who by that June had begun building a "porcelain knob manufactory" in Trenton, Young moved to New Jersey.[2] In the fall of the year, Young, with his three sons, Edward, John, and William junior, and with Richard Millington and John Astbury, two other potters, took over Hattersley's factory. It seems fitting that what is probably one of the earliest forms the factory produced would be inscribed to its patriarch, William Young, generally considered to be the father of the whiteware industry in Trenton. The pitcher must have been treasured by Young and his descendants, for it was carefully passed down in succeeding generations until family members donated it to the New Jersey State Museum.

In common with that of the Cartlidge factory, the mainstay of Young's production was porcelain trimmings, including doorknobs, escutcheons, and doorplates. The firm also supplied a limited amount of tableware, such as the plates and pitchers it exhibited in Philadelphia in 1854 at the Franklin Institute. In comparing the Young company entries with those of its competitors, the judges were guardedly favorable in their remarks: "The pitchers are not as smooth in the interior as the preceding lots, but in general, the ware is equally good."[3] Evidence that Young's firm had difficulties with its early porcelain experiments is found in a pitcher intended to be the same shape as the subject of this entry but badly warped and distorted in the firing.[4] A paper label formerly on the bottom of the pitcher purportedly read: "This jug was made by William Young about the year 1852 on Perry Street . . . this was the first white ware made in Trenton."[5] That the misshapen pitcher was not discarded lends credence to the legend on the label. Another pitcher, about four inches larger and with traces of its original gilding, is inscribed in the paste of the bottom: W. Young Co./Trenton/NJ/No. 1.[6] The "No. 1" strengthens the theory that the pitcher was the first form made by the factory. Also known is a similarly shaped example made of yellow earthenware and marked by the Trenton factory of James Taylor and Henry Speeler, which was engaged in making "Queensware, Rockingham and Cane colored fireproof ware" from 1853 until 1855.[7] The Young firm either copied the Taylor and Speeler shapes or used the same molds.

Stylistically, this tree-trunk pitcher fits in with the emphasis on naturalism that was part of the Rococo-revival style. The relief design is an ivy vine that clings to a tree stump whose wood knots, picked out in gold, add to its realism; the handle is in the form of a branch. The pitcher is undoubtedly English in inspiration. In 1846, the Staffordshire partnership of William Ridgway, E. J. Ridgway and Abington patented a similar design, but without the ivy vine. Several other English potteries produced different versions of the same pattern.[8]

1. Goldberg 1983, p. 18. I have relied on that history of Trenton potteries, which Mr. Goldberg generously lent me, for this and other biographical material on William Young, drawn largely from the William Young Daybooks and other manuscript material in the Trentoniana section of the Trenton Public Library.
2. Ibid., p. 15.
3. Franklin Institute, "Report on the Twenty-fourth Exhibition," p. 60.
4. Illustrated in Marvin D. Schwartz and Richard Wolfe, *A History of American Art Porcelain* (New York: Renaissance Editions, 1967), p. 31.
5. The pitcher is now at the New Jersey State Museum (acc. no. CH354.1).
6. Illustrated in Eleanor H. Gustafson, "Museum Accessions," *The Magazine Antiques* 122 (October 1982), p. 734.
7. Goldberg 1983, p. 24, quoting *Trenton State Gazette*, 31 May 1853.
8. Henrywood 1984, p. 70.

29
Pitcher, 1854–57

American Porcelain Manufacturing Company, Gloucester, New Jersey
Porcelain; H. 8¼ in. (21 cm.)
Marks (impressed, on bottom): APMC°
The Brooklyn Museum, The Arthur W. Clement Collection (43.128.199)

THIS IS ONE of two known pitchers, both featuring relief-molded decoration and a distinctive scroll handle, marked with the initials of the American Porcelain Manufacturing Company, situated in Gloucester, New Jersey, just across the Delaware River from Philadelphia. The pictorial decoration, its modeling somewhat imprecise, depicts two boys, one seated and the other kneeling, surrounded by various objects, among which a bellows, a bucket, and, behind the seated boy, one of a set of ninepins are identifiable. While the pattern could be considered merely a scene showing two youths at play, it has been referred to often by the name "Idle Apprentices," because the bellows, implying the presence of a nearby forge, suggests that the two are neophyte smiths taking a break from their work.

The pitcher is virtually an exact copy of English examples, though English versions are generally made of earthenware.[1] Under the spout of the pitcher is a satyr's mask; below the rim and on the front are ornamental scrolls of varying sizes. The scene, one frequently found on English relief-molded pitchers and mugs, may derive from an unidentified print. A related pitcher, decorated with roses and other flowers in relief and bearing the same mark, is described and illustrated by Edwin AtLee Barber in his anthology of American ceramics.[2] Its current whereabouts are unknown. The only other known object marked by the Gloucester factory is a plate (see cat. no. 31).

1. Henrywood 1984, pp. 215–16.
2. Barber 1893, p. 184.

30
Pitcher, 1854–57

Attributed to the American Porcelain Manufacturing Company,
Gloucester, New Jersey
Porcelain; H. 13 7/16 in. (34.1 cm.)
Unmarked
The Metropolitan Museum of Art, Purchase,
Mr. and Mrs. William A. Moore Gift and Sansbury-Mills Fund,
1982 (1982.312)

IN GLAZE and body, this pitcher relates more closely to the two known objects marked by the American Porcelain Manufacturing Company (see cat. nos. 29, 31) than to products from any other mid-nineteenth-century American factory. Of a baluster form, with a waist more slender than that of any of its counterparts, it is perhaps the most elegant of all known relief-molded porcelain pitchers made in America at that period. Its crisply formed decoration contains several classical and patriotic allusions. Anthemion leaves cover the neck; a laurel wreath surrounds a spread eagle perched on arrows visible behind a banner on the front. An identical pitcher is in the collections of the Newark Museum.[1] A yellow earthenware version—unmarked, as is this one—is in a private collection.

1. For illustration, see catalogue, *The Jacqueline D. Hodgson Collection of Important American Ceramics*, Sotheby-Parke-Bernet sale no. 3594, 22 January 1974, lot no. 35.

31
Plate, 1854–57

American Porcelain Manufacturing Company, Gloucester, New Jersey
Porcelain; Diam. 8⅛ in. (20.6 cm.)
Marks (impressed, on bottom): punched star / APMC^{o} within rectangle
John H. Nally

APART FROM two pitchers, this rare survival is the only object marked by the American Porcelain Manufacturing Company. The clay body is exceedingly white and the glaze shiny and smooth. The simple decoration, in the Rococo-revival style then prevalent, consists of pierced and scrolled cartouches in each of the four quadrants. This use of relief-molded scrolls around the openings and along the plate's rim is consistent with the decoration found on a marked pitcher at the Brooklyn Museum (see cat. no. 29).

32
Tea set, 1853–59

Kurlbaum and Schwartz, Philadelphia
Porcelain; H. teapot, 7⅞ in. (20 cm.), sugar bowl, 6⅞ in. (17.5 cm.),
cream pitcher, 7 5/16 in. (18.6 cm.), cup, 2¾ in. (7 cm.);
Diam. saucer, 5½ in. (14 cm.)
Marks (impressed, on bottom of saucer): K & S
Philadelphia Museum of Art, Gift of Charles G. Kurlbaum (03–389b, d);
Gift of Mrs. Robert John Hughes (39–26–1, 2, 3)

Whereas relief-molded decoration seems a characteristic of most of the porcelain made in mid-nineteenth-century America, this tea set has smooth sides and delicate ornamentation in gold. A band of tiny, finely painted ivy leaves and scrollwork decorates each piece; additional gold is seen on the finials, on the teapot's spout, and in a ring inside the rim of each of the set's four teacups. The gilding is especially notable for being thinner in application and more metallic in appearance than that found on the porcelain of earlier decades.

In both their clay body and glaze, these tea vessels made at mid-century by the Philadelphia porcelain firm of Charles A. Kurlbaum and John T. Schwartz (sometimes spelled Schwartze) are the finest American examples known. They were recognized as such even in their own time. In 1853, when the firm showed specimens of its production in its home city at the annual Franklin Institute exhibition, the judges awarded the firm a First Premium, saying: "The body is perfectly vitreous."[1] In the exhibition of the following year, the judges praised the quality of the porcelain even further, in consideration of a "pure white body, nearly as compact and fine grained as the finer European ware, and with a rich transparent glaze free from flaws."[2] Though they found the shapes of the firm's exhibition pieces to be of good style, the judges deemed them "not original."[3] That was an astute observation, for this teapot, sugar bowl, and cream pitcher are almost identical to forms probably made in France, at Limoges, which had by that time become a porcelain-manufacturing center. They have the same inverted pear shape and the same type of pear finials and gentle scroll handles as counterparts carrying a raised Haviland mark dating from the mid-1850s to the 1860s. Presumably, they were produced at a factory in Limoges to be sold in America by the Haviland Brothers firm.[4] Limoges porcelain of the same period marked with the name of Thomas A. Rees, another New York retailer, is also known.[5] The wares from France were probably familiar to many discriminating Americans, since the Haviland china store in New York City sold quantities of them.

The teapot, the slop bowl (not shown), and four cups and saucers of the service were a gift to the Philadelphia Museum of Art by Charles G. Kurlbaum, whose father was one of the firm's partners.

1. Myers 1980, p. 103, quoting "Report on the Twenty-third Exhibition," Franklin Institute, 1853.
2. Ibid., quoting "Report on the Twenty-fourth Exhibition," Franklin Institute, 1854.
3. Ibid., quoting "Report on the Twenty-third Exhibition," Franklin Institute, 1853.
4. See Gaston 1984b, "Mark 3," pp. 31, 33; pls. 14, 15. See also d'Albis and Romanet 1980, pp. 133–34.
5. The impressed name of Rees appears on a Limoges porcelain tea set that was a wedding gift in an American family in 1856 and is now at the Strong Museum, Rochester, N.Y. (acc. no. 81.594). Thomas A. Rees was associated with David Haviland, cofounder of his family china-importing firm, from 1846 until 1853. See d'Albis and Romanet 1980, p. 133. From 1853 until 1859, Rees is listed in the New York City directories as an importer of French china. I thank Margaret Caldwell for this information.

33
Plate, 1853–59

Kurlbaum and Schwartz, Philadelphia
Porcelain; Diam. 9⅝ in. (24.5 cm.)
Marks (impressed, on bottom): K & S
Philadelphia Museum of Art, Gift of Mrs. Robert John Hughes (39-26-25)

THIS PLATE, another, polychrome-decorated, at Philadelphia, and the saucers of a gold-decorated tea service are the only known marked examples of porcelain manufactured by the Philadelphia firm of Charles A. Kurlbaum and John T. Schwartz, or Schwartze. The plates are further distinguished in being the only known examples of polychrome decoration executed at the Kurlbaum and Schwartz factory.[1] The gift of the donor of part of the service (see cat. no. 32), they may have been intended to hold cakes at tea.

Four leaf sprays adorn the molded rim of this object; in the center is an exquisitely rendered bouquet of flowers. The arrangement of fuchsia, dahlia, blue and white morning glories, and forget-me-nots is vibrant in color and evokes the lushness and exuberance also found in the still-life painting of the German-born artist Severin Roesen, who was working in this country at the time. Still-life painters were not plentiful in America in the 1850s, and Roesen was one of the earliest to have a career in that genre. His training,

which began in Cologne during the 1840s, is thought to have included porcelain and enamel painting.[2] Kurlbaum and Schwartz, both chemists, were probably not involved in the actual workings of the factory. No china painter employed by them has been identified, and the sole reference to their decorators was made by Edwin AtLee Barber, in an account of the firm: "It is said that expert china painters and gilders were brought to Philadelphia from Germany."[3]

1. A pair of vases at the Henry Ford Museum, Dearborn, Michigan (acc. no. 70.103A, B), having gilt-bronze handles and polychrome decoration of flowers and pink bands has been attributed to Kurlbaum and Schwartz. For illustration, see Bishop and Coblenz 1979, fig. 243. Although the floral decoration shows some stylistic consistency with that of the plates, the attribution is not supported by any documentation.
2. See William H. Gerdts, "American Still-Life Painting: Severin Roesen's Fruitful Abundance," *Worcester Art Museum Journal* 5 (1981/82), p. 7. Roesen was briefly in Philadelphia about 1858, but there is no evidence to link him with the Kurlbaum and Schwartz firm.
3. Barber 1893 (rev. ed.), p. 557.

34
Pitcher, 1861–62

Probably William Bloor's East Liverpool Porcelain Works, or,
United States Porcelain Works, East Liverpool, Ohio
Porcelain; H. 10⅝ in. (27 cm.)
Unmarked
Inscribed (on front): Capt./L. A. Pierce./From/W. W. Chandler
The Metropolitan Museum of Art, Friends of the American Wing Fund,
1982 (1982.192)

ALTHOUGH William Bloor's East Liverpool Porcelain Works (also known as the United States Porcelain Works) was in operation for less than two years, the porcelain manufactured there was of a good-quality clay body and, as this pitcher demonstrates, had a glaze that was clear and shiny.[1] Even though the vessel walls have a thickness approaching that of standard white hotelware, the gilding is delicately executed. In that his East Liverpool establishment was the first west of Philadelphia to produce porcelain, Bloor's achievement can be viewed as remarkable.

This pitcher is attributed to Bloor's porcelain works on the basis of its similarity to a cream pitcher, also unmarked and smaller in size, in the Museum of Ceramics at East Liverpool. Common to both is a braced handle, a molded wreath on either side, and leafy details in relief under the spout. Further, the floral decoration in gold within the molded wreath on the larger example and that on one side of the cream pitcher are the same. The other side of the cream pitcher is inscribed: "Presented to/J. A. Riddle/by/Riddle Lodge/No. 315 of F. A. M." It was undoubtedly part of the hundred-and-fifty-one-piece dinner and tea service documented as having been made of "American china by William Bloor" in 1862, to be presented by the local Masonic Order, of which Bloor was a member, to Judge Riddle, of nearby Wellsville.[2]

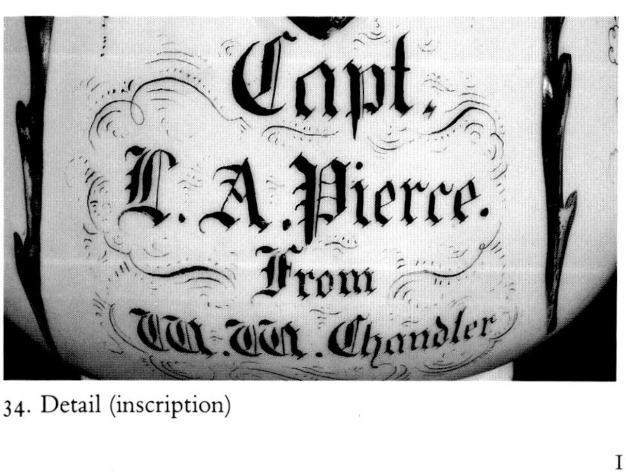

34. Detail (inscription)

The Bloor attribution for the subject of this entry is strengthened by the identity, business address, and dates of the two men—Captain Lawson A. Pierce and William W. Chandler—whose names are inscribed in gold on the front of the pitcher (ill.). Both Pierce and Chandler were railroad agents in Cleveland during the 1850s and 1860s: Pierce, for the Michigan Central line; Chandler, for the Cleveland and Pittsburgh.[3] Pierce is first mentioned in the Cleveland city directories in 1853 and Chandler in 1856. Whereas the last listing for Chandler is in 1863/64, Pierce's continues well into the 1870s. The Cleveland and Pittsburgh Railroad began service to East Liverpool in 1856; it was still East Liverpool's only connection by rail to the rest of the nation at the time that the pitcher was made.[4]

1. The pottery was called both the East Liverpool Porcelain Works and the United States Porcelain Works. An advertisement in an East Liverpool newspaper dated 28 November 1861 refers to William Bloor's East Liverpool Porcelain Works. See Gates and Ormerod 1982, p. 16. Conversely, a printed price list in the collections of the Museum of Ceramics at East Liverpool is headed "Porcelain and Parian China, Manufactured by William Bloor, at the United States Porcelain Works, East Liverpool, Ohio."
2. *Wellsville Patriot*, 20 May 1862. (This reference was provided by the courtesy of William C. Gates, Jr., of the Ohio Historical Society.) A large porcelain tureen in the Museum of Ceramics at East Liverpool has the same inscription and was also undoubtedly made by Bloor's porcelain firm.
3. I am grateful to J. Garrison Stradling for sharing with me his research on the census and directory information on Pierce and Chandler.
4. Information provided by J. Garrison Stradling, letter to author, 6 September 1982.

35
Portrait plaque of General Zachary Taylor, ca. 1848–50

Charles Cartlidge and Company, Greenpoint (Brooklyn), New York
Modeled by Josiah Jones
Parian; H. 6⅝ in. (16.8 cm.), W. 5 in. (12.7 cm.)
Unmarked
The Metropolitan Museum of Art, Purchase, Mrs. Iola Haverstick Gift, 1985 (1985.224)

In addition to its production of porcelain house trimmings and utilitarian tableware (see cat. nos. 20–24), the Charles Cartlidge company also made a series of portrait busts and profile bas-reliefs of eminent Americans—George Washington, Zachary Taylor, Daniel Webster, Henry Clay, Chief Justice John Marshall, and Archbishop John Joseph Hughes among them—of parian, a form of porcelain specially suited to sculptural work.[1] They were primarily from the hand of Josiah Jones, Cartlidge's brother-in-law. A skilled Staffordshire designer who had arrived in New York in 1847, Jones assisted Cartlidge in setting up his Greenpoint factory and became chief modeler when it opened the following year.

No patriotic subject could have been more timely than Zachary Taylor, whose successful presidential campaign of 1848 coincided with the first year of Cartlidge's production and whose term in office ended only eighteen months after his swearing-in ceremony. "Old Rough and Ready" had won public acclaim (and his nickname) through his victories during the Mexican War. His profile portrait shows a man, jaw set and eyes fixed in a determined expression, with a heavy face, thick neck, and unkempt hair and sideburns, all suggesting a personality more attuned to a career in the military than in politics.

A few of Jones's portraits were made from life, but the majority were based on engravings or were modeled on existing sculptures by noted artists of the period.[2] Early in his association with Cartlidge, Jones chose Taylor for the subject of a bust that Cartlidge described in a letter of 1848: "The bust of General Taylor is finished. It will be made in bisque porcelain and will be about nine inches high. . . . The features are a little too spare, but they are more intellectual, while . . . the 'fundamental features' are well preserved."[3] Jones's bas-relief of Taylor appears to have been copied from a bronze medal made by the sculptor Charles Cushing Wright after a design by Salathiel Ellis, which dates to 1848.[4]

The plaque was formerly owned by Charles Cartlidge's granddaughter Alice C. Ferguson. It was in her possession in 1895, the same year that Edwin AtLee Barber's monograph on the Cartlidge factory, in which it was illustrated, was published. It is the only such portrait plaque known.

1. Barber 1895, "Historical Sketch," p. 50.
2. Barber 1893 (rev. ed.), pp. 445–46.
3. Ibid., p. 446.
4. For illustration, see *National Portrait Gallery Permanent Collection Checklist* (Washington, D.C.: National Portrait Gallery, 1987), p. 275, acc. no. NPG.77.247.

36
Stirrup cup, 1848–56

Charles Cartlidge and Company, Greenpoint (Brooklyn), New York
Modeled by Josiah Jones
Parian; H. 3⅛ in. (7.9 cm.), L. 4¾ in. (12.1 cm.)
Unmarked
Mary M. Rowan

AMONG the decorative forms that Josiah Jones designed for the factory of his brother-in-law Charles Cartlidge were a number of objects that point to Jones's early years as a Staffordshire potter. These included statuettes, castles and miniature cottages, mugs with small frogs and lizards in high relief on the interior, and what historian Edwin AtLee Barber described as "drinking cups, or rhytons, in the form of the head of a fox or hound, such as were used by English sportsmen when tossing off their claret in the field."[1] The rhyton, or stirrup cup, has its origins in Mycenaean, Persian, and Chinese pottery. Traditionally used to contain the drink quaffed by a mounted rider before departing for the hunt, it became popular in the mid-eighteenth century in England, where examples made of earthenware or porcelain maintained its vogue well into the 1800s. Most commonly known in the form of the head of a hunting hound or, like this American example, that of a fox, stirrup cups are usually naturalistically colored. Since the form was made without a handle or a foot, the entire contents had to be drunk before it could be set down.

This exceedingly thin-walled, uncolored vessel, which has been broken and repaired sometime in this century, boasts the fine features attainable through slip-casting, the technique associated with parian. It descended in the family of Charles Cartlidge through his daughter Ann Cartlidge Tyndale and is now in the possession of a Cartlidge great-great-granddaughter. Its yellowed patina, the result of much handling, shows that the cup has been treasured over the generations.

1. Barber 1895, "Historical Sketch," p. 40.

37
Portrait medallion of Sarah Tyndale, 1854

Charles Cartlidge and Company, Greenpoint (Brooklyn), New York
Modeled by Josiah Jones
Parian; H. $2\frac{11}{16}$ in. (6.8 cm.), W. $1\frac{13}{16}$ in. (4.6 cm.)
Marks (incised, on back): Madam Tyndale/18 of February/1854
Anne M. Ewing

THIS SMALL portrait medallion is the only blue-and-white parian object of Cartlidge manufacture that has yet come to light, a tangible document of one hitherto unrecognized facet of the factory's production. In his monograph on the Cartlidge firm, Edwin AtLee Barber refers to the company's medallions in low relief, including cameos in "two or more colors" that were designed for "mounting in articles of jewelry, such as shawl pins, brooches, lockets and buckles, and for inserting in fine cabinet work."[1] Both the two-color cameo relief and its utilization as a piece of jewelry have antecedents in the English jasperware medallions made in the late eighteenth century by Josiah Wedgwood. Here, the background color—a strong, deep

blue having a fairly uneven tone—has been painted on the surface, endowing it with a smooth sheen. The ground is not covered to the edges, a possible indication that some metal mount was to have been added as a decorative border or a frame.

The medallion shows a profile portrait of a mature, somewhat stout and modestly dressed woman with hair in tight curls at the side of her face and the rest pulled back in a braid. Considering the minute scale, the details are surprisingly sharp and finely rendered. The subject is Sarah Tyndale, of Philadelphia, whose son Harold married Ann Cartlidge, Charles's daughter, in 1847. Sarah was the widow of Robinson Tyndale, in the early nineteenth century a highly respected Philadelphia dealer in china and glass. The Tyndale firm, which continued in the family for several generations, is known to have been an importer of the wares of John Ridgway.[2] Cartlidge's tenure as an agent for Ridgway in New York City may account for the acquaintance between the two families.

In his 1895 monograph on the Cartlidge factory, Barber discusses and illustrates one of the Sarah Tyndale medallions, which he says were "produced in several sizes and in various colors." He continues, "One of these is finished in dark blue and white, while others were white on a black ground, and several were produced in white paste, in the form of miniature bas-reliefs, all of which are owned by various members of the Cartlidge and Tyndale families."[3] The piece, identified as Madam Tyndale on the back, is specifically dated (an exception in Cartlidge's known oeuvre), but a search of family birth and marriage records does not reveal the significance of 18 February 1854. Nor is the reason for the choice of Sarah Tyndale as a subject readily apparent. The medallion descended in the family to its present owner, the great-granddaughter of Ann and Harold Tyndale.

1. Barber 1895, "Historical Sketch," p. 42.
2. Bill from John Ridgway to R. Tyndale, 7 February 1835, Society Collection, Historical Society of Pennsylvania.
3. Barber 1895, "Historical Sketch," p. 50.

38
Pitcher, 1847–48

Fenton's Works, Bennington, Vermont
Parian; H. 8⅝ in. (22 cm.)
Marks (impressed, on bottom, on applied molded medallion):
Fenton's Works; / Bennington, / Vermont.
The Metropolitan Museum of Art,
Gift of Dr. Charles W. Green, 1947 (47.90.192)

THIS PITCHER, atypical in Fenton's known parian production, is distinguished by the restraint of its simple design. The piece is graceful in shape, its rounded body flowing into a slender neck. The line is accentuated by the smooth, uncluttered surface interrupted only by a lone snowdrop whose stem echoes the curve of the pitcher. An identical form, its snowdrop design registered in England in January 1848 by Henry Fitz-Cook, has been published.[1] Another pitcher, bearing the mark of the English firm of J. Dimmick, dates to about 1862, after the Bennington factory had closed.[2]

If it were not for its Fenton mark, the subject of this entry might easily be mistaken for the English counterpart undoubtedly copied by Fenton's modeler. Similar in appearance and method of application to those commonly found on English relief-molded pitchers and further evidence of the object's antecedents is the mark—a molded, rectangular cartouche incorporating the factory name and location—which is virtually identical to that used by the Jones and Walley factory in Cobridge, England. With the firm name given as Fenton's Works, it is thought to have been used only

in the less-than-two-year period from 1847 to 1848 during which Fenton was the factory's sole owner. There is no reason, however, to suppose that it was automatically discontinued when the name of the company changed. Though Fenton took a business partner, he was still in sole charge of production. His works' later mark—a folded ribbon with the initials U.S.P. (United States Pottery) and two two-digit numbers, each doubtless referring to a particular size and pattern—probably in use from about 1850 to 1858, appears on identical pitchers. Similar ribbon marks are also found on English pottery.

1. Barret 1958, pls. 84, 85. A diligent search has failed to yield any further information on either pitcher or designer.
2. Hughes 1985, no. 160.

39
Pitcher, 1847–53

United States Pottery Company, Bennington, Vermont
Parian; H. 10 in. (25.4 cm.)
Marks (impressed, on bottom, on applied molded medallion):
Fenton's Works; / Bennington, / Vermont.
The Bennington Museum, Bennington, Vermont (75.92)

In 1853, Christopher Webber Fenton's pottery made an impressive display at the Crystal Palace Exhibition in New York City. Horace Greeley, in his published account of the fair, praised the firm's products: "The Parian Ware of this Company is remarkably fine, especially in the form of pitchers. They are light in material, [and] of graceful outline."[1] Numerous English relief-molded pitchers were shown at the New York exhibition, but Greeley found this Bennington pitcher worthy of particular notice. Moreover, it was the only example of Fenton's parian to be pictured in an exhibition publication (ill.).[2]

39. Pitcher illustrated

The pitcher, of an eight-paneled baluster shape, is decorated in relief with roses that seem to grow out of the twisted vine of the handle and climb toward the spout. Under the spout, the surface is molded to resemble a tree trunk. Though an unlimited number of identical vessels could be made from a properly maintained mold, the original model and the mold cast from it were expensive. A factory seeking ways to cut costs could vary a mold to produce pieces slightly different in appearance, a practice exemplified by this pitcher. Its octagonal form and overall shape appear again in a Bennington pitcher decorated with applied oak leaves and acorns, its background stippled and colored in blue and its handle in the form of a branch. The result is an almost entirely different object.[3]

Climbing-rose pitchers are known completely unglazed or, like this example (which, because of the numerous imperfections and blemishes on its surface, may have been one of the earliest examples produced from the mold), with a slight smear glaze achieved by the vaporization of some substance within the firing kiln, much as the glassy glaze on stoneware is produced by the introduction of salt into a high-fired kiln. The form is also known in glazed white graniteware.[4]

1. Greeley 1853, p. 122.
2. Silliman and Goodrich 1854, p. 79.
3. Barret 1958, pl. 53.
4. Ibid., pl. 92.

40
Bust of Christopher Webber Fenton, 1851–53

United States Pottery Company, Bennington, Vermont
Probably modeled by Daniel Greatbach
Parian; H. 14⁹⁄₁₆ in. (37 cm.)
Unmarked
The Bennington Museum, Bennington, Vermont,
Bequest of Mrs. Henry D. Fillmore, 1968

THIS three-quarter-life-size portrait bust is of the owner and founder of a porcelain and earthenware company that achieved considerable success in the mid-nineteenth century. The subject's father, Jonathan Fenton, Jr., was a potter working in New Haven as early as 1792. By 1801, he had moved to Dorset, Vermont, where until 1835 he and his two sons were engaged in the manufacture of stoneware.[1] It was there that Christopher learned the potting trade. Some time before 1837, Christopher became associated with the Norton family of potters, who had settled in Bennington, Vermont, and he married the daughter of Luman Norton, patriarch of the clan. In 1837, he secured a patent for firebrick that was sold through the Bennington stoneware factory of his brother-in-law Julius Norton. Between 1842 or 1843 and 1847, Christopher Fenton and Julius Norton were partners in a venture to manufacture buff-colored stonewares covered with the mottled brown glazes developed in England at the Rockingham factory. At that time, undoubtedly at Fenton's behest, they hired a man who had worked at the Staffordshire factory of W. T. Copeland and began to experiment on the means of developing a local parian. In 1847, Fenton established his own pottery, where, with the help of his Copeland modeler, he produced decorative objects in parian as well as utilitarian articles in yellow or white earthenware. In 1849, he took on a business partner named A. P. Lyman and renamed his works the United States Pottery Company. The pottery went out of business in 1858, and Fenton and Decius W. Clark, another associate, left Bennington for Peoria, Illinois, where Fenton founded the American Pottery Company. He remained in Peoria until his death, in 1865.

Fenton's plant in Bennington and that of Charles Cartlidge in Greenpoint, New York, were the first in this country to attempt parian sculpture. This bust of Fenton, made when the practice was relatively new, is a remarkable testament to his factory's achievement. The bust is not without problems: the porcelain body is decidedly tinged with gray, a large crack that developed in the neck during the firing has been filled in with a plaster substance, and the many blemishes on the surface undoubtedly represent not the subject's complexion but the technical difficulties encountered during the bust's realization. Fenton is portrayed in the manner of a Roman senator, the folds of his robes and the thick waves of his hair so regular as to appear almost stylized. His depiction is realistic, with his brow creased and his mouth appar-

"Porcelain and Flint Ware, Exhibiting at the Crystal Palace." Illustration from *Gleason's Pictorial Drawing-Room Companion*, 22 October 1853. Collection of Mr. and Mrs. J. G. Stradling

ently about to smile. The work is obviously a faithful likeness, as comparison with a portrait owned by Fenton's niece and reproduced in a history of ceramics reveals.[2] The modeling is attributed to Daniel Greatbach, an English craftsman who began his career in this country at the American Pottery Company in New Jersey before going to Vermont in 1850.[3]

In 1853, the bust was part of the centerpiece in the United States Pottery Company's large display at New York's Crystal Palace Exhibition of the Industry of All Nations. There it elicited a mention in Horace Greeley's review of the exhibition displays:

> Upon the centre of the floor stands a monument, ten feet in height. The first or lower section represents the "lava ware," or variegated stone; the second section their "flint ware;" the third, open columns inclosing a bust of Fenton, the designer of the articles on exhibition; the fourth section crowns the monument, and is a Parian female figure presenting a bible to a child on a monument by her side.[4]

The description of the extraordinary centerpiece was repeated word for word in an unsigned article in *Gleason's Pictorial* of 22 October 1853. In the accompanying engraving (ill.), the bust, which should have been visible inside the eight-columned enclosure, was omitted. After the exhibition Fenton moved the large monument in its entirety to the porch of his house on Pleasant Street in Bennington, where he was then living.[5]

1. For the historical data on Christopher Webber Fenton and his family, see Watkins 1950, pp. 141–45, 211–19.
2. Illustrated in Barber 1893 (rev. ed.), p. 441.
3. Ibid., p. 170.
4. Greeley 1853, p. 121.
5. Barber 1893, p. 170.

41
Figure of a praying child, 1849–58

United States Pottery Company, Bennington, Vermont
Parian; H. 13¼ in. (33.7 cm.)
Unmarked
Wadsworth Atheneum, Hartford, Connecticut. Gift of Mrs. Albert Hastings Pitkin in memory of her husband (1918.1106)

STATUARY PORCELAIN, as parian was called in 1843 when the English factory of W. T. Copeland first produced it, was primarily intended for the portrait busts and figures then fashionable for home decoration. The unglazed material had the color and texture of unpolished marble, it could be cast to achieve an unusually high degree of detail, and it was far less expensive than its stone counterparts. Eager to take advantage of its popularity, the Bennington factory of Christopher Webber Fenton succeeded with the help of an English modeler in producing parians that graced many an American parlor. A factory price list dated 1852 printed the titles of figures available in its "Parian Marble," including "Adoration, Cupid, Indian Queen, Hope, and Sailor Boy and Dog."[1] Other subjects were animals, birds, portrait busts of famous men, and such sentimental compositions as this one of a small child at prayer, which probably copies Luigi Pampaloni's original marble sculpture. Made in marble and in porcelain, the image became popular in America, where it was considered an apt subject for grave monuments. It was used on the memorial to Henry Ruggles in Brooklyn's Greenwood Cemetery.[2] The praying-child model is known in various sizes: one smaller, one the same as this version but in white graniteware, and one slightly larger, made of yellow earthenware and flint enamel glazes, in that instance olive green.[3]

1. Reproduced in Barret 1958, p. 10.
2. I am indebted to William H. Gerdts, professor of art history, The Graduate School and University Center of The City University of New York, for the information on Pampaloni as the source of the figure and on the figure's use as a grave monument—in Greenwood Cemetery, for example.
3. Barret 1958, pl. 360; Barber 1893, p. 169.

42
Figure of a poodle, 1849–58

Probably United States Pottery Company, Bennington, Vermont
Parian; H. 8¼ in. (21 cm.)
Unmarked
The Metropolitan Museum of Art, Gift of Dr. Charles W. Green, 1948
(48.25.2)

AMONG THE so-called Fancy Articles offered by the United States Pottery Company in a printed price list dated 20 July 1852 was a "Dog with basket, per doz. 13.00."[1] Presumably, the reference was to a figure such as this: a standing dog, clipped in the ornamental manner then fashionable, holding in his mouth a straw basket filled with fruit. Some examples like this one feature a mustache; others, more elaborately clipped, sport a topknot. The Bennington factory produced the poodles in other clay bodies, notably white graniteware and yellow earthenware, having varying mottled and colored flint enamel glazes. The source of the design was England, where similar figures made in glazed earthenware and usually fashioned in complementary pairs were in great demand from the late eighteenth century.

Other animals popular in the period were lions, stags, does, and reclining cows. Though no marked poodle is known, Bennington flint enamel stags, does, and cows, each supported on a substantial plinth, often have the factory mark that incorporates an 1849 patent date.

1. Reproduced in Barret 1958, p. 10.

43
Pitcher, 1852–58

United States Pottery Company, Bennington, Vermont
Parian; H. 8$\frac{3}{16}$ in. (20.8 cm.)
Marks (impressed, on bottom, on applied molded medallion):
UNITED STATES / POTTERY CO. / BENNINGTON, Vt.
The Metropolitan Museum of Art, Gift of Dr. Charles W. Green, 1947
(47.90.15)

THE MODELERS of most of the relief-molded parian pitchers made at the United States Pottery Company relied heavily on English examples, either adapting from them or copying them exactly. This pitcher, depicting in relief a waterfall cascading past mineral and vegetal formations, appears to be a uniquely American design. On the front is a representation of rock outcropping interspersed with plant life; the

handle resembles the branch of a tree. The 1850s saw the previous century's rococo design revived in public taste. Naturalism expressed three-dimensionally—whether in the form of cornstalks, oak leaves, or roses and vines—was a characteristic of the Rococo-revival style, but to fabricate a pitcher in the image of a waterfall is undoubtedly naturalism carried to the extreme.

This vessel, made in three different sizes, has often been called the Niagara Falls pitcher. The falls have always been a tourist attraction. In 1855, when John Roebling built the first bridge across the Niagara River from Niagara Falls, New York, to Niagara Falls, Ontario, the site would have become even more popular, perhaps providing the inspiration for this piece.

44
Pitcher, 1852–58

United States Pottery Company, Bennington, Vermont
Parian; H. 7¼ in. (18.4 cm.)
Marks (impressed, on bottom, on applied molded ribbon):
U.S.P. No. 14. / 12.
The Metropolitan Museum of Art, Gift of Dr. Charles W. Green, 1947
(47.90.195)

THE POND-LILY and foliage motifs that decorate this pitcher were popular designs on English relief-molded pitchers of the mid-nineteenth century. A composition of blossoms, buds, and lily pads is arrayed around the fullest part of this pitcher; a stylized arrangement of pads and buds forms a garland near the rim. Variations on the theme are found in English prototypes as early as 1849.[1] One, made by the Staffordshire firm of Cork and Edge and titled "Lily no. 2," is included in the catalogue of the British Section at the Paris Exposition Universelle of 1855.[2] The exact model for the Metropolitan's pond-lily pitcher, however, appears to be one produced by the factory of W. T. Copeland in what was called the Nymphea pattern, which was officially recorded by the British registry office on 30 May 1851.[3]

This is a good example of the blue-and-white parian produced at Bennington. The pitted background and the applied coloring that leaves the raised areas of design white create a dramatic effect. Like many Bennington parian pitchers, it was available in several sizes. The plaster mold survives in the Albert H. Pitkin collection at the Wadsworth Atheneum, Hartford, Connecticut.

1. A jug with lily-pad decoration, possibly manufactured by Worthington and Green and pictured in an engraving in *Journal of Design and Manufactures* (April 1849), is illustrated in Henrywood 1984, p. 209.
2. Ibid., p. 194.
3. Hughes 1985, no. 103.

45
Mug, ca. 1854–62

Probably William Bloor, Trenton, New Jersey, or East Liverpool, Ohio
Parian; H. 5¼ in. (13.3 cm.)
Unmarked
The Newark Museum, Purchase 1984,
W. Clark Symington Bequest Fund (84.5)

LOUIS (LAJOS) KOSSUTH was one of the principal figures of the Hungarian revolution of 1848, which temporarily rid his country of Austrian domination. In 1851, Russian troops intervened on the side of the Austrians and the Hungarian republic fell. Kossuth, whose deeds had been noted around the world and who was lionized as a great champion of liberty, went into exile. He had aroused great sympathy for his cause among Americans, and when he debarked in New York Harbor in December 1851 the nation welcomed him warmly. He toured American cities to deliver impassioned speeches on behalf of the Hungarian cause and was honored everywhere by receptions, dinners, and parades—events that received considerable coverage in the local newspapers. In an attempt to capitalize on his popular appeal, American factories incorporated his portrait on various items, including quilts, glass flasks, and ceramic mugs such as this object decorated in relief on one side with Kossuth's portrait and on the other with that of George Washington.[1] Kossuth is depicted in full military uniform, the braided fastenings of his jacket and the fur collar on his overcoat rendered in fastidious detail. His likeness corresponds to a Massachusetts newspaper description written in anticipation of his arrival in America: "A thick moustache nearly covers his mouth except when he speaks or smiles, and unites the beard and whiskers in full flock of dark hair, falling down from his chin."[2] Though the portrait of Washington on the reverse is somewhat awkwardly rendered, he, a hero of his country's revolution, is an appropriate subject to be paired with Kossuth.

Because the Kossuth mug has a counterpart bearing the impressed mark W BLOOR,[3] its manufacture is attributed to the same man, who is also known for having made a similarly marked porcelain equestrian figure of Kossuth. (The figure descended in Bloor's family well into this century, but its current whereabouts are unknown.)[4] Though Bloor is considered to be one of the most important figures in the history of whiteware manufacture in America, he is one of its most elusive. He was a peripatetic potter. Trained in his native Staffordshire, he began his American career in 1848 in association with William Brunt, Sr., a potter in East Liverpool, Ohio, where Bloor may have begun to experiment with producing a local whiteware.[5] He purportedly next sought his fortune in the California gold rush of the early 1850s before going by 1854 to Trenton, New Jersey, where with Henry Speeler and James Taylor he spent three or four years as a potter. Toward the end of the decade, he moved to East Liverpool and in 1861 founded the United States Porcelain Works. The venture was short-lived. In 1863, after possible service in the Union army, he reestablished himself in Trenton, building the Etruria Pottery (later the Ott and Brewer firm) with partners Joseph Ott and Thomas Booth. In 1871, Bloor sold his shares to his partners and sometime thereafter returned once more to Ohio. In 1873, he joined George Martin and two of William Brunt's sons in founding a ceramics company in East Liverpool.

His involved biographical history makes it difficult to ascertain whether Bloor made this mug in Trenton or in East Liverpool. There are several reasons to favor each place, but no documentary proof supports either. Kossuth's year-and-a-half visit to America, which ended in June 1853, ushered in the period during which Bloor joined Speeler and Taylor in Trenton in forming their own earthenware firm, which may also have produced porcelain. That supposition is based on the report of the Franklin Institute exhibition of 1856, which records that the Speeler, Taylor and Bloor

company received a silver medal for china, graniteware, and earthenware. No further details elaborate on the kind of "china" the partners exhibited. Evidence that they made high-quality porcelain—and parian in particular—is a parian pitcher of blue clay body, relief-molded in the Good Samaritan pattern and hand-incised on the bottom with the legend "Speeler, Taylor & Bloor / Trenton" in script. The pitcher is still owned by descendants of William Bloor.[6] Another privately owned pitcher of identical pattern but of a cream color is, like the Kossuth mug at East Liverpool, marked W BLOOR. A Trenton attribution for the subject of this entry is strengthened by a group of related Bloor parians at the Newark Museum.[7] A mug in the collection is identical to this in all respects except that the decoration consists of a courting couple instead of the Kossuth and Washington portraits.

Contrary evidence, however, points to an East Liverpool origin for the mug and a date of a few years later. Bloor's making of parian at the United States Porcelain Works in that city is documented in a surviving price list that enumerates his different parian forms, including matchboxes, vases, statuettes, jugs, and "shaving cups."[8] What the price list calls a shaving cup may correspond in form to the Kossuth mug. Moreover, a number of parian objects in the collections of the Museum of Ceramics at East Liverpool—matchboxes, curtain tiebacks, and jugs, one jug bearing the diamond mark Bloor used on a pitcher of known East Liverpool manufacture—exhibit relief decoration similar to that of this object.

It is possible, of course, that such mugs could have been produced in both Trenton and East Liverpool, which would make this one's place of origin unconfirmable. Molds utilized in the forming and relief-decorating of small parian objects were so easily transportable that potters and modelers often carried them along when they moved from one factory to another. The molds by which the Kossuth mug was formed and decorated may have been employed first in Trenton and then in East Liverpool, especially the smaller, sprig molds by which this relief decoration of grapevine and portraits was achieved. The use of those molds was revived only months after Bloor's death in 1877 by East Liverpool workmen at the Brunt, Bloor and Martin company, the last pottery with which Bloor was associated. That October, a trade journal carried a report on the firm's activities: "Some of the workmen in this factory are getting up parian goods on their own account. A specimen shown is a very elegantly shaped vase, blue body, and white relief, ornamented with medallions of Washington and Kossuth, and grape-vine decorations."[9] That provocative mention of a vase was the last reference to it, and the object itself has never come to light.

1. For a discussion of patterned, blown-molded flasks on which portraits of Kossuth are depicted, see McKearin and Wilson 1978, pp. 469–72.
2. Ibid., p. 470, quoting *Nantucket Inquirer,* 14 November 1851.
3. The mug is in the collections of the Museum of Ceramics at East Liverpool, Ohio, the gift of Walter B. Hill, son of an East Liverpool friend of Bloor's.
4. J. Garrison Stradling kindly provided this information.
5. "William H. Bloor," *Bulletin of the American Ceramic Society* 16 (January 1937), p. 26.
6. I am grateful to Mr. Stradling for bringing the Franklin Institute reference and the marked pitcher to my attention.
7. The collection was given to the Newark Museum in 1915 by Miss C. J. M. Husson, whose brothers, Appollinaire and Edmund, went into business in 1865 with Taylor and John F. Houdayer, a French Canadian who had bought Speeler's interest in the pottery. The new company was incorporated as the Trenton Pottery Company.
8. *Price List of Porcelain and Parian China, Manufactured by William Bloor, at the United States Porcelain Works, East Liverpool, Ohio* (n.p., n.d.), a copy of which is in the Museum of Ceramics at East Liverpool.
9. "East Liverpool Affairs," *Crockery and Glass Journal* 6 (25 October 1877), p. 15. I am obliged to Mr. Stradling for this reference.

46
Pitcher, 1861–62

William Bloor's East Liverpool Porcelain Works, or,
United States Porcelain Works, East Liverpool, Ohio
Parian; H. 9⅛ in. (23.2 cm.)
Marks (incised, on bottom, on applied molded lozenge): IV / W / Bloor / 3
New Jersey State Museum,
The Cybis Collection of American Porcelain (CH71.332)

A PRINTED PRICE LIST, titled "Porcelain and Parian China Manufactured by William Bloor, at the United States Porcelain Works, East Liverpool, Ohio," contains an entry under "jugs" for a Tulip pattern in seven sizes, ranging in price from eighteen dollars a dozen for the largest to four dollars a dozen for the smallest.[1] This object incised with W. Bloor's mark is unquestionably one of those offered. On both of its sides is a relief arrangement of leaves and tulip blossoms in varying stages of bloom that seem to be growing from the bottom of the jug, and there is additional relief decoration just below the rim and on the front. The theme is carried through to the braced handle, which is in the form of a tulip leaf.

The tulip motif was a popular design with English manufacturers. The Staffordshire factory of W. T. Copeland produced a version in stoneware for which a patent was registered on 12 September 1854.[2] The prototype for this example, however, is more likely to have been a pitcher made at James Dudson's pottery. Though it differs only slightly in composition, its heavily pebbled background has not been duplicated on the East Liverpool example.[3] Bloor must have felt that the piece would be more marketable if it could be considered of English manufacture, because the factory mark (ill.) he chose for it emulates the standard,

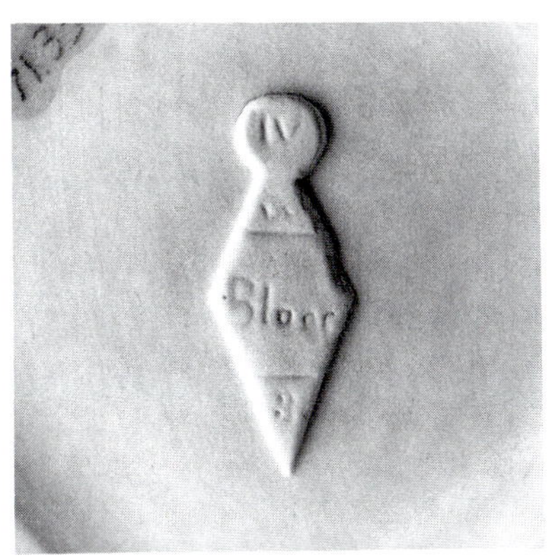

46. Detail (mark)

diamond-shaped device used in England to show that a design has been officially registered. The combination of letters and numbers on English marks can be read to determine the medium and the exact day of registration. Bloor's diamond mark consists of a circular device at the top incised with the Roman numeral IV, which refers to the category of pottery and porcelain. In place of the English registry abbreviation ("Rd") and the numbers and letters for the date, Bloor has substituted his own name. The numeral 3 at the bottom probably denotes that this was the third largest size in which the pitcher was made; according to the price list, a dozen of those would have cost twelve dollars. A larger pitcher in the Museum of Ceramics at East Liverpool, its background color a streaky, light lavender blue, has the same type of mark. The numeral 1 at the bottom shows that it was the largest size made. Another pitcher, whose entirely illegible mark appears to be of a similar shape, is made of yellow earthenware covered with a mottled brown glaze of the Rockingham type.[4] The medium suggests that it may be the product of another East Liverpool firm; if so, it can be inferred that molds were used by more than one factory and were possibly sold when a plant closed or perhaps were taken to a new place of employment by a transient workman.

1. Price list in the collections of the Museum of Ceramics at East Liverpool, Ohio.
2. Henrywood 1984, fig. 137.
3. Ibid., figs. 2, 3, 4, 173.
4. National Museum of American History, Smithsonian Institution, Washington, D.C. (acc. no. 76.11).

47
Pitcher, 1875–79

Dallas Pottery, Cincinnati, Ohio
Parian; H. 9⅝ in. (24.5 cm.)
Marks (impressed, on bottom): DALLAS
The Metropolitan Museum of Art,
Mr. and Mrs. Edward J. Scheider Gift, 1987 (1987.170.1)

THE POTTERY founded by Frederick Dallas in 1865 on Hamilton Road in Cincinnati, Ohio, is perhaps best known for its influence on the early years of Cincinnati art pottery. During the late 1870s and early 1880s, it was at the Dallas kilns that the women of the Cincinnati Pottery Club fired their decorated wares. (Maria Longworth Nichols, a club member who had financed one of the kilns, was to found one of the most successful of all American art potteries, which she called the Rookwood Pottery.)

While Dallas's artistic faience and cream-colored earthenware is well known, the factory's production of parian is virtually unrecorded. Consequently, a document like this parian pitcher with the pottery's name impressed on its foot rim assumes great importance. The first reference to parian production at the Dallas factory appeared in February 1875 in an article in a trade periodical. The writer reported the Dallas manufacture of various articles in "Parian marble, embracing fourteen sizes and varieties of pitchers, candle-sticks, match-boxes, molasses-jugs, and etc." He went on to say:

> This is the only establishment in the West that makes Parian goods, and Mr. Dallas is deserving great credit for his enterprise in introducing it. The material used in the manufacture of these goods is brought from Pennsylvania and Maryland. After a careful and critical examination, we have no hesitation in saying that they are fully equal in every respect to the imported Parian ware.[1]

The firm continued its production of parian at least until 1879. In that year, it was awarded a bronze medal for its "display of Parian Marble-ware" at the Cincinnati Seventh Industrial Exposition.[2] The following year, no mention of parian appeared in the firm's published advertisements. In 1881, Frederick Dallas died, and his firm closed shortly afterward. These data establish that the probable date for this piece is about 1875 to 1879.

Three forms of pitchers, all having different floral motifs, are the only Dallas Pottery parian shapes currently known. The subject of this entry displays a calla-lily plant within a woven basket. Another, decorated with tulips in relief and featured in the firm's advertisements, is not unlike the example produced in East Liverpool by William Bloor (see cat. no. 46). A third has a representation of iris plants on a ribbed background. Apparent in all three is the style of the Aesthetic movement then prevalent in America; the motifs, particularly the calla lily and the iris, are directly from that design vocabulary. Though the three pitchers are monochrome pieces in a creamy white, all have the unusually crisp details of design that can be achieved only through the slip-casting technique required for the parian medium.

1. "Cincinnati Enterprise," *The Crockery Journal* 1 (27 February 1875), p. 7.
2. "Cincinnati Exposition," *Crockery and Glass Journal* 10 (16 October 1879), p. 10.

48
Pitcher, 1875

Union Porcelain Works, Greenpoint (Brooklyn), New York
Designed by Karl L. H. Müller
Parian; H. 8³⁄₁₆ in. (20.8 cm.)
Marks (incised, at right side, under spout): KLHM / 1875
T. E. Goodwin

A PITCHER of this form, undoubtedly inspired by a Renaissance metal antecedent and exhibited in 1876 by the Union Porcelain Works at the annual American Institute Fair in New York City, earned this praise from an unidentified reviewer: "The poet's pitcher, in plain white porcelain, ornamented with wreaths and vines, and medallion heads is a chaste and beautiful affair."[1] The pitcher's name derives from the finely rendered profile relief portraits of poets that encircle the body within medallions, each inscribed below with the poet's name—Homer, Virgil, Ossian, Dante, Shakespeare, and Milton—and each adorned above with relevant motifs or vignettes in meticulous relief. No exact English prototype is known, but a pitcher in the Elizabethan pattern introduced several decades earlier by the Cobridge firm of E. Jones is of a related paneled and broken-waisted shape.[2]

Müller, the designer, favored subject matter incorporating themes of poets or playwrights. The source for the subject of this entry may be the "Vase in Silver, The Poets," which Müller exhibited in 1863 at the Fourth Annual Exhibition of the Artists' Fund Society.[3] He designed several other pieces of related subject matter, including a bust of Shakespeare; a Centennial pedestal with motifs based on the story of Electra (see cat. no. 58); a vase having the figures of Comedy and Tragedy on the handles and depicting the American actress Charlotte Saunders Cushman as the character Meg Merrilies in the play *Guy Mannering*, which was exhibited at the American Institute Fair in 1876 and is known today only from a contemporary description; and two representations of the famous actor Edwin Forrest—one a small portrait plaque and the other a bust as William Tell.[4]

Although several poets pitchers cast from the same mold are known, this one was unquestionably the first made and was probably the prototype on which the others were based. It is the only one incised with the designer's initials and the date 1875. Those fea-

tures relate it to a bar pitcher (see cat. no. 61), also a prototype for an object put into production in time for the nation's Centennial Exposition and also marked with Müller's initials and the same date.

1. "The American Institute Fair," *Crockery and Glass Journal* 4 (28 September 1876), p. 14.
2. Illustrated in Henrywood 1984, fig. 91.
3. Artists' Fund Society of New York, *Catalogue of the Fourth Annual Exhibition* (New York: G. A. Whitehorne, 1863), p. 16.
4. For the Shakespeare bust and the Meg Merrilies vase, see "The American Institute Fair," *Crockery and Glass Journal* 4 (28 September 1876), p. 14; the Edwin Forrest portrait plaque is at the Metropolitan Museum (acc. no. 1987.230); for the Forrest bust, see Barber 1893, fig. 116.

49

Statuette, ca. 1876

Union Porcelain Works, Greenpoint (Brooklyn), New York
Designed and modeled by Karl L. H. Müller
Parian; H. 12¼ in. (31.1 cm.)
Marks (incised): U.P.W. / Greenpoint. / N.Y. (on back, near anvil bottom);
K. Müller (on top of base)
The Brooklyn Museum, Gift of Franklin Chace (68.87.55)

THE BROTHERS Karl and Nicholas Müller were both trained in Koblenz, Germany, where they worked in a goldsmith's shop before going on to Paris to study and then emigrating to America about 1850. Motivated by the great American vogue for statuettes in parian and in bronze, which began in the 1850s and continued for several decades, they set up shop in New York City to produce clock cases and statuettes in various media that would appeal to the popular market.[1] Nicholas did the casting to Karl's designs, which were centered on themes of specific American interest, including figures of baseball players, "Newsboy in Winter," "Newsboy in Summer," and "statuettes of 'The American Workman' as blacksmith and sculptor."[2] The "blacksmith" is undoubtedly the white-metal figure (Fig. 1) inscribed with Karl Müller's signature and the date 1867 that he patented as "Design for Figure and Base" on 4 February

Figure 1. Karl L. H. Müller. Statuette, 1867. Patinated white metal, H. 11⅛ in. (28.3 cm.). Collection of Marco Polo Stufano

Figure 2. Karl L. H. Müller. "Carl Müller's Design for Figure and Base." Patent no. 2919, 1868. Cartographic and Architectural Branch, National Archives and Records Administration

1868 (Fig. 2). The sculptor may have modeled a first version in 1865: a figure of his titled "The Blacksmith" appeared that year in the statuary gallery of the Artists' Fund Society exhibition held at the National Academy of Design.[3] A blacksmith figure was also displayed at the Brooklyn Art Association's exhibitions of 1865 and 1868.[4]

Müller joined the Union Porcelain Works in 1874 and shortly afterward modeled the subject of this entry in parian after the versions he had made and patented the previous decade. The blacksmith, still garbed in his work clothes, is portrayed at rest. His sleeves are rolled up, his leather apron is tied at his waist, and the tools of his trade—a nail, a horseshoe, a pair of pliers, and a hammer—lie at his feet. He has draped his coat over the anvil against which he leans as he lights his pipe from a poker (now missing). The relaxed pose, differing from those of Müller's sculptor and baseball figures, which are shown in the action of their professions, may have been what prompted one critic to comment: "[The] attitude is not quite to our mind. It is too 'elegant.'"[5]

The parian blacksmith descended in the family of Thomas C. Smith, owner and founder of the Union Porcelain Works.

1. Capellocampo [pseud.], "Four American Artists," *New York Evening Post*, 29 August 1868. In 1868, Müller patented two "designs for clock cases" (pat. nos. 2943 and 3249). See photostats Ph1335.1, 2, Downs Manuscript and Microfilm Collection, The Henry Francis du Pont Winterthur Museum, Winterthur, Delaware. Müller later incorporated some of their motifs in his porcelain designs.
2. Capellocampo, "Four American Artists." Outside of a few contemporary references and exhibition catalogues, Müller's sculptural career is largely undocumented.
3. Artists' Fund Society of New York, *Catalogue of the Sixth Annual Exhibition* (New York: G. A. Whitehorne, 1865), p. 17.
4. Clark S. Marlor, *A History of the Brooklyn Art Association with an Index of Exhibitions* (New York: James F. Carr, 1970), p. 283.
5. Bogart 1979, p. 90, quoting "Fine Arts," *New-York Daily Tribune*, 29 May 1868, p. 2.

50
Bust of James Carr, ca. 1876

New York City Pottery (James Carr)
Modeled by W. H. Edge
Parian; H. 21⅜ in. (54.3 cm.)
Unmarked
The Newark Museum, Gift of Mrs. M. E. Clark, 1928 (28.4)

James Carr's pottery, at 442 West Thirteenth Street in New York City, was in business from 1853, producing utilitarian objects, mostly in yellow earthenware. As a result of experiments he conducted in a variety of clay bodies, Carr developed a parian medium and, probably in the early 1870s, began to make figural busts and statuettes a preferred part of his firm's repertoire. By the time of the Philadelphia Centennial Exposition, his parian representations of subjects such as Jesus Christ, George Washington, Ulysses S. Grant, and Henry Ward Beecher were so successful that they dominated the firm's display. An appeal on the part of American ceramics exhibitors, who felt that the products of their native industry had been overlooked, caused the judges to award Carr's factory a gold medal for its parian "of a hard, well-vitrified body, brilliant and of fine texture."[1]

In that same year, the Carr pottery entered similar parian figures in the American Institute Fair in New York City. Again, they made a stellar showing, causing one journalist to report: "In parian goods Mr. Carr makes a strong exhibit. . . . We may soon look for American parian statuary to successfully compete with that of foreign makers."[2] A year later, at the same fair, his display earned another favorable review: "Parian ware seems to be a favorite of Mr. Carr, and he shows many very clever and attractive specimens made at his pottery. . . . The finish of

these parian goods is very fine, and they give promise of great excellence in this line of manufacture."[3]

Many of the pottery's figural works were modeled by W. H. Edge, whose name appeared on several examples, such as the representations of Washington and Grant.[4] There is a paucity of documentation on Edge's career as a sculptor.[5] He is known to have come from Trenton to the New York City Pottery around 1876.[6] His employment by Carr follows the pattern established at the Union Porcelain Works and the firm of Ott and Brewer, where sculptors were hired to design exhibition pieces for the factories' displays at the Philadelphia Centennial Exposition.

Comparison with a period photograph of James Carr shows that this almost three-quarter-life-size bust is a remarkably faithful likeness.[7] The factory owner is presented not in the classical manner then favored, but in contemporary attire, complete with a stiff collar and a bow tie, and with his curly white hair and beard naturally portrayed.

Because Edge is the only sculptor known to have been employed at Carr's firm and because the bust is similar in style to his few marked works, this likeness of the pottery owner, while unsigned, was undoubtedly modeled by him. The work was given to the Newark Museum by Carr's youngest daughter. A similar bust, also unmarked, remains in family possession.

1. Tyndale 1880, p. 284.
2. "The American Institute Fair," *Crockery and Glass Journal* 4 (5 October 1876), p. 14.
3. Ibid. 6 (4 October 1877), p. 10.
4. The representation of Washington is at the Henry Ford Museum, Dearborn, Michigan (acc. no. 61.71.3); that of Grant, at the Metropolitan Museum (acc. no. 68.103.3).
5. Edge's name is also associated with decoration. Included in Tyndale's report was the comment: "The etchings under the glaze (designed by Mr. W. H. Edge) are commended for technical merit." Tyndale 1880, p. 284.
6. Barber 1893 (rev. ed.), p. 457.
7. Ibid., p. 458.

51
Vase, 1878–85

John Moses and Company, Trenton, New Jersey
Parian; H. 12⅞ in. (32.7 cm.)
Marks (incised, on bottom): John Moses / & Co
The Metropolitan Museum of Art,
Purchase, Mrs. Roger Brunschwig Gift, 1987 (1987.192)

THIS REMARKABLE OBJECT documents for the first time that the firm of John Moses and Company, of the Glasgow Pottery in Trenton, New Jersey, made parian, a practice that would have remained unsuspected if the vase had not come to light. Relatively large by parian vase standards and very thin, it is an ambitiously conceived piece. Its baluster form is decorated with a series of sprays of white leaves in slight relief on a deep blue stippled background, though some of the leaves are almost obscured by an exquisitely wrought three-dimensional grapevine draped on either side. Both the decorative technique and the motifs displayed in the vase relate to works produced some thirty years earlier at the United States Pottery Company in Bennington, Vermont.

51. Detail (mark)

John Moses and Company's Glasgow Pottery was well known for its thriving production of white graniteware and cream-colored earthenware fashioned into heavy utilitarian vessels for table and toilet use. The factory was perhaps most noted for the teacups and saucers it made as souvenirs of the nation's Centennial Exposition in Philadelphia.

In 1879, ceramics historian Jennie J. Young reported that the firm was conducting experiments, chiefly with Pennsylvania kaolin, "with a view to making porcelain." She added, "Many trial pieces have a pure translucent body and excellent glaze."[1]

This vase, with its hand-incised signature on the bottom (ill.), may well have been one of the pieces that caught her eye.

The execution of the vase must have required considerable and very costly handwork. Technical problems are implicit in tears near the upper rim and in several firing cracks on the base. Though those difficulties would have rendered the object economically unfeasible, preventing its entering regular production, it nevertheless stands as evidence of the continuing development of parian manufacture in the late nineteenth century while at the same time preserving the decoration of an earlier parian tradition.

1. Young 1879, p. 462.

52
Pair of plaques, ca. 1885–87

D. F. Haynes and Company, Baltimore, Maryland
Probably modeled by James Priestman
Parian; Diam. 5½ in. (14 cm.)
Unmarked
Division of Ceramics and Glass, National Museum of American History, Smithsonian Institution, Washington, D.C. Gift of Portia M. Filbert, 1986 (cat. no. 1986.446.30a, b)

THESE CIRCULAR parian plaques—allegorical compositions of Day and Night—copy originals executed by the Danish sculptor Albert (or Bertel) Thorvaldsen, who was especially skilled in the art of bas-relief. In 1824, the duke of Devonshire installed the Thorvaldsen plaques in Chatsworth's Gallery of Sculpture. The gallery, housed in Devonshire's county seat, was devoted to the "chef-d'oeuvres of the most distinguished British and foreign sculptors."[1] Thorvaldsen's revival of the classical manner of executing sculpture eventually found an enthusiastic audience in both England and Europe in the second half of the nineteenth century. In America, he soon became known through the reproductions and engravings that were in vogue at that time.

The original Thorvaldsen bas-reliefs of Day and Night were copied in parian in Denmark by both the Royal Copenhagen Porcelain factory and the firm of Bing and Grøndahl. They were also adapted as designs on a relief-molded stoneware jug of English manufacture, probably by the Staffordshire factory of the Dudson Brothers.[2] The Thorvaldsen plaques, discussed and illustrated in London art journals published in 1844 and 1852,[3] were lauded for being among the "most exquisitely poetical conceptions of a mind whose constitution was eminently of a poetical order."[4]

Day, carrying a bouquet and with a torch-flourishing putto riding on her shoulder, is represented as a winged, classically draped female figure, "full of life and light, scattering bright flowers on the jeweled earth."[5] Night, though similar in garb and pose, is more serene. She is accompanied by an owl, the bird of the night, and her eyes and those of the two infants she clasps in her arms are closed. A border of stylized acanthus leaves lends an additional element of classical design to each plaque. The figures stand out on a brown background, the color acquired either by dipping or, more probably, by painting.

Other parian plaques James Priestman made for the Baltimore firm of D. F. Haynes are adaptations of Thorvaldsen reliefs of personifications of the sea-

sons.[6] The plaques of Day and Night descended in the family of the Baltimore potter Edwin Bennett, who also employed the services of modeler Priestman.

1. "'Night.'—'Morning.' from the Bas-Reliefs by Thorwaldsen," *Art Journal* (London), 1 January 1852, p. 21.
2. Illustrated in Henrywood 1984, fig. 180.
3. "The Living Artists of Europe: No. II, Albert Thorwaldsen," *The Art-Union* 6 (1 February 1844), pp. 40–41.
4. *Art Journal* (London), 1 January 1852, p. 21.
5. Ibid.
6. Barber 1893, p. 324.

53
Pair of plaques, ca. 1885–86

D. F. Haynes and Company, Baltimore, Maryland
Designed by James Priestman
Parian; H. 9¼ in. (23.5 cm.), W. 6½ in. (16.5 cm.)
Unmarked
Division of Ceramics and Glass, National Museum of American History, Smithsonian Institution, Washington, D.C. Gift of D. F. Haynes & Company (cat. nos. 96,682; 96,683)

THESE OVAL PLAQUES in extraordinarily high relief are perhaps the best-known parian objects made by David Franklin Haynes's Chesapeake Pottery and modeled by James Priestman, a master craftsman whose career is largely undocumented. Priestman is listed in the Baltimore city directories (where his profession is given as carver) for only two years, 1883 and 1886.[1] The subjects of the plaques—on one, the heads of a cow and a calf, on the other, the head of a bull—project toward the viewer with a startling three-dimensionality, possibly a result of Priestman's training as a carver. The heads were apparently studies modeled from life of "typical animals in the noted herd of Mr. Adams,"[2] which may account for their verisimilitude. The plaques were given to the Smithsonian Institution by the D. F. Haynes firm shortly after they were made. Matted in plush, they remain in their original rectangular frames.

1. In 1883, Priestman's address was 28 Pleasant Street; in 1886, 104 North Greene Street.
2. Barber 1893, pp. 324–25.

54
Baseball vase (pair), 1875–76

Ott and Brewer, Trenton, New Jersey
Designed and modeled by Isaac Broome
Parian; H. 38¾ in. (98.4 cm.)
Marks: BROOME. Des. & Sculp' 1875-/No. II (incised, at midsection base); March 1st 1876 (incised, on midsection bottom) (1); Unmarked (2)
Detroit Historical Museum (56.77.1) (1)
New Jersey State Museum, The Brewer Collection (CH354.22) (2)

In preparation for the nation's Centennial Exposition, several large firms, including Ott and Brewer's Etruria Pottery in Trenton, New Jersey, James Carr's New York City Pottery, and the Union Porcelain Works of Greenpoint, New York, hired sculptors to design and model their exhibition pieces. Ott and Brewer enlisted the services of the sculptor Isaac Broome, a Canadian who had arrived in Philadelphia about 1850 and embarked on a multifaceted career, studying art, exhibiting in Philadelphia at the Pennsylvania Academy of the Fine Arts, and, much later, working in terracotta in Pittsburgh, where he taught china painting and started his own tile factory. The most memorable works he ever modeled were those he executed after 1875, during the approximately three-year period of his Ott and Brewer employment. Among them, this pair of baseball vases holds pride of place.

The artists and artisans who produced works specifically for the Centennial Exposition drew largely on historic events for inspiration and adapted them to forms loosely derived from classical art. No traditional theme, however, could have been more appropriate to the celebration of America's hundredth birthday than this pair of vases representing the national sport. The idea came from John Hart Brewer, one of the owners of the pottery.[1] In Broome's realization of Brewer's imaginative concept, he utilized subject matter that, despite the contemporary and immensely popular theme, incorporated several elements of classical derivation. These consist of the wreath of laurel encircling the body of each vase and, at the bottom, what resembles Roman fasces tied together but on closer inspection turns out to be baseball bats held by a nineteenth-century leather belt. The overall cone shape may loosely allude to that of a bat with a circle of small baseballs at its grip. On the base are three finely modeled, freestanding baseball players: a pitcher, a "striker" (batter), and a catcher. Depicted in shallow relief on the upper part of the cone are three complementary figures at a different stage of motion: behind the batter, for instance, the player is running between bases. The cover for the vase is half a baseball, the stitching defined in relief. Standing guard from its perch on top is a proud American eagle.

The exposition officially opened in Philadelphia on 10 May 1876. In early June, one of the vases was moved from the Ott and Brewer display in the ceramics exhibition area to the Art Gallery in Memorial Hall, thus elevating the status of the vase from a mere ceramic figural piece to a sculptural work of art.[2]

The originality and quality of the vases were praised by many critics and writers of the day, including ceramics historian Jennie J. Young. In a minutely detailed account, Young extolled the pair's virtues, saying that the baseball players were "modelled after a thoroughly American ideal of physical beauty, embodying muscular activity rather than ponderous strength." She added, "These vases are the work of a genuine artist, who has surrounded a general design of great merit with many finely executed and suggestive details."[3] Not all observations were as favorable. In 1879, when one of the pair was exhibited at the American Institute Fair in New York, a journalist, though conceding that it "attracted much attention from its originality and national character," found that "anatomically considered, [the figures]

are far from being perfect. For instance, the 'pitcher's' fingers are disproportionately long and large."[4]

John Hart Brewer kept one of the original pair for his private collection of American ceramics, which is now at the New Jersey State Museum. The whereabouts of the other were unknown until recently.[5] It was probably the vase that Brewer offered "as a championship emblem" in 1887 to the National Baseball League, which had been founded two years earlier.[6] In a letter agreeing to accept the vase as the pennant trophy, league president N. E. Young wrote: "I have no doubt that the club that is so fortunate as to receive the vase will be very proud of it and value it highly."[7] That October, the Detroit Wolverines captured the National League pennant and were likely presented with the Ott and Brewer vase.[8] It is logical to assume that the trophy never left Detroit. It was housed later at the Detroit Institute of Arts and, again, at the Detroit Historical Museum, in whose collections it has remained.[9] The date 1875 on the vase refers to the year the model was made; the date 1 March 1876 was hand-inscribed before the vase was fired, a short two months before it was put on display at Philadelphia.

1. Young 1879, p. 465.
2. Stradling 1976, p. 149, citing *Crockery and Glass Journal* 3 (16 June 1876), p. 14.
3. Young 1879, p. 465.
4. "Pottery at the American Institute Fair," *Art Amateur* 1 (November 1879), p. 127.
5. My colleague Ellen Paul Denker learned of the vase's existence in Detroit during her tenure as an assistant curator at the New Jersey State Museum.
6. "The Potteries: Trenton," *Crockery and Glass Journal* 25 (9 June 1887), p. 24.
7. Ibid.
8. Bill McGraw, "Baseball and Detroit, 1887: One Hundred Seasons Ago," *Detroit Free Press*, 5 April 1987, p. 20.
9. Neither the Institute of Arts nor the Historical Museum has any documentation of the vase's history in its holdings.

55
Statuette, ca. 1875–76

Ott and Brewer, Trenton, New Jersey
Designed and modeled by Isaac Broome
Parian; H. 14⅞ in. (37.8 cm.)
Marks (on base, painted in black): PROF. ISAAC VROOM / TOM MULLEN / 1875 / F. KENNEDY
Private collection

On 24 November 1876, a local newspaper noted that the Ott and Brewer Centennial display in Philadelphia had included "a set of the statuettes of base ball players, such as surround the vase described [cat. no. 54]."[1] The three realistic figures that surround each of the two baseball vases modeled by Isaac Broome (referred to as "Vroom" in an inscription possibly added sometime later) were copied for display and sale as individual statuettes. According to family tradition, the model for all three figures was Roebling Ericson Broome, Isaac's only son.[2] This example—the catcher, bare-handed, as was customary in the early years of the game—depicts the subject catching the ball the pitcher has just thrown. The modeling of the facial features, the muscular limbs, and the uniform is exceedingly well rendered. Details in relief of the clothing and the shoes, the stitching in particular, have been further accentuated by color rubbed into selected areas, causing them to stand out clearly against the smooth, creamy white parian. The statuettes were described by one noted ceramics historian of the period as being "full of life and spirit."[3]

As claimed in an undated illustrated circular probably published about 1877 by Ott and Brewer to promote their parian production (Fig. 27, p. 34), "All our subjects are popular, and the work of an experienced American Artist." The text continued: "We have avoided the glossy surface common to Parian

ware, the color of our goods being mellow and marble-like shows the expressions of each feature with fine effect. For sharpness and distinctness of outlines, correctness and quality of tone, we think no figures in the market can surpass them."[4]

Since these statuettes were cast from molds, any number of them could have been produced. How many were made is not known, but this example and the batter and the catcher in the collections of the New Jersey State Museum are the only ones that have yet come to light.[5] In the price list that accompanied the circular, the three figures were offered at twenty-five dollars each. (The large baseball vase of the preceding entry cost two hundred and fifty dollars.) Whereas all the firm's other advertised works—such as two models of baseball players, this time young boys, each titled "Happy Hours"—could be purchased directly from the pottery, the three statuettes that included this catcher were sold exclusively through Tiffany and Company of New York.[6]

1. Stradling 1976, p. 149, quoting *Philadelphia Public Ledger*, 24 November 1876.
2. Information provided by James Kersey, Broome's grandson, to the New Jersey State Museum.
3. Elliott 1878, p. 341.
4. Ott and Brewer, undated art circular, collection of David and Barbara Goldberg.
5. Acc. nos. CH354.23.1; CH354.23.2.
6. Ott and Brewer, undated price list, collection of the New Jersey State Museum (acc. no. CH85.33.6).

56
Bust of Cleopatra, 1876

Ott and Brewer, Trenton, New Jersey
Designed and modeled by Isaac Broome
Parian, colored; H. 21 in. (53.3 cm.)
Marks (on base): BROOME, Sculp' 1876 (incised); OTT & BREWER/ TRENTON, N.J. (impressed)
New Jersey State Museum, The Brewer Collection (CH354.24)

AT THE Philadelphia Centennial Exposition, Ott and Brewer exhibited numerous off-white parian portrait busts designed by Isaac Broome, including those of George Washington, Abraham Lincoln, and Ulysses S. Grant. When the celebration ended, on 10 November 1876, Broome began on several other works, Shakespeare and Franklin among them.[1] Of all the portrait busts he designed and modeled, it was the *Cleopatra* that caused the most stir, partly because of the glamorous subject, but more, perhaps, because the object was made in colored parian, the tints achieved by the addition of oxides of iron and other metals to the clay. The piece may have had its first public showing in 1878, at the Paris Exposition Universelle.[2] Visitors accustomed to portrait busts made primarily in cool white or cream must have been startled at the sight of the seductive black face and neck above an elaborately decorated gold bodice and with an exotically patterned gold headdress.

The era's preoccupation with antiquity was most notable at the Philadelphia fairgrounds in the terracotta exhibits, which contained reproductions and adaptations of Greek, Roman, and Egyptian forms.[3] Recent archaeological excavations and attendant reports in the press had kindled the interest of collectors and connoisseurs as well as consumers. The Broome *Cleopatra*, though it does not actually copy an ancient model, is in the style of classical sculpture and also conjures up images of the ancient Egyptian world. The model for the face was Miss Mary Thompson, thought to be one of Trenton's most beautiful women.[4]

The Cleopatra bust was discussed at great length in contemporary accounts. One unnamed journalist, after returning from a visit to Broome's studio in 1877, wrote:

> Mr. Broome has just completed his masterpiece in the line of busts. This is one of Cleopatra, in heroic size, and it comes nearer our ideal of what the beautiful Egyptian queen really was than any other representation we have ever seen. The head-dress, draperies, etc., are exact copies of the Cleopatra of the Temple at Philo, and are perfect in the most minute details. The features, while they preserve accurately the Egyptian cast of countenance, are softened and rounded after the Grecian style, and are most striking in their haughty beauty. This Cleopatra looks the queen, at the same time we could see beneath the royal air traces of the fascinating softness of the woman. To the scholar, or to the artist, this bust is a study and a gem. It is the largest parian bust which has ever been made, and it is wonderful how it could be cast so perfectly, for it is without a flaw.[5]

The following year, *Cleopatra* won a gold medal for the Ott and Brewer company at the Exposition Universelle. Nevertheless, the work was not universally praised. When it was exhibited in 1879 at the American Institute Fair in New York City, one critic, dismayed by its great size, found it "exaggerated and unnatural, reminding the spectator more of a fabled inhabitant of Brobdingnag than of a queen who once lived and ruled."[6]

When the firm was acquired by Charles H. Cook, in 1894, the molds for *Cleopatra* and a number of other Broome figure busts remained at the factory. (Several of them, reissued later and signed by Broome at that time, are marked with the 1914 date and also with 1876, the year the original pieces were modeled.) In 1914, Cook presented the *Cleopatra* mold to Walter Scott Lenox, for whom Broome, although well on in years, was then working. Cook's sole stipulation was that only three copies of the bust would be made—one for himself, one for William S. Hancock, and one for Lenox—after which the mold was to be destroyed.[7]

1. Stradling 1976, p. 156, quoting *Philadelphia Public Ledger*, 24 November 1876.
2. Though *Cleopatra* has traditionally been thought to have been made for and exhibited at the Centennial, there is much documentary evidence to support that the bust was completed only after the exposition in Philadelphia had already closed. See Stradling 1976, p. 156, and "American Parian," *Crockery and Glass Journal* 5 (22 March 1877), p. 15.
3. See Frelinghuysen 1986, pp. 200–203.
4. "Cleopatra Bust for Art School," *Trenton Times-Advertiser*, 24 October 1915, p. 2.
5. "American Parian," *Crockery and Glass Journal* 5 (22 March 1877), p. 15.
6. "Pottery at the American Institute Fair," *Art Amateur* 1 (November 1879), p. 127.
7. Hancock was in charge of the Cook firm's retail sales. After his death, in 1915, his copy was purchased at his estate sale and presented to the Trenton School of Industrial Arts.

57
Pair of vases, 1877

Ott and Brewer, Trenton, New Jersey
Designed and modeled by Isaac Broome
Parian, colored; H. 7¾ in. (19.7 cm.)
Marks, smiling face: Ott & Brewer / Trenton / N.J. (incised, on bottom); BROOME. / 1877 (incised, on base); serious face: OTT & BREWER (impressed, on side) / TRENTON. N.J. (incised, on side) / COPYRIGHTED (impressed, on side); BROOME. / 1877 (incised, on base)
Private collection

On each of these vases, the enigmatic subject is a finely modeled head poking through a cracked egg. Broome's inspiration in using the egg metaphor in his design may have been a sculpture exhibited by the Florentine artist Emanuele Caroni at the Centennial Exposition, which Broome, himself having objects on display, must have seen. The Caroni work, called *Birth of Cupid*, or *Birth of Love*, depicts a winged infant emerging from a broken egg.[1] On the Broome vases, each of the masklike faces with its close-fitting skullcap and ruffled collar appears consciously to reflect some specific emotion, but the expressions seem at once spontaneous and lifeless. The origin of Broome's design for these unusual vases is not known. He may have conceived them as interpretations of Harlequin and Pierrot, derived from their commedia dell'arte forebears, Arlecchino and Pedrolino. If so, the reference coincides with the revival of the Italian sixteenth-century comedy tradition that took place in Europe during the latter part of the 1800s. That form of entertainment interested numerous artists and authors of the period.[2] As romantic characters conjuring up images of fantasy and innocence, much in the manner of circus clowns, the figures had universal public appeal.

The Ott and Brewer firm's experiments with colored clay bodies made a valuable contribution to the porcelain field. In the year these monochrome, brown-bodied vases were made, one journalist described the pottery's parian production in great detail, commenting on its use of colors: "The blue, brown, drab, and other tints one sees in some works made of parian are produced by mixing it with the oxide of iron, cobalt, and other metals."[3] A version of one of the pair in a glazed green body is at the New Jersey State Museum.[4] A pair made in a creamy white, glazed and with facial highlights painted in overglaze colored enamels, is in a private collection.

The subjects of this entry, each dated 1877, are marked both by the pottery and by the modeler and designer Isaac Broome during the sculptor's period of employment as Ott and Brewer's designer. The word "copyrighted" on one is an unusual occurrence in nineteenth-century American ceramics. An illustrated art circular in which some of the firm's sculptural works were offered for sale pointed out that the

pieces were protected by law so that the customer could "avoid plaster or other copies being thrown on the market."[5]

1. I am grateful to William H. Gerdts, professor of art history, The Graduate School and University Center of The City University of New York, for suggesting this possibility.
2. Albert Boime, *Thomas Couture and the Eclectic Vision* (New Haven and London: Yale University Press, 1980), pp. 293–326.
3. "Trenton Earthenware Manufactories," *Crockery and Glass Journal* 6 (25 October 1877), p. 25.
4. The Brewer Collection (acc. no. CH354.26).
5. Ott and Brewer, undated art circular, collection of David and Barbara Goldberg.

58
Centennial pedestal (pair), 1876

Union Porcelain Works, Greenpoint (Brooklyn), New York
Designed by Karl L. H. Müller
Porcelain; H. 40 13/16 in. (103.7 cm.)
Marks: K L / Indian on horseback / H. M. (incised on one side, near top-section base, within circle); U.P.W. / eagle's head with S in beak (similarly, on other side); N.Y. (raised letters near top of lower section); UNION / PORCELAIN / WORKS / NY / x92 (inside base, stamped in red) (1); K L / Indian on horseback / H. M. (incised, on one side, near top-section base, within circle); U.P.W. / eagle's head with S in beak (similarly, on other side); N.Y. (raised letters near top of lower section); UNION PORCELAIN WORKS / GREENPOINT / L.I. / 187[obliterated] (inside base, painted in red) (2)
The Metropolitan Museum of Art, Purchase, Anonymous Gift, 1968 (68.99.1) (1)
Division of Ceramics and Glass, National Museum of American History, The Smithsonian Institution, Washington, D.C. (cat. no. 74.18) (2)

THIS PAIR of pedestals, each made in four separate pieces, were executed for the Union Porcelain Works display at the Centennial Exposition in Philadelphia.[1] They were among the most ambitious works ever to have been attempted in porcelain. At the Centennial, supporting the two large Century vases (see cat. no. 59), they must have been impressive indeed, though the period description of them in place is brief: "At two corners of the large glass case are pedestals upon which a classic story is told in bas-relief."[2]

Figure 1. Detail (mourning women vignette)

Classical allusions were considered appropriate inspiration for the objects exhibited at the nation's hundredth anniversary celebration, and many Centennial pieces, notably those produced by the Greenpoint firm, incorporated such motifs or forms in their displays. At the top of each of these pedestals (the form itself dating to ancient times) are masks of Greek drama, a single mask of Comedy and three double masks of Tragedy, below which are depicted four vignettes, divided by Ionic pilasters, that possibly represent episodes in the story of Electra. Because the figures and scenes do not fit into the standard iconographic repertoire, their exact reference is not readily apparent. They probably represent a pastiche from several different literary sources, or possibly the designer, Karl L. H. Müller, constructed the vignettes

Figure 2. Detail (Orestes vignette)

directly from legends of antiquity rather than borrowing from known pictorial precedents. The four depictions may be interpreted as Electra being aided by the old tutor to smuggle her brother, the young Orestes, to safety; Electra offering libations at the tomb of her father, Agamemnon, with Orestes, now an adult, appearing in answer to her prayers; a scene of women mourning in front of the tomb, with the statue of Apollo looking on (Fig. 1); and Orestes, with Electra and their old nurse, contemplating the body of Clytemnestra, whom he has just slain (Fig. 2). The depictions may be interpretations of events as they were variously related by Sophocles, Euripides, and Aeschylus. The lower band, separated from the upper by pairs of striding griffins, contains a relief representation of a tale told by Sophocles: the adult Orestes, now unrecognized, returns to his father's palace to avenge Agamemnon's murder at the hands of Clytemnestra and her lover, Aegisthus, gaining access to their presence by telling them that Orestes has been killed in a chariot race.[3] Several classical architectural features—egg-and-dart molding, dentiling, stylized trailing vines, and wavelike motifs—add further decorative authenticity.

The fashion of representing white figures modeled in shallow relief against a light-colored background, generally blue, is called jasperware, popular in England in the late eighteenth century, when it was introduced by Josiah Wedgwood and his contemporaries. From the first days of its production, jasperware has been a mainstay of the Wedgwood pottery, which has manufactured it without interruption to this day. The effect is achieved by varied processes: white reliefs applied to a solid-colored body or to a white body that has been dipped in color or to a white body that is then painted around them. Here, the ground tint, an unusual pale apricot unknown in the Wedgwood oeuvre, has probably been painted on the white body after the reliefs were in place, for the outline around the figures is uneven and the background hue varies in intensity.

Although the pedestals are massive in scale, the pale tint, the delicacy of the figures, and the organization of the decoration into several sections bestow on the pair a pleasing elegance. One other Centennial pedestal is known. In a private collection, it differs from these in its background color, a greenish brown, and in having on its plain midsection band the painted title "ELECTRA."

1. On each pedestal, the larger upper section was cast in two parts—the molded top and the relief-decorated section immediately below—and then cemented together.
2. Stradling 1976, p. 151, quoting *Crockery and Glass Journal* 3 (25 May 1876), p. 15.
3. The vignettes were interpreted by the kindness of Joan Breton Connelly, assistant professor of fine arts, New York University.

59
Century vase (pair), 1876

Union Porcelain Works, Greenpoint (Brooklyn), New York
Designed by Karl L. H. Müller
Porcelain; H. 22¼ in. (56.5 cm.)
Marks (on each): Century Vase / Exhibited at Centennial / Exhibition at Philadelphia / Manufactured 1876 / By Union Porcelain Works / Greenpoint (on bottom, painted in black); UPW / eagle's head with S in beak (on bottom, on applied molded disk)
The Brooklyn Museum, Gift of Carll and Franklin Chace in memory of their mother, Pastora Forest Smith Chace, daughter of Thomas Carll Smith (43.25) (1)
High Museum of Art, Atlanta, Georgia, Virginia Carroll Crawford Collection (1986.163) (2)

MUCH OF THE American porcelain produced during the hundred years prior to the nation's Centennial derived from contemporary European ceramics in both shape and decoration. In anticipation of exhibiting at the Philadelphia exposition, however, several American firms hired skilled foreign artists and sculptors to design and decorate their wares in a patriotic mode. Of these, the Union Porcelain Works, under the artistic direction of Karl L. H. Müller, is credited for some of the most original porcelains made in the United States during the last quarter of the nineteenth century.

Müller, a German-born sculptor who had studied at the Royal Academy in Paris and later at the National Academy of Design in New York, devised many Centennial pieces, several of them large in scale. Most notable among these were a pair of three-and-a-half-foot-high biscuit-porcelain pedestals (see cat. no. 58) and, originally accompanying them, this pair of objects, called Century vases by the firm (sometimes known as Centennial vases, an allusion to the country's hundredth anniversary). They are perhaps the most famous of the porcelain products made by the thriving pottery.[1]

While the vases' shape derives loosely from classical sources and some of their decoration draws on various European traditions, their iconography and vigorous quality reveal a thoroughly American character. The design was intended to illustrate the progress of the United States during its first century. On each of the pair, North American bison heads serve as handles; smaller animal heads (including ram, bison, and walrus) in full relief are arranged at intervals around the body; adorning either side is a bisque profile portrait in relief of George Washington within a diamond-shaped reserve and, on the neck, a gold eagle surmounted by gold stars and lightning bolts on a rich blue ground; each of six biscuit relief panels around the base depicts a different event in American history. Flanking the Washington portraits above and below are eight slightly truncated, triangular reserves painted around the vases, which contain vignettes of American progress (ill.).

Though credit for the concept for these magnificent objects has been given to Charles H. L. Smith, son of Thomas C. Smith, owner of the Union Porcelain Works,[2] the actual design and probably the painting as well are undeniably by Müller's own hand. George Washington was a subject he frequently used throughout his career. In 1857, he showed what was described in the Cosmopolitan Art Association Catalogue of Works of Art of Sandusky, Ohio, as a "Large Bronze Medallion of George Washington."[3] In 1864, he also exhibited a medallion of Washington at the Fifth Annual Exhibition of the Artists' Fund Society in New York.[4] His portrayal of Washington on these vases shows a marked similarity to a crayon drawing made by the French artist Charles Balthazar Julien Févret de Saint-Mémin, who spent the years from 1794 to 1814 in America. An engraving after the portrait

taken in 1866 by Robert Dudensing was published in the United States.

Positioned on their porcelain pedestals, the large and ornately decorated vases would have been the focal point of the Union Porcelain Works display. Because no pictures of the firm's booth survive, a contemporary description provides the only account of the impressive installation:

> The finest ware is displayed in a large glass case in the centre of which rises a pedestal crowned with a finely executed and remarkably life-like bust of Mr. Thos. Smith, which was cast on his own premises. . . . At two corners of the large glass case are pedestals upon which a classic story is told in bas-relief. These support a pair of vases upon whose bases, also in bas-relief, we find Penn treating with the Indians, a log cabin with the early settler, ax in hand, resting from his toil, and the story of the tea-riot in Boston harbor, and a soldier standing by his cannon. Above these there are some representative paintings of the progress of the arts. The telegraph is illustrated by a pole upon which a workman is placing the last of a number of wires; the steamer, a sewing machine and a reaper are also shown. . . . When visitors examine this display, they will see what can be done in art pottery on this side of the water.[5]

59. Detail (vignette)

The firm also exhibited the Century vases in New York City at the American Institute Fair later that same year and again in 1879.[6] They became the virtual emblem of the factory's work throughout the nineteenth century and even into the early years of the twentieth.[7]

Three other large-size versions and numerous smaller ones (see cat. no. 60) are known. These two, the only large pair known, are the most decorated by far of the vases. Of the three others grand in scale, the first, in the collections of the Smithsonian Institution's National Museum of American History, depicts similar scenes of modern industry within diamond-shaped reserves amid overall painted decoration in the Gothic style; the second, in the New Jersey State Museum, has no scenic decoration but displays a patterned arrangement of leaves and birds' heads; the third, in a private collection, having underglaze blue decoration in certain areas but no overglaze embellishment, appears never to have been finished.[8]

1. The Philadelphia firm of Galloway and Graff, a terracotta company, also exhibited a Century vase at the 1876 fair. See J. S. Ingram, *The Centennial Exposition, Described and Illustrated* (Philadelphia, 1876), ill. facing p. 227.
2. Young 1879, p. 476.
3. See Yarnall and Gerdts 1986, 4, pp. 2519–20.
4. Artists' Fund Society of New York, *Catalogue of the Fifth Annual Exhibition at the Galleries, No. 625 Broadway, N.Y.* (New York: 1864), p. 16.
5. Stradling 1976, p. 151, quoting *Crockery and Glass Journal* 3 (25 May 1876), p. 15. Not mentioned in the review were the Indian chief and Frances Mason's sweet-potato dinner present in the bas-relief decoration or, in the painted scenes of progress, the canal boats loading at a grain elevator or a potter fashioning a plate with the use of a jigger (template).
6. "The American Institute Fair," *Crockery and Glass Journal* 4 (28 September 1876), p. 14; "Pottery and the American Institute Fair," *Art Amateur* 1 (November 1879), p. 127.
7. The vase appears in an illustration of the Union Porcelain Works factory buildings and a selection of its artwares in an 1884 account of the business. See Stiles 1884, p. 763. The firm advertised extensively in the *American Pottery Gazette*, which singled out the Century vase as an example of its artwares. See "The Centennial Vase," *American Pottery Gazette* 8 (September 1908), pp. 13, 20.
8. National Museum of American History, Smithsonian Institution (cat. no. 74.17); New Jersey State Museum (acc. no. CH73.68).

60
Century vase, 1877

Union Porcelain Works, Greenpoint (Brooklyn), New York
Designed by Karl L. H. Müller
Porcelain; H. 12⅝ in. (32.1 cm.)
Marks: K. MULLER (incised, under Washington's shoulder on one relief);
U.P.W. (incised, near base, on log cabin vignette);
UPW / eagle's head with S in beak (on bottom, on applied molded disk); U.P.W. / 1877 (on bottom, painted in black)
The Metropolitan Museum of Art, Friends of the American Wing Fund, 1987 (1987.12)

THIS VASE, one of about fourteen known small Century, or Centennial, vases, is approximately ten inches shorter than the pair that made such a showing at the Union Porcelain Works booth at the Centennial Exposition (see cat. no. 59). About half the smaller versions are uncolored, but this vase displays vibrant, leafy overglaze painted decoration. Its designs and its palette of green, blue, and peach are more exuberant and sophisticated than are those of most of its kind. It is further distinguished by being one of only two known dated examples. The presence of the date—1877—may signify that it is an exhibition piece, a hypothesis strengthened by its quality. It may have been among the Century vases that the Union Porcelain Works exhibited in 1877 at the American Institute Fair in New York City or it may have been part of the factory's displays in 1878 at the Paris Exposition Universelle. It is even more meaningful among all Century vases in being incised with the designer's signature under the shoulder of the subject (ill.), in the tradition of portrait medals made earlier in the century. The inscription, combined with some handworked detailing on the portraits on either side of the vase, would seem to indicate that Müller personally worked on the piece. The majority of the known small Century vases appear in pairs, but the whereabouts of the mate to this one are unknown.

60. Detail (signature)

61

Pitcher, 1875

Union Porcelain Works, Greenpoint (Brooklyn), New York
Designed by Karl L. H. Müller
Porcelain; H. 9¼ in. (23.5 cm.)
Marks: U.P.W. / N.Y.-/1875 (incised, on barrel end); K L / Indian on horseback / H M (on bottom, on applied molded disk)
Private collection

Pitcher, ca. 1876

Union Porcelain Works, Greenpoint (Brooklyn), New York
Designed by Karl L. H. Müller
Porcelain; H. 9⅝ in. (24.5 cm.)
Marks: U.P.W. (incised, on barrel end); UNION PORCELAIN WORKS / GREENPOINT / N.Y. (on bottom, painted in black)
Inscribed (on front): C.G.M.
The Metropolitan Museum of Art, Purchase, Anonymous Gift, 1968 (68.103.2)

AN ANNOUNCEMENT in a trade publication of 11 November 1875 read: "Messrs. T. C. Smith & Son, proprietors of the Union Porcelain Works, Greenpoint, L. I., have just designed and finished a decorated bar pitcher, which is conceded to be the most attractive article of its kind in the market." The unnamed journalist then described the unusual piece in considerable detail:

> . . . The mouth is made to represent a sea lion with tusks, beard, etc., and forms the spout of the pitcher, the whole being handsomely decorated. On one side is a figure of King Gambrinus introducing lager into the United States, and offering Brother Jonathan his first glass of the foaming beverage. The Buck Goat is seen surmounting the beer keg. On the reverse side are figures of Bill Nye and Ah Sin, the "Heathen Chinee," who has just been caught with the three aces falling from his sleeve. The handle is composed of some nondescript animal, who seems to be endeavoring to crawl into the pitcher. This article will undoubtedly take with the trade, and is just the thing.[1]

Of these two objects, the completely white one, owned privately, may be the first of the so-called Heathen Chinee pitchers (the name stemming from a Bret Harte poem of 1870) to have been made at the Union Porcelain Works and may even have been an experimental piece. It resembles all the other known examples, but with slight variations. Of these, the most striking is the handle: the animal at the top, possibly a polar bear, is almost identical to that of the decorated version, but the handle terminal is treated far differently from the stylized leaves that appear on the other and on subsequent pitchers of the same form. The problems inherent in the structure of this earlier version can be seen in the break, filled in with plaster, between the base of the handle and the beginning of the scroll that extends upward from it. The marks, too, differ on the prototype pitcher. Whereas all other examples display merely the molded initials of the factory (U.P.W.), this inscription—U.P.W. / N.Y. / 1875 on the end of the keg standing next to the mythical Flemish king—is hand-incised. Moreover, the designer's own cipher appears on the bottom of the pitcher.

The figure of Brother Jonathan on this and on all the ensuing examples may be adapted from the similarly titled work that Müller exhibited as "Statuary" at the International Art Institution of New York in 1859.[2] According to a tradition in the Smith family, the circular spout on every pitcher, which prevented ice from escaping into the glass, was patented by Thomas C. Smith.[3]

The second subject, from the Metropolitan's collections, is fully decorated in overglaze colors, its white bisque figures in relief on a blue ground recalling the blue-and-white jasperware made by Wedgwood in England from the late eighteenth century. The walrus spout and the polar-bear handle are painted naturalistically, and the piece is further enlivened by flower sprays within a geometric neo-Grec border. The identity of the person for whom this example was made and whose initials, *C.G.M.*, appear under the spout is unknown. Other pitchers of this type feature overglaze decoration of the kind popular during the late 1870s and early 1880s, including Japanese bamboo and stylized Egyptian palm trees.

The shape, an offshoot of the "Sweetheart" pitchers made in the early 1850s by the United States Pottery Company in Bennington, Vermont, was later adopted by the Union Porcelain Works for several of their products. The subjects of this entry were perhaps intended to celebrate the exploration of the Pacific Northwest; the walrus and polar bear references may have been intended to invoke the climate of the state of Washington. More telling, however, is the scene from Harte's "Heathen Chinee," a poem that reflects the discrimination practiced against the large influx of Chinese laborers to the United States during the second half of the nineteenth century.[4]

Pitchers of this form seem to have been among the most popular articles produced by the Union Porcelain Works during the decade from the mid-1870s, and were first exhibited in 1876 as part of the firm's displays at the Centennial Exposition. The latest dated example known (1886) is at the Henry Ford Museum, Dearborn, Michigan.[5] All but identical pitchers bearing the mark "G. P. Co." are also known. They are later examples probably made by the Greenwood Pottery Company in Trenton, New Jersey. The question of whether the factory purchased the Union Porcelain Works molds or was merely copying the design has never been answered.[6]

1. "A Unique Bar Pitcher," *Crockery and Glass Journal* 2 (11 November 1875), p. 16.
2. Yarnall and Gerdts 1986, 4, p. 2515.
3. Typescript inventory of Union Porcelain Works wares owned by Thomas C. Smith's grandsons Carll S. and Franklin Chace, dated 11 March 1943, accession files, Decorative Arts Department, The Brooklyn Museum.
4. For further discussion of the effect the Chinese immigration had on the decorative arts in the last third of the nineteenth century, see Ellen Paul Denker, *After the Chinese Taste: China's Influence in America, 1730–1930* (Salem, Mass.: Peabody Museum of Salem, 1985), pp. 38–40. Mrs. Denker cites another example by the Union Porcelain Works that seems to epitomize the hostility encountered by Chinese immigrants: An unusual porcelain figure group probably dating to the 1880s at the Smithsonian Institution's National Museum of American History (acc. no. 75.122), it shows two boys, one white and one black, looking on complacently as a Chinese boy struggles to get into the nest of the great American eagle.
5. Acc. no. 61.78.3.
6. See "The Mystery Pitcher," *Maine Antiques Digest*, March 1982.

62
Liberty cup and saucer, 1876

Union Porcelain Works, Greenpoint (Brooklyn), New York
Probably designed by Karl L. H. Müller
Porcelain; H. cup, 4 9/16 in. (11.6 cm.); Diam. saucer, 6 13/16 in. (17.3 cm.)
Marks (on bottom, painted in red on cup; in black, within diamond, on saucer): 1876/UNION PORCELAIN WORKS/GREENPOINT/N.Y.
The Metropolitan Museum of Art, Gift of Mr. and Mrs. Franklin Chace, 1969 (69.194.5,6)

In chronicling the Union Porcelain Works' rich display at the Philadelphia Centennial Exposition, a journalist noted: "As a souvenir, an elegantly designed and executed cup and saucer has been prepared, upon which Justice sits in bas-relief, while Liberty forms the handle."[1] The elaborate decoration and the large

scale of the cup suggest that it was intended not for use but for display. As with many of the exhibition objects designed for the Centennial, the piece combines classical and patriotic motifs. In the classical manner, a border of stylized laurel leaves and berries encircles the saucer; extending around the cup are the seated figures of a classically garbed Justice on one side and Hermes, the god of commerce and protector of traders, with his caduceus, on the other. Between the figures are symbols in relief of the nation's bounty—the cornstalk of the North and the cotton plant of the South. The handle consists of the richly clothed Liberty standing on the American eagle. The white relief decoration on the background's soft matte blue recalls the blue-and-white jasperware that Wedgwood and his contemporaries began to make in England in the late eighteenth century. On the borders, the decorative gilding is among the finest work of its kind of the period; the rich, deeper blue heightens the patriotic feeling and, especially in combination with the lavish use of gold, imbues the piece with a regal aura.

Of the number of known versions of the Liberty cup, this one is distinguished in that its decoration, while the most elaborate of all, neither descends into fussiness nor overwhelms the beauty of the form. Further proof of its quality is that it was cherished enough to be retained by firm owner Thomas C. Smith and his family for two generations before coming to the Metropolitan.

1. Stradling 1976, p. 151, quoting *Crockery and Glass Journal* 3 (25 May 1876), p. 15.

63
Ice pitcher, ca. 1876

Union Porcelain Works, Greenpoint (Brooklyn), New York
Porcelain; H. 12 in. (30.5 cm.)
Marks (incised, on wicker basket): U.P.W.
New Jersey State Museum,
The Cybis Collection of American Porcelain (CH70.250a, b)

AROUND THE TIME of the nation's Centennial, Americans took great interest in the culture and art of ancient Egypt. Perhaps in an effort to associate the United States with one of the most sophisticated civilizations of all time, ceramists employed stylized and colorful Egyptian palmettes and other devices to decorate many a period object. More obvious allusions included Ott and Brewer's bust of Cleopatra (see cat. no. 56) and this pitcher, by the Union Porcelain Works, which depicts on each side in a bisque relief scenes from the Old Testament—on one side, the pharaoh's daughter finding the basket containing the baby Moses in the bullrushes; on the other, the death of Moses. Emerging from the handle is a mysterious head, possibly that of the pharaoh, and the front of the pitcher is ornamented with painted decoration in the Egyptian style. Other ancient motifs are two sea creatures on either side of the spout and the ram's head that supports it. A walrus head as the finial perhaps hints that the vessel is to be used for cold beverages.

Silver-plated ice pitchers were fashionable during the second half of the nineteenth century, and they had to be designed so as to maintain the coolness of the beverage they contained. That was achieved largely by the use of multiple walls. In 1854, a patent for a double-walled metal vessel was secured by James H. Stimpson of Baltimore, Maryland. In 1859, he improved his invention by making the vessel's inner wall of porcelain.[1] What evolved was a range of silver-plated pitchers of a highly decorative nature that became immensely popular during the next two decades. As a catalogue published by the Meriden Britannia Company in 1871 advertised, "The silverplated porcelain lined Ice Pitchers are not only the cheapest and best for service, but are the only pitchers now made to meet the popular demand, there being over forty thousand (40,000) now in use."[2]

Constructed on Stimpson's principle is this wholly porcelain example whose double walls provide insulation much in the manner of today's thermos bottles. The Union Porcelain Works was probably one of the factories that produced the porcelain liners for the silver-plate manufacturers. Even if it was not, its designers were unquestionably familiar with the form. This pitcher, with its slightly sloping sides and caryatid handle, echoes the overall shape of silver-plated counterparts and borrows many of the motifs often found on them. A pitcher similar but without the sea creatures on either side of the spout is in the collections of The Metropolitan Museum of Art.[3] Marked by the factory and for the year 1876, it is the basis for the dating of this object.

1. Edmund P. Hogan, *An American Heritage: A Book about the International Silver Company* (Dallas, Tex.: Taylor Publishing Company, 1977), p. 138.
2. Ibid.
3. Acc. no. 1980.70.

64
Tea set, 1876

Union Porcelain Works, Greenpoint (Brooklyn), New York
Designed by Karl L. H. Müller
Porcelain; H. teapot, 6¾ in. (17.2 cm.), sugar bowl, 4½ in. (11.4 cm.),
cream pitcher, 3⅞ in. (9.8 cm.), cup, 2⅜ in. (6 cm.);
Diam. saucer, 5 in. (12.7 cm.)
Marks (on bottom, painted in red): U.P.W. / S
The Brooklyn Museum, Gift of Franklin Chace (68.87.29–32)

THIS TEA SET can be seen as an eighteenth-century rococo conceit interpreted by a creative designer working in late-nineteenth-century America. The traditional tea-set forms have taken on new character through their teeming depictions of real and imaginary flora and fauna. Each of the three principal pieces (teapot, sugar bowl, and cream pitcher) is supported by four rabbits. On all three, the handles consist of a pitcher plant joined to the body by varying fanciful creatures: birds perch atop those of the sugar bowl; two foxes play on that of the teapot. Near the base of the teapot is a small lizard; the spout is supported by a kind of winged grotesque. Some of the motifs refer to the putative contents of each vessel: a goat on the cream-pitcher handle, an African sugarcane picker the finial on the sugar bowl, and a pigtailed Chinese on the teapot cover.

All the pieces of the set have appropriately elaborate overglaze decoration. The three-dimensional figures are rendered naturalistically, while the flat surfaces are painted in a multicolored pattern oriental in derivation. The orange-red ground is literally covered with fine garlands of flowers interspersed with birds and butterflies. Circular and irregularly shaped reserves edged with gold scrolls contain miniature vignettes of branches of flowers, again with butterflies and birds and even dogs. The design is ascribed to Karl L. H. Müller, the Union Porcelain Works' artistic director. Thirty years after the set was made, one reporter commented: "The entire conception is of course one made without a thought for the commercial side. It is really the expression of the artist, pure and simple, executed in a fine quality of delicate china."[1] He was viewing the objects from the perspective of three decades; after more than eleven, his words still ring true.

How many similar sets the Union Porcelain Works made is not known. An unglazed stoneware version is in the collections of the Metropolitan Museum.[2] Possibly the prototype for the porcelain shapes, it was likely the "unglazed" set exhibited at New York City's American Institute Fair in 1876.[3] The stoneware set and the subject of this entry were both given to the institutions that now house them by Mr. and Mrs. Franklin Chace. Mr. Chace is a grandson of Thomas Carll Smith, the founder of the Union Porcelain Works. Period descriptions attest to the existence of at least two other Union Porcelain Works tea sets, one where "birds of various kinds, in brilliant plumage, appear among a mist of flowers on a background of rich matt blue," and another with "vine tracery in lavender."[4] Including this set, identified as being "an odd shade of salmon," all three porcelain examples were exhibited at the Centennial Exposition. There they were called "tete-a-tete tea services" and elicited "admiration from the delicacy of the ware and shape, and for beauty of design."[5]

1. "Interesting Items about Potters and Glassmakers," *American Pottery Gazette* 8 (November 1908), p. 31.
2. Acc. no. 69.194.7–14. See *19th-Century America: Furniture and Other Decorative Arts*, exh. cat. (New York: The Metropolitan Museum of Art, 1970), no. 201.
3. See "The American Institute Fair," *Crockery and Glass Journal* 4 (28 September 1876), p. 14.
4. "Interesting Items about Potters and Glassmakers," p. 31; Stradling 1976, p. 150, quoting *Crockery and Glass Journal* 3 (25 May 1876), p. 15.
5. Stradling 1976, p. 150.

65

Cup and saucer, ca. 1876

Union Porcelain Works, Greenpoint (Brooklyn), New York
Porcelain; H. cup, $1\frac{15}{16}$ in. (4.9 cm.); Diam. saucer, 5 in. (12.7 cm.)
Marks (on bottom): UNION / Porcelain Works. (on saucer, stamped in black); U.P.W. / S. (on cup, painted in black)
John H. Nally

THIS DIMINUTIVE cup and saucer were once part of a complete tea set of which they and the slop bowl, in another private collection, are the sole survivors.[1] The service to which they belonged may have been one of those exhibited by the Union Porcelain Works at the Centennial celebration in Philadelphia—one decorated with birds in brilliant plumage (see reference at cat. no. 64).[2] Moreover, the shape of the cup is identical to that in the subject of the previous entry.

The Union Porcelain Works was the first American pottery to produce a true hard-paste porcelain that could compare favorably with what was being made in France. On this cup and saucer, the ornamentation, among the most lavish and elegant of any work known from the factory, is predominantly French in influence and, to a greater degree than any of the firm's other known examples, substantiates the porcelain works' claim to be manufacturing "French china."[3]

Stylistically, the objects recall Paris porcelain of almost a half-century earlier. The distinctive ground color of Sèvres blue, a recognizably French attribute, provides an excellent foil for the ornate embellishment; the abundance and application of the gilding on both pieces is accorded the same importance it enjoyed in France in the first half of the century, when the art was at its zenith. Typical also of that bygone period is the display of oval reserves containing painstakingly rendered exotic birds and butterflies amid flowers and foliage.

1. The privately owned slop bowl is identical in shape to that from a Centennial set in gray stoneware at the Metropolitan Museum (acc. no. 69.194.13). For illustration, see *19th-Century America: Furniture and Other Decorative Arts*, exh. cat. (New York: The Metropolitan Museum of Art, 1970), no. 203.
2. See n. 4, cat. no. 64: "Interesting Items about Potters and Glassmakers," *American Pottery Gazette* 8 (November 1908), p. 31.
3. Undated Union Porcelain Works trade card, collections of The New-York Historical Society, New York City.

66
Vase, 1879

Union Porcelain Works, Greenpoint (Brooklyn), New York
Porcelain; H. 8⅝ in. (22 cm.)
Marks (on bottom, painted in black):
1879 / UNION PORCELAIN WORKS / GREENPOINT / N.Y.
The Metropolitan Museum of Art, Gift of Florence I. Balasny-Barnes, in memory of her sister, Yvette B. Gould, 1984 (1984.443.9)

A VASE in the form of a naturalistically rendered pitcher plant supported by a tortoise was probably the idea of the Union Porcelain Works' imaginative chief designer, Karl L. H. Müller. The plant was a design motif favored by the Greenpoint firm, as its appearance in several examples demonstrates—notably for the handles of the teapot, sugar bowl, and cream pitcher of a set (see cat. no. 64) that the factory produced for the Philadelphia Centennial Exposition. According to notes made by two grandsons of company founder Thomas C. Smith, specimens of the species grown in Smith's greenhouse served as the model for vases of that form.[1] Since the pitcher plant is commonly found in North American swamps, it may have been chosen as a peculiarly native botanical motif. That the plant is essentially a vessel in itself—a rarity in natural vegetation—and has connotations of nectar and coloration that are highly suitable to design adaptation may also account for its popularity in decorative schemes.

The firm's display at the Centennial Exposition included a similar example, described in a contemporary report: "The pitcher plant has been put to another and appropriate use as a bouquet holder, and is upheld by a frog."[2] Other vases exist, dated 1877 and 1879. The same general form is also known in a smaller size and, in rarer cases, with a monkey at the base and a smaller monkey at the rim.[3] Though such vases are usually painted in vivid, naturalistic colors, there are some that remain plain white and undecorated.

1. Typescript inventory of Union Porcelain Works wares owned by Thomas C. Smith's grandsons Carll S. and Franklin Chace, dated 11 March 1943, accession files, Decorative Arts Department, The Brooklyn Museum.
2. Stradling 1976, p. 151, quoting *Crockery and Glass Journal* 3 (25 May 1976), p. 15.
3. Ibid.

67
Plate, 1882–90

Ott and Brewer, Trenton, New Jersey
Belleek; Diam. 6 3/16 in. (15.7 cm.)
Marks (on bottom): BELLEEK / O & B / TRENTON within crescent moon / NJ (stamped in red); 67 (on paper label)
David and Barbara Goldberg

Many of the designs executed during the 1870s and 1880s at the Belleek factory in Ireland remained in production for many decades and some are still being made. This plate is a smaller version of an Irish example (ill.) that was part of a tea service in what was called the Thorn pattern in the firm's 1904 catalogue, the earliest visual record of Irish Belleek.[1] Of the entire service, Ott and Brewer copied only the plate. Though at first glance it appears to be an exact reproduction of the original (both have scalloped rims and a central relief-molded design of a spiderweb and spiders), the flowering prunus blossoms that embellish every second lobe on its rim are subtly different, and it varies to a greater degree in having a decorative inner border of heart-shaped leaves alternating with sprigs of simple flowers. Further, its gold, red, and black palette is more sophisticated than that of known Irish counterparts, which are characteristically decorated in gold and pastel-luster colors.

The Trenton firm made many porcelains in emulation of Irish prototypes, including tea wares in Ivy and Grass patterns (see cat. no. 68), some of which display the restricted color range of this meticulously painted little plate. Its design, dating to the mid-1880s, ascribes to many of the principles of the Aesthetic movement. These include the Japanesque inspiration explicit in the angular prunus blossoms of the exterior border and, on the interior, in the stylized treatment of the natural ornament, the motifs repeated for added decorative effect. The plate may once have been owned by Edwin AtLee Barber, noted historian of the American ceramics industry and an important early collector.[2]

1. The catalogue is reproduced in Degenhardt 1978, pp. 167–90.
2. See *Illustrated Catalogue of China, Pottery, Porcelains and Glass [Collected by] the Late Edwin AtLee Barber*, estate sale, Samuel T. Freeman & Co., Philadelphia, 10 and 11 December 1917, lot 523.

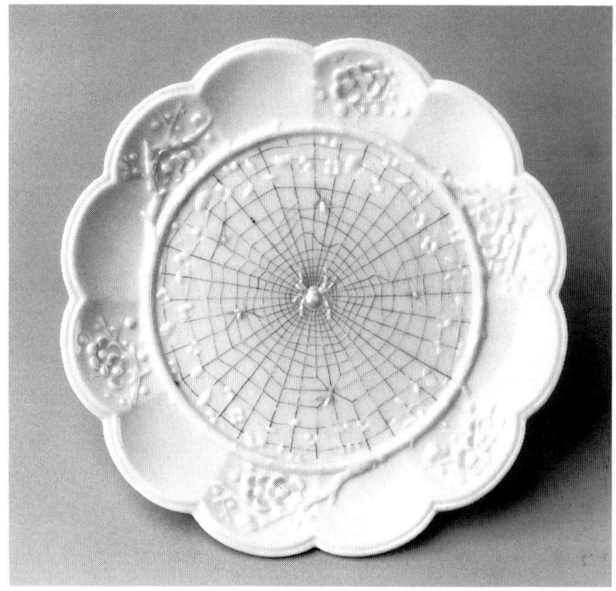

Plate, 1878. Belleek Pottery, Fermanagh, Ireland. Diam. 6⅞ in. (17.5 cm.). Collection of Miriam and Aaron Levine

68
Salt and pepper, 1882–90

Ott and Brewer, Trenton, New Jersey
Belleek; H. pepper, 3¹⁄₁₆ in. (7.8 cm.), salt, 1⁷⁄₁₆ in. (3.7 cm.)
Marks (on bottom, stamped in red):
BELLEEK / O & B / TRENTON within crescent moon / NJ
David and Barbara Goldberg

As does the scalloped plate with the spiderweb and prunus blossoms (see cat. no. 67), this salt dish and pepper shaker manifest a delicacy and refinement not found on all American Belleek. On these small and exceedingly thin vessels, the decoration of cattails, sprigs of wheat, and blades of grass is delicately painted in varying shades of gold and green, with details finely rendered in black and deep red. The blades of grass appear to be growing out of the foot of the salt dish and to be bound together with a grass tie just below the bowl. Although the decoration has its origins in Irish Belleek Grass tea wares, the forms themselves are exclusively American.

69
Tête-à-tête set, 1882–90

Ott and Brewer, Trenton, New Jersey
Belleek; H. teapot, 3⅞ in. (9.8 cm.), sugar bowl, 3½ in. (8.9 cm.),
cream pitcher, 2⁹⁄₁₆ in. (6.5 cm.); L. tray, 16 in. (40.6 cm.); W. tray, 15 in. (38.1 cm.)
Marks (on bottom, stamped in black):
O & B / BELLEEK within crescent moon
The Metropolitan Museum of Art, Purchase,
Mr. and Mrs. H. O. H. Frelinghuysen Gift, 1983 (1983.69.1–4)

TÊTE-À-TÊTE SETS were among the most favored objects of all the celebrated Belleek porcelain produced by the Ott and Brewer firm. The inclusion of those little treasures in the first public display of Ott and Brewer Belleek porcelain in Boston in September of 1883 is a testament to the company's pride in them.[1] Mentioned with particular emphasis in reviews of the event were the daintiness and lightness of the vessels. Though the sets were strong enough to withstand the rigors of normal daily use, they

were said to weigh less than two pounds complete.[2] The shapes, with their suggestion of surface relief, mimic the outline and texture of seashells. The paper-thin walls of the components rival the delicacy of their Irish counterparts. It is forms such as these that so admirably demonstrate the eggshell quality for which Belleek is deservedly famous.

This American interpretation copies almost directly an Irish Belleek pattern known as Tridacna, after a member of the shell family, and carries the allusion further in the shape of the accompanying tray, that of a mammoth mollusk. The set's rich adornment in raised gold and bronze (described variously as in the Kensington—referring to the South Kensington art school in London—or the Royal Worcester style), in which the Ott and Brewer firm excelled, was accorded high acclaim by the public and was also lauded by the critics. One local author mentioned the technique in glowing terms: "The bronze, gold and silver decorations in the Royal Worcester design are obtained from English and American coins, and it is generally admitted by experts that the shell tete a tete sets, both in the quality of the ware and artistic decorations are superior to anything in the pottery line ever on sale in this country."[3] Far from discouraging buyers, the substantial price attached to such ensembles (between fifty and seventy-five dollars) apparently increased their desirability. As it was said, "The richer they are the more they are sought for by high class trade."[4]

1. "Boston Exhibition," *Crockery and Glass Journal* 18 (20 September 1883), p. 29.
2. "The Potteries: Trenton," *Crockery and Glass Journal* 17 (7 June 1883), p. 10.
3. "Rivaling English Ware: What Ott and Brewer Have Done," *Trenton Times*, 15 October 1883, p. 1.
4. "The Potteries: Trenton," *Crockery and Glass Journal* 18 (15 November 1883), p. 16.

70
Vase, 1882–90

Ott and Brewer, Trenton, New Jersey
Belleek; H. 9¾ in. (24.8 cm.)
Marks (on bottom, stamped in red):
BELLEEK / O & B / TRENTON within crescent moon / NJ
Private collection

Dark colors, providing matte backgrounds on which metallic designs of various hues were applied, resulted in a more dramatic effect than could be attained by more conventional decoration on the natural cream-colored Belleek body. This vase, with its attenuated square neck and its adornment of a flying crane amid flowering bamboo, attests to the pervasive influence of oriental art on the American Belleek of the period. The ornament has been executed in a highly skilled manner: soft gold clouds have been sponged over the moss-green surface in true oriental fashion, the flowers are of finely modulated golden hues and have contrasting silver centers, and the raised paste chasing in the delineation of the crane's feathers and the petals' veins is particularly refined. The decoration on the front contrasts admirably with the spareness of that on the back: a single floral spray with a stem as thin as a penciled line.

199

71
Double ewer, 1882–90

Ott and Brewer, Trenton, New Jersey
Belleek; H. 9 in. (22.9 cm.)
Marks (on bottom, stamped in red):
BELLEEK / sword piercing crown / O & B
David and Barbara Goldberg

THIS DOUBLE EWER in the shape of a melon is one of the more eccentric forms produced at the Ott and Brewer pottery. The exquisitely wrought design consisting of water-lily buds, blossoms, and pad-shaped leaves that covers most of the surface issues from plants that seem to be growing out of the base. The same type of decoration is found on Belleek porcelain made by the Willets Manufacturing Company, also of Trenton (see cat. no. 76). Here, the leaves, stems, and blossoms, all outlined in gold, are suitably colored: greens and browns for the leaves; pinks and reds for the blossoms. The application of the color, perhaps by means of a sponge, has resulted in texture evocative of the living plants. Imparting a sense of depth to the design is the sensitive use of grisaille for complementary water-lily motifs. The theme is carried to the upper part of the vase by realistically textured branches that have been hollowed out and cut off at oblique angles to create the two irregular spouts. The elaborate handle is in the form of intertwined twigs. Both the theme and the naturalistic decoration in relief recall Japanesque designs made popular by the Royal Worcester pottery in England.

72
Pitcher, 1887–93

Willets Manufacturing Company, Trenton, New Jersey
Probably designed by Walter Scott Lenox
Belleek; H. 9⅛ in. (23.2 cm.)
Unmarked
Ann Willets Lapham Frazer

THE NAUTILUS has been used as an ornament since the seventeenth century. In the late 1600s, goldsmiths and silversmiths created elaborate mounts made of precious metals for the shells, often encrusting them with jewels and baroque pearls. The convuluted relic of the sea assumed new attributes when it was fashioned from the comparably delicate Irish Belleek porcelain: an ornament of the nautilus resting on a stem of coral became one of the Belleek factory's most highly prized decorative achievements. Not unexpectedly, the Willets factory capitalized on the shell's popularity and suitability to the medium. This object varies from Irish prototypes in that it is a pitcher (the natural opening of the shell acting as the spout) and has a putto seated on the swirling ribbon that forms the handle. Willets produced numerous forms that were almost direct copies of their Irish counterparts, intricate woven baskets (see cat. no. 73) and delicate shell dishes on periwinkle feet among them.

The roles played in the making of this pitcher by Walter Scott Lenox, at the time head of the Willets decorating department, and William Bromley, Sr., an Irish craftsman who had come to the firm from Ott and Brewer to help Willets develop its own Belleek porcelain, have been the subject of much debate. Based on Lenox's illustrious reputation in the field of design and Bromley's expertise as a modeler and maker of Belleek porcelain clay, it seems likely that Lenox designed the pitcher and Bromley modeled it.

While this object and its known related examples are major documents in the history of American Belleek porcelain, the archetypal nautilus pitcher, inscribed and dated "WB / May 4th 1887 / WSL," is in the Lenox China archives. It may have been a presentation piece from Lenox to Bromley. Lenox, who had also been employed by Ott and Brewer, left that pottery for Willets in January 1884; Bromley developed the firm's Belleek, initially called Art Porcelaine, in March of 1887. The piece is the first known dated example of Willets Belleek production. Another version, now in the collections of the Newark Museum, was formerly owned by Edwin AtLee Barber, to whom the Willets firm is said to have given it.[1] The subject of this entry descended in the Willets family.

1. Acc. no. 48.4. Information contained in letter to author, 27 January 1988, from Ulysses G. Dietz, curator of decorative arts, Newark Museum.

73
Basket, 1887–93

Willets Manufacturing Company, Trenton, New Jersey
Belleek; H. 3½ in. (8.9 cm.), L. 10⅛ in. (25.7 cm.), W. 8⅜ in. (21.3 cm.)
Marks (on bottom, on applied disk):
BELLEEK / W formed by a coiled serpent / WILLETS
Arthur V. Colletti

THE WILLETS FACTORY made some of the most elaborate pieces of American Belleek known today, such as this openwork basket and an ornate mirror frame (see cat. no. 74), each a good example of the quality achieved by the firm. Though these virtuosic objects best illustrate the plasticity of the Belleek medium, the versatility of the material in no way obviates the extraordinary skill required of the craftsmen.

The baskets were executed in the manner of Irish Belleek prototypes. Each one was handwoven from "straws" of clay on a plaster-of-paris mold in the shape of the finished basket. Working on the upside-down mold, the craftsman first wove the base from rods consisting of three spaghetti-thin strands of clay. Separating the three, he proceeded downward to form the sides of the basket, placing a layer of strands on the mold in a swirled pattern and fashioning over it a subsequent layer perpendicular to the first. While the body was drying, the rim, the feet, and any applied floral or leaf ornament were made, also by hand and usually by the same craftsman. The little florets and leaves that garnish the rim of this Willets example exhibit the minute differences that are the hallmark of a handmade object.

74
Mirror frame, 1887–93

Willets Manufacturing Company, Trenton, New Jersey
Belleek; H. 17½ in. (44.5 cm.), W. 13⅜ in. (34 cm.)
Marks (on back, stamped in red):
BELLEEK / W formed by a coiled serpent / WILLETS
The Newark Museum, Purchase 1979, The Members' Fund (79.12)

THE MOST SPECTACULAR tour de force in American Belleek yet come to light is this porcelain mirror frame completely encrusted with minutely crafted flowers, leaves, and branches, each detail of which was fashioned by hand. The frame is constructed of a porcelain skeleton formed by a wreath of branches to which abundant flowers of varying species and sizes are applied around the sides and the bottom; the upper part is covered with a delicate flowering vine that leaves the underlying branches visible. The ultrashiny glaze imparts to the porcelain the pearly luster that is one of the inherent qualities of Irish Belleek. Such objects as this required exacting skill and unlimited patience on the part of the craftsman. The result is so extraordinary that if it were not for the factory's Belleek mark, the piece might easily have been mistaken for its Irish counterpart.

These flower-bedecked Belleek frames, first made in Ireland, were produced in this country in Trenton by the Ott and Brewer factory as well as by Willets. This example is one of the most extravagantly decorated of all known American versions. It has a history of ownership in Trenton, in the family of Charles L. Zenker, former manager of the Willets factory.[1]

1. Information contained in letter to author, 27 January 1988, from Ulysses G. Dietz, curator of decorative arts, Newark Museum.

75
Footed dish, ca. 1887–1905

Willets Manufacturing Company, Trenton, New Jersey
Belleek; H. 3½ in. (8.9 cm.), W. 11¾ in. (29.9 cm.)
Marks (on bottom, stamped in black):
BELLEEK / W formed by a coiled serpent / WILLETS
New Jersey State Museum, Gift of the Friends of the New Jersey State Museum,
Acquisitions '78 Fund (CH80.79.2)

ALTHOUGH the smooth surface and creamy color of Belleek porcelain lent themselves admirably to polychrome enamel and metallic decoration of all styles, another fashion exemplified by this dish relies on the medium's innate qualities: the porcelain in an undecorated state allows the form to emerge as the primary design ingredient. This unusual dish, standing on its four shell feet, started out as a simple oval bowl. In a more daring statement, it was then cut and curled away from the rim while it was still leather-hard. While at first glance the piece appears to have a boldly ruffled edge, the torn handling of the material lends it a capricious air.

This manipulated treatment is best known through comparably thin-walled, distorted red-earthenware vessels thrown by the highly individual Mississippi potter George E. Ohr, who was working from the early 1880s until about 1906 or 1909.[1] To determine exactly where the practice originated is difficult. Willets began to manufacture an eggshell porcelain in 1887 and continued to produce what was still being called Willets Belleek long after 1909, when the firm went into receivership and was reorganized as the New Jersey Pottery Company.[2] Ruffled, punched, and pulled forms were likely in production at both Willets and Ott and Brewer by the mid-1880s; Ohr, presumably, did not produce work in his tortured style before 1895.[3] He may well have been aware of Trenton's innovative wares, for they were marketed throughout the country. He also made a point of absorbing as much information on ceramics as he could and, to that end, traveled far and wide, undoubtedly visiting the country's leading ceramics centers. Ohr's originality cannot be denied, but the Trenton firms and their avant-garde objects, such as this footed dish, may have had a greater influence on his work than is recognized.[4]

1. For further information on Ohr, see Robert W. Blasberg, *The Unknown Ohr* (Milford, Pa.: Peaceable Press, 1986) and Garth Clark, "George E. Ohr: Avant-Garde Volumes," *Studio Potter* 12 (December 1983), pp. 10–19.
2. A bill dated 27 May 1913 in a private collection has the New Jersey Pottery Company letterhead, which includes mention of its production of "Willets Belleek."
3. "George E. Ohr: Avant-Garde Volumes," p. 12.
4. That possibility was suggested by Ellen Paul Denker and Bert Randall Denker, Kaplan 1987, no. 110.

76
Vase, 1887–1905

Willets Manufacturing Company, Trenton, New Jersey
Belleek; H. 10⅜ in. (26.4 cm.)
Marks (on bottom): W formed by coiled serpent / WILLETS (stamped in red); conjoined JC (painted in purple)
John H. Nally

THE Willets Manufacturing Company, the second American pottery to succeed in manufacturing Belleek porcelain, considered the fine wares it produced to be an art line, an adjunct to its bread-and-butter output of white granite and opaque porcelain dinnerware and toilet sets. Its commitment to that objective can be read in its naming the new medium Art Porcelaine and in its assertion that each product would be a unique work of art, to "command extravagant prices because a guarantee is furnished that no exact duplicate of the decoration will be ever sold again."[1] Period trade publications consistently reported on the quality of the Willets decorators (then supervised by Walter Scott Lenox), comparing their work with that being done at Royal Worcester in England, at Dresden in Germany, at Vienna in Austria, and at Sèvres in France.

Sad to say, virtually all the decorators of the period—at the Willets plant and elsewhere—have remained anonymous. They were rarely discussed as individuals in contemporary published accounts and they seldom signed their work. This outstanding vase may represent one of the few known cases where that obscurity has been penetrated. On the bottom of the vase, along with the printed factory mark, appear the painted conjoined initials *JC*, undoubtedly those of the artist. One may speculate that they stand for James Carr, founder of the New York City Pottery. Though his work in the field of decoration is not documented, the lettering of the signature shows a great similarity to his known marks.[2] Another possibility is that the initials belong to James Callowhill, a decorator who entered the American ceramics industry in the 1880s with his brother, Scott, having trained at Worcester, where vases in a similar mode were produced.

The leaves and stems of the water plant that begin at the base of the vase are rendered in mottled reds and greens, the stems carefully outlined by fine lines consisting of a series of gold dots. Aquatic plants—a highly popular motif added to the ceramics repertoire during the 1880s—are also found on decorated Belleek porcelain objects made at Ott and Brewer (see cat. no. 71). The brilliant yellow ground on this vase is unusual, since the firm's decoration was as a rule executed on the glazed ivory body. That atypical feature impressed a reporter from Trenton's *True American* who visited Willets' department of art porcelain in 1887. There he saw "an exquisite line of vases in an array of magnificent grounds." He was also greatly taken with the "ormolo, raised and chased gold and gilding, figures in relief, and all that is most ornate and lovely in modern art."[3]

1. Advertisement, Willets Manufacturing Company, *Crockery and Glass Journal* 25 (2 June 1887), p. 25.
2. Barber 1904, p. 79.
3. *True American*, 22 May 1887. I am grateful to Ellen Paul Denker for bringing this reference to my attention.

77
Teapot and sugar bowl, 1889

Knowles, Taylor and Knowles, East Liverpool, Ohio
Belleek; H. teapot, 3¾ in. (9.5 cm.), sugar bowl, 3⁹⁄₁₆ in. (9.1 cm.)
Marks (on bottom, stamped in purple): TRADE MARK / K.T. & K.
on circular band, eagle within, wreath surrounding / BELLEEK
Private collection

THESE OBJECTS, undoubtedly part of a full tea service (or, based on their small size, a tête-à-tête set), are the only known marked pieces of Belleek porcelain made by the East Liverpool firm owned by Isaac W. Knowles, his son Homer S. Knowles, and his son-in-law John N. Taylor.[1] The first announcement that the Knowles, Taylor and Knowles firm was making Belleek porcelain appeared in the *Crockery and Glass Journal* of 10 January 1889, where it was noted that the partners, at their newly built porcelain factory, "are now producing white granite, vitreous, translucent hotel china, Belleek and art goods."[2] The firm's eggshell porcelain was made under the direction of Joshua Poole, formerly plant manager of the Irish works. In common with many of the wares produced in Trenton at the Willets and Ott and Brewer factories, the teapot and the sugar bowl duplicate the color and thinness of the Irish porcelain, though their shape, that of a melon with surfaces scored and pebbled to resemble the rind, is unknown in Irish Belleek. As an unnamed journalist, writing of Knowles, Taylor and Knowles' Belleek and art goods in April 1889, commented, "One of their novelties—the Melon shape set—is particularly pretty."[3] Only a few months later, an article in the same journal found the objects to be among "the handsomest pieces of pottery produced in America."[4] The Melon shape, along with tea forms in the Cactus and Venice patterns, was listed among the company's Belleek in a catalogue issued in 1889.[5]

In June 1889, Knowles, Taylor and Knowles hired a designer and decorator who had formerly worked at the English Royal Worcester Porcelain Works.[6] Though these melon-shaped examples do not reveal any unusual technical command on the part of the decorator, their leaves and vines in tints of pale blue and varying shades of gold are proof that his presence on the staff made decoration in the Royal Worcester style available on the fine porcelain products produced at East Liverpool.

Despite the evident quality of its Belleek, the firm was able to produce that fine porcelain for just under a year. In November 1889, the factory was destroyed by a fire in which, according to newspaper accounts of the disaster, much of its stock was lost.[7] The conflagration and the enforced cessation of work it imposed account for the scarcity of Belleek objects made by Knowles, Taylor and Knowles. When the factory was rebuilt the following year, the partners discontinued production of true Belleek and developed a new line of bone china, called Lotus Ware (see cat. nos. 78–80), to replace it.

1. Unmarked examples of Belleek in the collections of the Museum of Ceramics at East Liverpool, Ohio, have been attributed to the same firm on the basis of comparison with these pieces.
2. "The Potteries," *Crockery and Glass Journal* 29 (10 January 1889), p. 24.
3. Ibid. (25 April 1889), p. 28.
4. Ibid. 30 (1 August 1889), p. 30.
5. Ibid. (8 August 1889), p. 28.
6. Ibid. 29 (6 June 1889), p. 28.
7. See "A Big Blaze in East Liverpool," *Crockery and Glass Journal* 30 (21 November 1889), p. 25; Cox 1942, p. 155.

78
Ewer, 1891–97

Knowles, Taylor and Knowles, East Liverpool, Ohio
Bone china; H. 9⅜ in. (23.9 cm.)
Marks (on bottom, stamped in green): K.T.K. Co. / crescent moon and star, within circle surmounted by crown / LOTUS WARE
The Metropolitan Museum of Art, Purchase, The Dietrich Foundation, Inc., Gift and Friends of the American Wing Fund, 1985 (1985.98)

After November 1889, when the Knowles, Taylor and Knowles porcelain plant burned to the ground, a new factory was begun. When it was completed, the firm did not resume production of its fine eggshell porcelain (see cat. no. 77), but instead introduced a new line of bone china named Lotus Ware, which was intended to rival the Belleek manufactured in Trenton. Some of the most successful objects made of the firm's Lotus Ware were those that exploited the natural purity and delicacy of the medium. This ewer, with its slender neck, high arched spout, and thin handle, is a good example. Referred to as the "Etruscan pitcher" in a surviving page from a company catalogue,[1] it has a body ornamented with applied jewel-like porcelain dots and delicate pierced encrustations that recall metalwork designs from the world of Islam. That unusual type of decoration, unique to Knowles, Taylor and Knowles, has been credited to Henry Schmidt, a German potter from the Meissen porcelain works employed briefly in New York City and in Trenton and who was referred to at East Liverpool as a "fancy worker" or an "artist."[2]

Much of the openwork designs were achieved by means of an instrument not unlike a cake decorator's bag and funnel, resulting in ornament that resembles sugar frosting on a cake made of white porcelain. The decorator, using clay of a jellylike consistency, would force it through the funnel, modifying the pressure to form the floral or openwork designs. A description in the words of Schmidt's assistant helps to illuminate the novel technique: "His openwork patterns were first worked out on a small plaster of Paris mold. He would do a quick penciling of his design on the mold and then etch it out slowly with a sharp tool so that, when he went to work on it with his cornucopia bag, these minute indentations served to support the moist clay while the design was drying. When the drying process was complete, the openwork would be removed from the mold by a slight jolt of the plaster form from the hand. He would next take the openwork design into his hand and apply a little fresh slip to its outer edges. Then he would attach the design to the vase or bowl on which he was working. This required much care. If too much pressure were applied, the pattern would be crushed and rendered useless."[3]

1. Two undated pages from a company catalogue survive in the collections of the Museum of Ceramics at East Liverpool, Ohio.
2. Henry Schmidt may be the Hermann Schmidt who is included in a listing of independent porcelain decorators in Dresden, Germany, compiled from Dresden city directories from 1855 to 1943/44 and published in Robert E. Röntgen, *The Book of Meissen* (Exton, Pa.: Schiffer Publishing, 1984), p. 322. See also Cox 1942, p. 156.
3. Cox 1942, p. 156.

79
Two pitchers, 1891–97

Knowles, Taylor and Knowles, East Liverpool, Ohio
Designed by Kenneth P. Beattie
Bone china; H. 5¾ in. (14.6 cm.)
Marks (stamped on base, in red on one; in green on the other): K.T.K. Co. / crescent moon and star, within circle surmounted by crown / LOTUS WARE
The Metropolitan Museum of Art, Gift of Florence I. Balasny-Barnes, in memory of her parents, Elizabeth C. and Joseph Balasny, 1986 (1986.443.4,8)

KNOWLES, TAYLOR AND KNOWLES developed a special art line of bone china called Lotus Ware and utilized the medium for a wide assortment of designs, some employing different methods of decoration, some using colored clay bodies. These two small bone-china pitchers made from the same mold are of a form that has been attributed to the firm's chief modeler, Kenneth P. Beattie.[1] In 1893, Knowles, Taylor and Knowles included similar pitchers in its display at the World's Columbian Exposition in Chicago. The shape, which can be traced to Near Eastern inspiration, has a wide, low belly tapering to a tall, narrow neck and spout. On the neck is a swirling vine of stylized flowers and leaves in slight relief; encircling the base are fine, vertical molded ribs.

In 1893, a year well within the period to which these little pitchers date, twelve decorating kilns were in use at the East Liverpool plant, denoting the importance of that aspect of its production.[2] On these two objects, the decorative treatment is startlingly different. One is made of the dark olive-green body obtained by mixing iron oxide with the clay, a process that made its debut as early as 1878 in European examples exhibited in Paris, where objects of that color were seen and admired by many Americans.[3] The relief-molded decoration of the pitcher, barely visible in the dark body, is further obscured by a hand-fashioned spray of flowers in white paste, a type of embellishment much prized by American buyers.

The second pitcher, of a white body with overglaze decoration in gilding and colored enamels, is further enriched by the application of tiny turquoise jewels made of raised enamel dots dramatically presented on a gold ground within reserves on each side of the bowl. Pale pink covers the neck's relief-molded stylized flowers highlighted in gold. These contrast sharply with the naturalistic roses seen in full bloom and bud and painted in soft pastel colors of pink, yellow, and green on the lower half of the pitcher, which relate closely to the work of Trenton painter William Morley (see cat. no. 93). He was perhaps the Will Morley of the Doulton factory in London, who along with his brother George is known to have been hired by Knowles, Taylor and Knowles to execute the painted and gold decoration of its Lotus Ware.[4]

1. Barber 1893, p. 203.
2. Ibid.
3. Blake 1880, 3, p. 134.
4. Maude M. Doyle, "Lotus Ware," *American Antiques Journal* 2 (November 1947), p. 5. Harry R. Thompson was another Knowles, Taylor and Knowles decorator of Lotus Ware. Apparently a close friend of plant manager Joshua Poole's, Thompson also painted a vase later given by his daughter Bernice Thompson Steinfield to the Henry Ford Museum, Dearborn, Michigan (acc. no. 61.74.1).

80

Vase, 1891–97

Knowles, Taylor and Knowles, East Liverpool, Ohio
Bone china; H. 9⅜ in. (23.9 cm.)
Marks (on bottom, stamped in green): K.T.K. Co. / crescent moon and star, within circle surmounted by crown / LOTUS WARE
Ohio Historical Society, Museum of Ceramics at East Liverpool (H1335)

COLORED GROUNDS for parian objects (see cat. nos. 56, 57) and for pâte-sur-pâte decoration (obtained by building up a paste of white slip on a glazed, colored body and then carving away the ornament) were immensely popular during the last quarter of the nineteenth century. According to Marc Louis Solon, French originator and master of the pâte-sur-pâte technique, he had been inspired by a Chinese vase of celadon-glazed porcelain having a design of flowers and foliage in white paste.[1] A ground of delicate celadon-green color, achieved by the addition of iron oxide to the porcelain paste and particularly valued because of its allusions to prized oriental porcelains of great age, was among several colors seen and admired in the displays of French and English potteries at the great international expositions of the period.

"The Knowles, Taylor & Knowles Company Lotus Ware." One of two surviving pages from an undated company catalogue, 8½ × 12 in. (21.6 × 30.5 cm.). Ohio Historical Society, Museum of Ceramics at East Liverpool

According to an extant page (ill.) from a catalogue the firm of Knowles, Taylor and Knowles issued in the 1890s, this vase, number 501, was of the Thebian pattern and was available in various colored bodies—white, olive, or, as here, celadon. On the vase, beautifully articulated white flowers and leaves seem to be clinging to the pale green body, a realistic effect enhanced by the unusual asymmetric handle that appears to twist in and out of the actual form. While the firm is known to have executed a small number of pâte-sur-pâte artwares, few of them have survived.[2] Instead, the embellishment of this object (and that of many of the more elaborate pieces of Lotus Ware turned out by the factory) is of white paste painstakingly formed by hand and then applied to the piece.

1. L. Solon, "Pate-sur-Pate," *Art Journal* (London), March 1901, p. 75.
2. Barber 1893, pp. 204–6.

81
Tea set, 1891–94

American Art China Company, Trenton, New Jersey
Belleek; H. teapot, 6 in. (15.2 cm.), sugar bowl, 4¾ in. (12.1 cm.),
cream pitcher, 3⁹⁄₁₆ in. (9.1 cm.)
Marks (on teapot and cream pitcher bottom, stamped in blue):
AAC Co monogram / BELLEEK CHINA
The Metropolitan Museum of Art, Friends of the American Wing Fund,
1984 (1984.153.1–3)

ALTHOUGH short-lived and today almost forgotten, the American Art China Company, founded by John C. Rittenhouse and George Evans in 1891, made some of the finest Belleek porcelain in the Trenton area. Prominent in the firm's surviving oeuvre is this tea set, a joyous expression in the Rococo-revival style. While other Trenton firms, including Morris and Willmore and the Ceramic Art Company, produced comparable sets also made of scrolled, shell-like forms (Fig. 40, p. 51), none possesses the lightness or fantasy found in this charming example.

Typically rococo is the whimsical, almost anthropomorphic quality of the individual pieces, which stems from their lobed feet, the fish-scale texture on part of their surfaces, and the manner in which the spouts of the teapot and the cream pitcher poke through the scrolls on the upper part of the vessels. That rococo influence is further demonstrated in the deliberate lack of symmetry in the relief and polychrome and gold-painted decoration that characterizes the design.

82
Vase, Ewer, 1893–1900

Columbian Art Pottery (Morris and Willmore), Trenton, New Jersey
Belleek; H. vase, 12¾ in. (32.4 cm.), ewer, 13 1/16 in. (33.2 cm.)
Marks (on bottom, stamped in red):
BELLEEK / conjoined MW / TRENTON on ribbon band / N.J.
Private collection

WILLIAM T. MORRIS AND FRANCIS R. WILLMORE, the English-born founders and proprietors of the Columbian Art Pottery, both worked at the Worcester Royal Porcelain Works in their native land before emigrating to the United States and locating in Trenton. Their Worcester conditioning is apparent in the shape and the decoration of these two objects. In shape, both pieces demonstrate the influence of Near Eastern forms evident in Western ceramics by the mid-1870s.[1] The vase handles, consisting of the angular, intertwining arabesques found in Islamic scrollwork, are particularly true to that source. The decoration is more conventional: on both objects, the smooth surfaces have been treated as if they were canvases, each filled with a softly painted landscape scene of muted palette and containing a single figure. The unknown decorator or decorators either copied period paintings or executed original compositions in the romantic manner popular in the 1880s and 1890s.

Illustration in *Industrial Trenton and Vicinity* (Wilmington, Del.: George A. Wolf, Publisher, for Trenton Board of Trade, 1900), p. 72. New Jersey State Library, Trenton

The ewer and the vase, which exhibit perhaps the finest painting technique known on Columbian Art Pottery porcelain, were undoubtedly a source of great pride to the factory and its owners. Together with a second vase also decorated in the Royal Worcester style and having reticulated handles, the two objects are featured in a presentation photograph (ill.) that accompanied a short description of the firm and its wares for inclusion in a publication on Trenton industries.[2] Both pieces descended in the family of William T. Morris before being acquired by the present owner.

1. Frelinghuysen 1986, pp. 216–18.
2. *Industrial Trenton and Vicinity* (Wilmington, Del.: George A. Wolf, Publisher, for the Trenton Board of Trade, 1900), p. 72. I am grateful to David Goldberg for bringing this reference to my attention.

83
Vase, 1878

Union Porcelain Works, Greenpoint (Brooklyn), New York
Porcelain; H. 11 in. (27.9 cm.)
Marks: U.P.W. (on briefcase, painted in purple); ESC 1878 (scratched on side of base); 1878 / U.P.W. / eagle's head with S in beak (on bottom, painted in red)
The Bennington Museum, Bennington, Vermont, Gift of Dr. J. McCullough Turner, Bethany, Connecticut (65.173)

THE SCENIC DECORATION painted in monochrome purple on the white porcelain body of this vase resembles a print or a pencil drawing more likely to be found in a sketchbook. The vignettes around the vase, read from bottom to top, chronicle an excursion made by train to the Green Mountains of Vermont that was organized in the spring of 1878 by Mr. and Mrs. R. C. Root. Little is known about the pair, except that Root was president of the Glastenburg and Lebanon Springs railroads, possibly a factor in the hosts' choice of entertainment.[1] In the first vignette, labeled START at middle bottom, Root, cane in one hand and doffed top hat in the other, welcomes his guests, who include Thomas C. Smith, owner of the Union Porcelain Works, and Mrs. Smith, aboard the railroad car "Duchess." Smith is identified by the briefcase he carries, which is marked with the initials *U.P.W.* Other vignettes portray the passing landscape, the industrial scenery, and the hotels where the guests spent the night after dining and being en-

Figure 1. Vignettes, with guest list

Figure 2. Vignettes, including return trip

At the Walloomsac
DUCHESS.
START

Figure 3. Detail (bottom)

tertained (Figs. 1, 2). On Thursday, 16 May 1878, the Bennington newspaper printed this notice: "A party of New York ladies and gentlemen were in town, stopping at the Putnam and [Wolloomsac] Houses on Tuesday and Wednesday evenings of this week. The party arrived from that city on Tuesday afternoon, and after spending the night, went to Rutland and returned yesterday, and to-day they set out upon their return."[2] The account then listed the names of the guests and reported that they had expressed themselves "delighted with the trip and their visit to this portion of the Green Mountain State."[3] The final vignette on the vase shows the weary group departing the train.

The diverting subject matter and the presence of Thomas C. Smith on the outing lead to the conclusion that Smith had the vase created at his factory to present to his hosts in appreciation of their hospitality. The likeness of Root that appears at the bottom of the vase with the caption "He was at the Bottom of it" (Fig. 3) substantiates that theory, as does Smith's custom of having a porcelain memento made in honor of a special event he had attended. On another occasion (coincidentally, also related to trains, that time a dinner party celebrating a railroad opening), he presented his fellow guests with teacups and saucers he had had made at his factory, each cup embellished with a picture of a train.[4]

The initials *E.S.C.* and the date 1878 on the side of the vase are an unusual feature.[5] The decorator's identity has not been established, though a search through the Brooklyn city directories of 1878 to 1880 reveals the possibility that he was Edwin S. Creamer, whose occupation was given as painter.[6] The same initials appear on one other Union Porcelain Works vessel dated 1880 and identical in shape to this railroad-excursion vase. Now in a private collection, it has three evenly spaced depictions of baseball players, each wearing a uniform of different color and pattern and with a different letter that combines with the others to read *ESC*.

Smith prized the anonymous artist's work enough to show it in 1878 at the Society of Decorative Art in New York, where "gems of the modern, foreign and American schools of painting and rare examples of various art industries" were displayed.[7] Among the four examples of Union Porcelain Works production exhibited was number 606, undoubtedly the subject of this entry. It was described as "Hard paste porcelain, made by Union Porcelain Works, Greenpoint. Decoration, A Trip to the Green Mountains.—Mr. Thomas C. Smith."[8]

1. "The Lebanon Springs Railroad," *Bennington Banner*, 11 October 1877.
2. *Bennington Banner*, 16 May 1878. I am grateful to J. Garrison Stradling for this reference, and I thank Eugene R. Kosche, curator of history, Bennington Museum, Bennington, Vermont, for sending me a copy of the newspaper notice.
3. Ibid.
4. See typescript inventory of Union Porcelain Works wares owned by Thomas C. Smith's grandsons Carll S. and Franklin Chace, dated 11 March 1943, accession files, Decorative Arts Department, The Brooklyn Museum.
5. Other than Karl L. H. Müller, head of the design department, few of the artists who worked for the Greenpoint firm have been identified, though several plates are known to have been painted by John M. Falconer. See Young 1879, fig. 455.
6. Creamer was listed in the directory of 1879/80 as a painter at 103 Java Street in Brooklyn, only a few blocks away from the porcelain factory. The designated occupation could also mean, of course, that Creamer was a housepainter.
7. *Catalogue of the Loan Exhibition in and of The Society of Decorative Art 1878* (New York: National Academy of Design, 1878), p. 31.
8. Ibid.

84
Cup and saucer, 1875–85

Union Porcelain Works, Greenpoint (Brooklyn), New York
Porcelain; H. cup, 3 in. (7.6 cm.);
Diam. saucer, 5¾ in. (14.6 cm.)
Marks (on bottom of each piece, stamped in green):
U.P.W. / eagle's head with S in beak
The Metropolitan Museum of Art,
Gift of Mr. and Mrs. Franklin Chace, 1969 (69.194.17, 18)

THE INTEREST of potters in the ceramics of the Orient reached its height in the decade after 1875, suggesting the probable date for this cup and saucer.[1] Here, the porcelain medium is seen to its greatest advantage. The thin walls and shiny glaze speak for themselves, but the medium's adaptability to virtuosic technique is emphasized in the diapered rice-grain decoration that is its principal feature. Borrowed from Chinese porcelains of the Ch'ien Lung period (1735–96), the pattern is created by a series of small perforations, each about the size and shape of a grain of rice, which, when filled and covered by a clear glaze, results in a highly translucent effect. The process called for exquisite care on the part of the craftsman, who could have ruined the entire piece by one slip of his knife. On the cup, the oriental influence is apparent also in the cut-back rim and the molded motif of the handle.

Beginning about 1845, pierced decoration was one hallmark of excellence in the nineteenth-century porcelain produced at England's Worcester potteries. Reticulated objects were exhibited by the Grainger factory in London in 1862.[2] Toward the end of the nineteenth century, the technique was being employed in France to demonstrate both the skill of the craftsman and the perfection of the medium. Examples in what was called Rice Porcelain exhibited by the Pouyat factory of Limoges at the Exposition Universelle of 1878 won considerable praise from the American delegation to the fair.[3]

Though the technique was elevated to its highest expression in the 1890s under the meticulous hand of George Owen, working at the Royal Worcester Company, this elegant ensemble made by the Union Porcelain Works at least ten years earlier displays a flawless white paste superbly complemented by the prowess of the native craftsman. The masterly pierced work holds its own among counterparts produced overseas by far older and more experienced houses.

1. For a discussion of the influence of oriental ceramics on American pottery and porcelain, see Frelinghuysen 1986, pp. 205–29.
2. Godden 1961, p. 128.
3. Blake 1880, p. 163; see also d'Albis and Romanet 1980, p. 119.

85
Teapot and cream pitcher, ca. 1880

Greenwood Pottery, Trenton, New Jersey
Porcelain; H. teapot 4¾ in. (12.1 cm.),
cream pitcher, 3⅜ in. (8.6 cm.)
Marks (on bottom, on paper label): Greenwood China / made by Jas. Tams / 1880 / & presented to / J. H. Brewer / for his collection
New Jersey State Museum, The Brewer Collection,
Gift of Mrs. John Hart Brewer (CH354.17.1, 2a, b)

THE ORIGIN of these pieces, the only known survivors of what must originally have been a complete set, is given on the paper label affixed to the bottom of the teapot. James Tams, like many of his colleagues in the Trenton potting industry, learned his trade in Staffordshire, Tams in the town of Longton. Emigrating to the New World in 1861, he began his American career in Trenton, working with his father, William, as a kilnman at William Young and Company (see cat. no. 28).[1] In 1861, William Tams went into business with James P. Stephens and Charles Brearley, forming a company that was later to be named the Greenwood Pottery. In 1865, after a short trip back to England, James Tams joined the firm. On the death of his father, he acquired William's share in the business, serving first as factory superintendent and, in 1868, when the firm was renamed, becoming president of the company. The partners maintained a steady production of white hotelware, as did most of their competitors, and the pottery went on to become one of the largest in Trenton. Tams, to acquire more artistic prestige, brought out a finer class of goods, which by late 1875 were being praised for "graceful, durable and ornamental" designs and shapes.[2] Particularly noteworthy was their embellishment, "from the simple colored and gold band to the finest antique or floral decorations."[3] Over the next few years, the Greenwood firm continued to improve the body of the porcelain and its decoration, and in the autumn of 1879, its display at the American Institute Fair in New York City was warmly received. One object was particularly complimented: "A dainty tea-set richly decorated in bright and dead gold, attracts considerable attention."[4]

Stylistically, the ornament on the teapot and cream pitcher—animals in a landscape within oval reserves,

a lavish use of gilding, and a distinctive ground color—relates to nineteenth-century French decoration. Trade journals of the day often commented on the resemblance between Greenwood goods and French china. The reviewer of one American Institute Fair found a pitcher, part of the firm's display, "one of the prettiest things that I have seen for many a day. The shape of the jug gives a panel on each side, and in one of these is painted, in excellent style, the head of a fox hound with nose 'a scent,' on the other panel is painted two lively looking sons of Reynard peering over a breastwork of brush, as if they were trying to throw the hounds off the scent. The ground and gilding are capitally done."[5] His description corresponds to the ornament of the subjects of this entry. The brown-and-white hunting dog in the teapot reserve looks backward as if it had just caught the scent of the running fox on the pitcher. The gold bands of each piece are composed of the matte and shiny gilding that was noted in the previously quoted review as "bright and dead gold." The detailing in black both in the bands at the spout and handles and in the delicate linear pattern is typical of the Renaissance-revival style that dates to the late 1860s and early 1870s—a decade before these pieces were made.

The two pieces were presented, probably by Tams, to John Hart Brewer, a partner in the large and successful Ott and Brewer firm and an important personage in the Trenton ceramics industry. During his career, Brewer amassed a sizable collection of local ceramics now preserved at the New Jersey State Museum. Many of the pieces were accompanied by Brewer's handwritten notes containing salient information. Without his careful records, much of the history of the individual objects, including this teapot and pitcher, would have been lost.

1. "James Tams Dies after Notable Life as Potter," *Trenton Evening Times*, 12 November 1910, p. 1.
2. "The Greenwood Pottery Company," *Crockery and Glass Journal* 2 (23 December 1875), p. 22.
3. Ibid.
4. "Native Ceramics at the American Institute," *Crockery and Glass Journal* 10 (9 October 1879), p. 24.
5. "Trenton Potteries," *Crockery and Glass Journal* 10 (30 October 1879), p. 20.

86
Vase, 1883–86

Greenwood Pottery, Trenton, New Jersey
Porcelain; H. 9⁵⁄₁₆ in. (23.7 cm.)
Marks (on bottom, stamped in purple): GREENWOOD on ribbon band / NE PLUS ULTRA on tripartite band / 61 within scrolled, octagonal device / WARE on band
Florence I. Balasny-Barnes

JUST AS THE Greenwood Pottery's ivory porcelain (see cat. no. 87) was produced to vie with the renowned objects made at the Worcester Royal Porcelain Works, so too the company's fine vases, with their floral designs of raised gold and bronze on a deep, shiny, mazarine-blue ground, were intended to compete with similar precedents. As this example demonstrates, the American firm succeeded so brilliantly in its aspirations that if the pieces were not marked by the maker, these "vases of fine translucent porcelain . . . might easily be mistaken for the rich productions of the Royal Worcester factories."[1] That comment, made by a journalist in 1884, is as true today as it was a century ago. Here, the especially fluid treatment of the chrysanthemum, a flower favored by Japanese artists, is visible in the shading from gold to dark bronze on the petals and in the graceful calligraphic line traced by their stems. The same sort of decoration exhibited at the Centennial Exposition by the English firm had aroused the admiration of all who saw it and possibly planted the seed of its popularity with the American market. The porcelain of the Worcester display, "of Japanese style, [with] metallic decoration in relief on dark-blue grounds," was particularly noted in the judges' report.[2] What distinguishes this vase from the other Greenwood examples adorned with Japanesque motifs in gold and bronze on a mazarine-blue ground is the presence of the small, delicate flowers painted in white slip, which call to mind the pâte-sur-pâte technique that was practiced to a small extent at the factory.[3] The vase's shape—Islamic in inspiration—is also found in examples having an ivory ground. The illustration of one now unlocated version shows it with a domed lid.[4] It may have been unique in that feature, for no known vase made in the same shape retains a cover. The embellishment sponged in gold near the top of the interior on the subject of this entry suggests that it stands as originally completed.

1. "The Potteries," *Crockery and Glass Journal* 20 (2 October 1884), p. 10.
2. Tyndale 1880, p. 44.
3. See Barber 1893, p. 227.
4. Ibid., fig. 98.

87
Vase, 1884–86

Greenwood Pottery, Trenton, New Jersey
Porcelain; H. 13 9/16 in. (34.4 cm.)
Marks (on bottom, stamped in purple): GREENWOOD on ribbon band / NE PLUS ULTRA on tripartite band / 61 within scrolled, octagonal device / WARE on band
Arthur V. Colletti

THE SIMILARITY of this two-handled vase to the decorated ivory porcelains produced by the Worcester Royal Porcelain Works during the late nineteenth century was no mere coincidence. When the Greenwood Pottery made a concerted attempt to break into the art-porcelain market, it strove to compete with and to copy Worcester counterparts. Invoking the unmatchable excellence of its own porcelainware, the firm named the new line Ne Plus Ultra, which a printed company trade card described as a "fac-simile of Royal Worcester, having an Ivory finish and Raised Gold and other Metallic and Bronze Decorations. Each piece is stamped on bottom with our stamp."[1] The art-porcelain wares, developed in 1883, were noted in the local press:

> A very important product of the industry consists of a line of very superior works of art, principally vases of various shapes and sizes, richly and artistically decorated in the Royal Worcester style, similar in design to Japanese decorations. These beautiful art pieces are especially valuable, not only on account of the superiority of the ware, and artistic skill embodied in design and decorations, but also on account of an established rule not to manufacture more than one piece of a kind, consequently it is impossible to find duplicate copies scattered throughout the land.[2]

This vase, larger than most known Greenwood Pottery pieces, emulates some of the best of Worcester's qualities: a satin-smooth ivory surface; rich gold ornamentation; Near Eastern inspiration, seen in the exuberant scroll handles; delicate enamel painting, here of hummingbirds and a trumpet vine in shades of blue and green; and the careful application of gilding and polychrome enamels to yield a smooth, flat surface.

To achieve decoration of the Royal Worcester type, the Greenwood Pottery hired workers from the English factory. Though their identities are for the most part unknown, one was named in the first mention of a Royal Worcester artisan employed at the Greenwood Pottery, which appeared in a trade journal of July 1883: "For some time past a Mr. Jones, formerly at the Royal Worcester Works, in England, as decorator, has been engaged in embellishing some special pieces of the Greenwood's goods in the rich style of decoration peculiar to the Royal Worcester and Crown Derby factories."[3] By the end of the year, the same periodical reported the results to be "identical with the rich pieces of work that come from that celebrated factory, the artists working on them having been brought directly from the Royal Worcester Works."[4]

So closely did the American examples resemble the English counterparts that the Worcester emigrants may have brought samples of their work to Trenton. Several vases from Worcester survive in the New Jersey State Museum, the gift of James Tams's great-granddaughter.[5] In August 1884, a contemporary periodical reported that the pottery was "at work on a new series of goods in which they are introducing fine bits of painting to vary the decorations in gold and bronze."[6] The subject of this entry may not have been made before then. The factory carried its emulation of Royal Worcester to the highest level, even in the trademark that appears on the bottom of these Ne Plus Ultra pieces. The mark is a near replica of its Worcester cousin, except that the English crown is replaced by a geometric banner incorporating the word "Greenwood" and the Ne Plus Ultra designation.

1. Trade card at the New Jersey State Museum, Department of Cultural History (acc. no. CH79.1.56h).

2. "The Growth of Pottery: Work of the Greenwood Pottery," *Trenton Times*, 10 November 1883, p. 1.
3. "The Potteries," *Crockery and Glass Journal* 18 (19 July 1883), p. 38.
4. Ibid. (20 December 1883), p. 78.
5. See acc. nos. CH79.1.8; CH79.1.26.
6. "The Potteries," *Crockery and Glass Journal* 20 (14 August 1884), p. 30.

88
Vase, 1884–90

Probably made by Faience Manufacturing Company,
Greenpoint (Brooklyn), New York
Decorated by Edward Lycett
Porcelain; H. 12¾ in. (32.4 cm.)
Signed on bottom: E Lycett / New York; E Lycett (scratched in script)
Unmarked
Inscribed: CWEA / 1869 1883 / JAN. 20. (on one side); CJA (on other side)
John H. Nally

Edward Lycett, whose signature appears twice on the bottom of this vase and who has been dubbed "the pioneer of china painting in America," enjoyed a varied, long, and successful career in the field of ceramics decoration. Before coming to this country in 1861, the English-born Lycett had been trained in his craft at the Copeland pottery in Stoke-on-Trent, as well as at the London china-decorating establishment of Thomas Battam, Sr.[1] During the early part of his American career, Lycett continued in the tradition of his English experience, painting terracotta vases in the Greek style in the independent shop he opened on Greene Street shortly after arriving in New York.

He was soon hard at work painting plaques for New York furnituremakers as well. He also executed elaborate monogramming and other distinguishing devices on imported porcelain blanks for his own clientele and for retail shops. After the Civil War, when travel became easier, Lycett left New York to work in Saint Louis, Missouri, and Cincinnati and East Liverpool, Ohio. He influenced local artisans wherever he went, a bequest that can be traced in the amateur china painting that became a widespread phenomenon in the next two decades. Returning to New York in 1884, he founded the Faience Manufacturing Company in Greenpoint, Brooklyn, and remained there for six years. He then retired to Atlanta, Georgia, where he died in 1910.

Most of the products of the Faience Manufacturing Company were of an ivory-colored earthenware body, or ivoryware, as it was called. As proprietor of the firm, Lycett conducted experiments with clays and glazes, developing a "pure white, hard porcelain, with no vestige of the cream tint that has been so difficult to overcome by potters generally."[2] Because color has been applied on selected areas to simulate the appearance of ivoryware, this vase made of porcelain gives the impression that both earthenware and porcelain have been combined in its execution. The exotic nature of its shape, with its prominent griffin handles and ribbed base, is consistent with the style of vases Lycett's company excelled in. Similarly, the rich gilding and lushly painted decoration attest to Lycett's artistic beginnings, especially the profusion of pink and yellow roses that were a favorite motif of his throughout his career.

A diligent search has failed to ascertain the significance of the intertwined initials *CWEA* and the dates 1869 and 1883 that appear on one side of the vase and the initials *CJA* on the other. Construction on the Brooklyn Bridge was begun in 1869 and completed in 1883, but whether that has any relevance to the marks on this vase or its presentation is mere conjecture.

1. The primary source for biographical information on Edward Lycett is Edwin AtLee Barber, "The Pioneer of China Painting in America," *The Ceramic Monthly* 2 (September 1895), pp. 5–20. The article also appeared in *The New England Magazine* of September 1895, pp. 33–48. See also Lydia Lycett, "China Painting by the Lycetts," *Atlanta Historical Bulletin* 6 (July 1941), pp. 201–14.
2. Barber, "The Pioneer of China Painting in America," p. 16.

1869 1883
JAN. 20

89
Teapot, 1888

Louisiana Porcelain Works, or, New Orleans Porcelain Works,
New Orleans, Louisiana
Porcelain; H. 8⅝ in. (22 cm.)
Unmarked
Inscribed: MH
Historic New Orleans Collection (1981.26.5)

THIS TEAPOT is one of a hundred and thirty-seven surviving pieces from a complete service for twelve that represents the only porcelain known to have been produced by the Louisiana Porcelain Works (also called the New Orleans Porcelain Works) of Joseph Hernandez and Bertram Saloy.[1] The documentation of the service is the firm's original bill of sale, dated 8 June 1888, to Professor Ashley Davis Hurt, headmaster of Tulane High School, for "1 Dinner Service, Monogram & Special Decoration #25. . . . $85.00."[2] A sentence in a letter from Hurt to his daughter Elizabeth further supports the attribution: "It is Limoges china made in New Orleans by Limoges workmen, of Limoges kaolin, and decorated by one of Haviland's best artists imported for this purpose."[3]

As demonstrated in the teapot, the close relationship between the pieces of the set and Limoges porcelain is self-evident. The shape, in the Cable pattern (so named because of the twisted motif here seen around finial and handle), was popular in Limoges porcelain manufactured in the 1870s. It also appeared with variations in the whiteware of numerous American factories for two decades. The decoration has a boglike setting that may have been chosen as a reference to the Louisiana landscape; the transfer-printed outlines of the motifs have been filled in with hand-painted pastel colors. On all the pieces of the service is the pale-blue-and-gold monogram of Mary Hurt, for whose birthday her husband ordered the service. In a letter to their daughter, Hurt explained the special configuration of the letters *MH*: "I had the *M* made more prominent than the *H* for it is especially for *M*." Poignantly, he continued, "As I told you before it has been immensely admired. You write me *fully* how it strikes your mother for I shall be anxious to know."[4]

The development of porcelain in New Orleans was a struggle from the very beginning. The first factory was established there in 1880 by Eugène Surgi and Abel D'Estampes with the hope of producing a line of products that in paste and artistry would rival the quality of those imported from France. Surgi, who came to America from France in 1845 and maintained his career as a civil engineer for most of his professional life, supplied the capital for the joint venture.[5] The expertise was the contribution of D'Estampes, superintendent of a large pottery in Vierzon, France, before emigrating to the United States in 1871.[6] Nevertheless, he proved to be a failure, and by August 1882 had been replaced by a Mr. Caeff, or Caeffe, who had once worked at the Union Porcelain Works in Greenpoint, New York.[7] (Caeff's tenure was also to be short-lived.) In that same year, a board of directors was formed, with Bertram Saloy, who owned the land on which the factory was built, serving as vice president. In the following months, many improvements were made, including the building of a new kiln. In 1883, having triumphed over the many difficulties that attend any new manufacturing enterprise, the firm finally began production of a line of porcelain. Among their products were "pretty novelties in pitchers. One especially, which bore upon its sides a crescent enclosing a star in low relief, emblematic of the Crescent City."[8]

In the first four years of its existence, the New Orleans Porcelain Works turned out a porcelain that was undoubtedly the thick variety known as hotelware. As reported in a trade journal in early 1884, it was "heavy ware—extra heavy indeed—just the class of goods that will be readily taken up by the cheap boarding houses and coffee stands in the market."[9]

The firm's measure of success was not sufficient to keep it in business, and it went into bankruptcy that spring. Saloy then acquired it at auction. By early 1886, in partnership with Joseph Hernandez, another local businessman, and under the practical direction of Paul Thevenet, who had worked at Limoges, Saloy revived the manufactory.[10] After the arrival of at least four skilled French workmen, it went on to produce a fine line of porcelain in the Limoges style popular in America since the 1850s. An extensive article in a local newspaper listed the company's plentiful variety of forms: "Pitchers of all sorts of artistic and novel designs, delicate tea and coffee cups, little mustard dishes and all the innumerable articles which go to make up a complete table service."[11] That sort of service is undoubtedly akin to the one represented by the subject of this entry.

1. The service, acquired from a descendant of the original owner, is at the Historic New Orleans Collection, New Orleans, La.
2. Original bill of sale, Historic New Orleans Collection.
3. Letter of 14 June 1888, Manuscript Division, Historic New Orleans Collection. Quoted in Pat Comiller, "Louisiana Limoges," *The Historic New Orleans Collection Newsletter* 2 (Winter 1984), p. 6.
4. Ibid.
5. *Biographical and Historical Memoirs of Louisiana*, 2 vols. (Chicago: Goodspeed Publishing Company, 1892), 2, p. 413.
6. "The Porcelain Works at New Orleans," *Crockery and Glass Journal* 13 (3 March 1881), p. 24.
7. "New Orleans Trade Reports," *Crockery and Glass Journal* 16 (31 August 1882), p. 36. In an effort to compete with the New Orleans Porcelain Works, D'Estampes formed a new company, which he called the French Porcelain Company. It too was a failure. See "New Orleans Reports," *Crockery and Glass Journal* 17 (5 April 1883), p. 8.
8. Ibid. (3 May 1883), p. 6.
9. "New Orleans Trade Reports," *Crockery and Glass Journal* 19 (3 January 1884), p. 34.
10. See "Fine Porcelain. The New Orleans Factory: The Pioneer of the Industry in America," *The Sunday States*, 27 June 1887, p. 8. A typescript of the article was provided by courtesy of the Historic New Orleans Collection. In the article, the Thevenet mentioned may have been a misspelling of Thouvenet, possibly a reference to a Thouvenet Spiquel & Company cited as operating in Limoges between 1887 and 1891. See d'Albis and Romanet 1980, p. 175.
11. "Fine Porcelain. The New Orleans Factory," p. 8.

90
Centerpiece, 1892

Ohio Valley China Company, Wheeling, West Virginia
Modeled by Carl Goetz
Porcelain; H. 25½ in. (64.8 cm.)
Unmarked
Philadelphia Museum of Art, Given by Ohio Valley China Company (93-376)

When the Ohio Valley China Company was reorganized in 1891 from the West Virginia China Company founded only two or three years earlier, it set out to make true hard-paste porcelain in the best European tradition.[1] In its brief, five-year existence, it succeeded; what it produced was of a quality among the finest then being made in America. In October 1891 the firm announced the hiring of two German craftsmen.[2] One of the two was undoubtedly the German-trained potter and chemist W. H. Zimmer, who was elected superintendent of the works that November to be responsible for developing a line of "translucent china."[3] By the following January, the factory surprised its competition by coming out with a "high grade of china on the French principle."[4] Only a few months later, it was producing what was described in a trade journal as "dinner and tea sets and novelties of translucent china equal to the Carlsbad," of a quality so superior that the reporter considered it likely that a china dealer, seeing these wares for the first time, would doubt that they had been manufactured in America.[5] The similarity to German wares

in "quality, color, and translucency" can be attributed to the recipes for making porcelain brought from that country by Zimmer.[6]

In 1892, the Ohio Valley China Company branched out into a line of art porcelain that was cited in that same year for its delicate character, superior quality, and elegance. The firm's teawares and dinnerwares, designed to "suit American tastes in Dresden, Vienna and Meissen styles," were sold in the best jewelry and china stores.[7] In June, the company introduced its first bisque wares.[8] This elaborate centerpiece, or fruit holder, the only known surviving example of the firm's art line, still stands as a remarkable example of American manufacture. Its combination of bisque and glazed porcelain is a European fashion that rarely appears in domestic objects. The exceedingly white clay body also contributes to its European air. The masterly piece of large size and complicated modeling is credited to Carl Goetz, a craftsman from Hildburghausen, Germany, employed for a time by the Wheeling firm.[9] In the supplement to his definitive *Pottery and Porcelain of the United States*, Edwin AtLee Barber described the centerpiece clearly, though he did not give its location.[10] He would have been familiar with the object, since he had undoubtedly been instrumental in its acquisition by the Pennsylvania Museum (now the Philadelphia Museum of Art) in 1892, the year he was named honorary curator of the newly formed Department of American Pottery and Porcelain.[11]

The pottery produced at least one other figural work comparably grandiose in concept. An object just under four feet in height featuring a globe, an eagle, the American shield, and a representation of Columbus, it occupied the central position in the company's display at the World's Columbian Exposition in Chicago in 1893.[12] Its present location is unknown; indeed, the piece may no longer exist. Whether or not the Ohio Valley China Company ever again attempted such an ambitious project is not recorded, but the fine porcelain objects it continued to produce were of highly marketable quality. Though the company began to founder in April 1894, when labor unions campaigned against its using imported workmen, it stayed in business through 1895. It shut down completely the next year.

1. Edwin AtLee Barber cites the company as beginning in 1890, but contemporary accounts in the *Crockery and Glass Journal* record that real estate and property of the West Virginia China Company were transferred to the owners of the Ohio Valley China Company in June 1891, though the plant had not yet begun operations. Not until January 1892 were samples of their porcelain ready for salesmen. See Barber 1893 (rev. ed.), p. 497; "The Potteries: Wheeling," *Crockery and Glass Journal* 33 (4 June 1891), p. 22.
2. "The Potteries: Wheeling," *Crockery and Glass Journal* 34 (15 October 1891), pp. 40, 42.
3. Ibid. (5 November 1891), p. 34.
4. "Potters and Glassmakers of the Ohio Valley," *Crockery and Glass Journal* 35 (28 January 1892), p. 21.
5. Ibid. (9 June 1892), p. 23.
6. "Making Real China," *Crockery and Glass Journal* 36 (10 November 1892), p. 30. "Carlsbad" was used to describe the porcelain made in that region of Bohemia. It was imported in large quantities by innumerable American dealers and was enormously popular in this country. Several of the importing firms maintained their own factories in Carlsbad, as they did in Limoges.
7. "The Potteries: Wheeling," *Crockery and Glass Journal* 36 (21 July 1892), p. 74.
8. Ibid. 35 (30 June 1892), p. 32.
9. Barber 1893 (rev. ed.), p. 497.
10. Ibid.
11. Barber's encouragement of the contemporary ceramics industry to donate works to Philadelphia was paralleled by the Women's Art Museum Association in Cincinnati, which solicited gifts from American potteries for the museum it was planning, thereby securing for public display a representation of current ceramic production. See *Art Palace of the West: A Centennial Tribute, 1881–1981*, exh. cat. (Cincinnati, Ohio: Cincinnati Art Museum, 1981), pp. 29–30.
12. For a detailed account of the piece, see "The Potteries: Wheeling," *Crockery and Glass Journal* 37 (27 April 1893), pp. 24–25.

91
Vase, 1889–96

Ceramic Art Company, Trenton, New Jersey
Belleek; H. 7½ in. (19.1 cm.)
Marks (on bottom, stamped in pink): painter's palette / conjoined CAC / BELLEEK
New Jersey State Museum, Gift of Mr. and Mrs. Joseph R. Comly (CH68.95.3)

The Ceramic Art Company was founded in 1889 by Walter Scott Lenox and Jonathan Coxon, Sr., former associates at Trenton's Ott and Brewer pottery, where Lenox was head of the decorating department and Coxon was superintendent. What set their new company apart from its competitors was that it concentrated solely on the making of artware instead of supplementing a commercial production with a small range of artistic vessels.

Both in its overall shape and its reticulated neck and two molded scroll handles, this vase dating to the first period of the firm's history is reminiscent of the Royal Worcester vases of Near Eastern inspiration. Its design scheme, however, is predominantly oriental in character, with varied patterns of leaves and flowers creating the impression of a richly woven Japanese textile. The leaves are treated in soft, matte enamels, those on the lower part of the vase white on a deep blue ground, those on the upper part pink on a ground shading from cream to yellow. The asymmetrically placed raised gold bamboo blossoms in gold-bordered scalloped reserves further enrich the vase. The eclectic combination of styles is consistent with the ideas of the Aesthetic movement, which had reached its height in America in the late 1870s and early 1880s. The oriental influence on the Ceramic Art Company wares coincides with the firm's employing prior to 1891 a Japanese artist named F. Fouji to join the ranks of its decorators. The piece is not signed, but it may well be the work of his hand. A local newspaper described his technique: "[He plies] his brushes over the delicate productions of the Ceramic Art Works, and spreads them with gold in quaint oriental designs."[1] The article continued: "It is interesting to stand beside him and see him gently stroke a fragile Belleek vase, with a pencil looking as fine as a hair, until the delicate design is completed."[2]

1. "An Artist From Japan," *Trenton Town Topics*, 31 January 1891, p. 4.
2. Ibid. The name also appears in contemporary articles as Fauji, Foudji, and Fudgi; in one reference, his first name is given as Gazo.

92
Bowl, 1897

Ceramic Art Company, Trenton, New Jersey
Porcelain; H. 2⅞ in. (7.3 cm.), Diam. 7⅞ in. (20 cm.)
Marks (on bottom): THE / CERAMIC ART Co / TRENTON, N.J., within wreath / NATIONAL PORCELAIN PAINTING / COMPETITION 1897. (stamped in green) / NJC (signed) within wreath (stamped in green)
New Jersey State Museum (CH84.4)

About the time of the nation's Centennial, a passion for china painting swept the country. For the next four decades, literally hundreds of thousands of women avidly took up their brushes.[1] The Ceramic Art Company enjoyed an active trade among those dedicated amateurs. In addition to supplying aspiring artists with vases and bowls in a plain creamy white state, the factory sold them a line of colored enamels. In 1889, the company's first advertisement recommended its porcelain body as "especially adapted to the wants of amateur decorators."[2] In the first of its catalogues, which appeared in 1891, the firm extolled the merits of its products, noting that the "constantly increasing number of cultured ladies who have taken up the study of ceramic decoration, has encouraged us to produce many of the novel forms presented in this volume."[3] The catalogue also pointed out the advantages of the firm's glaze: "It produces on the surface of our china a mellowness of texture that is unrivaled for the development of the fullest color effects in ceramic enamels. Another point of excellence is that in firing the enamels there is never any possibility of discoloration, a quality that will be fully appreciated by all amateurs."[4]

By joining with other retailers, manufacturers, and individuals in sponsoring occasional china-painting competitions, the company also promoted its wares to growing numbers of devoted dilettantes. During

the summer of 1896, for example, it contributed one of the prizes in a contest among "the members of the several leagues of mineral painters throughout the United States," held in Cincinnati, Ohio.[5] The prize—a selection of pieces of its white Belleek ware—was offered for "the best decorated piece of American Belleek."[6] Perhaps encouraged by the success of the Cincinnati venture, the company inaugurated a National China Painters' Bowl Competition, producing a number of wide, shallow bowls (an awkward choice, considering the purpose), which they invited potters and artists to paint and gild to their own design for judging. Again, the contest was probably a means of advertising the products of the Ceramic Art Company.[7] For three days in early November, the entries were displayed at the Waldorf-Astoria Hotel in New York to be viewed by contestants, potters, and the general public.[8] The event must have been of some importance in the ceramics world, for the noted potter Charles F. Binns was brought over from England to deliver a lecture, "The Potter's Art," at the hotel, surely as an adjunct to the exhibition.[9]

Figure 1. Competition bowl, 1897. Made by the Ceramic Art Company, Trenton, New Jersey. The Metropolitan Museum of Art, Friends of the American Wing Fund, 1987 (1987.26)

Figure 2. Competition bowl, 1897. Made by the Ceramic Art Company, Trenton, New Jersey. New Jersey State Museum, The Cybis Collection of American Porcelain (CH72.236)

The subject of this entry is one of the decorated competition bowls, all of which were marked with a special stamp designed specifically for the contest. The mark consists of an upper wreath incorporating the mark of the Ceramic Art Company and a lower wreath left empty (this one filled by the decorator's cipher), separated by the legend "National Porcelain Painting Competition 1897." The initials on this example have not been identified, but the graceful pattern of ovals and scrolls in a soft, pleasing palette demonstrates the amateur artist's skill in raised enamel painting, which is visible in the flowers, the gold and enamel jewels, and the gilding. Another bowl, in the collections of the Metropolitan Museum, is Renaissance in feeling, with its repeated motif of a stylized ram's head and ornate scrolls in a monochromatic blue green highlighted in gold (Fig. 1). Still another style is represented in an example at the New Jersey State Museum (Fig. 2), which typifies a naturalistic mode of china painting, as demonstrated in the orange and green nasturtium blossoms and leaves. Regrettably, the trade press neither recorded the results of the competition nor identified the winner.

1. For a complete account of the china-painting movement in America, see Brandimarte 1988.
2. *Crockery and Glass Journal* 30 (7 November 1889), p. 18.
3. *The Ceramic Art Co.* 1891.
4. Ibid.
5. "Prizes for Amateur China Painters," *Crockery and Glass Journal* 44 (30 July 1896), p. 28.
6. Ibid.
7. It has been suggested that the company devised the competition as a means of finding talented china painters to employ. See Robinson and Feeny 1980, p. 84. In view of the firm's thriving decorating department and the highly public nature of the competition, the theory seems most unlikely.
8. "Trenton Potteries," *Crockery and Glass Journal* 46 (4 November 1897), p. 33.
9. For a summary of the lecture, see *Crockery and Glass Journal* 46 (11 November 1897), pp. 20–21.

93
Vase, 1900–1905

Ceramic Art Company, Trenton, New Jersey
Decorated by William H. Morley
Porcelain; H. 18½ in. (47 cm.)
Signed on reserve, at upper right: W. H. MORLEY
Marks (on bottom, stamped in green):
conjoined CAC within wreath / LENOX
New Jersey State Museum, W. T. C. Johnson Foundation Fund (CH86.22)

WILLIAM H. MORLEY, who painted this vase and the largest number of signed Ceramic Art Company objects, was perhaps the best known of all of the artists who worked for Walter Scott Lenox. The vase represents the smaller of two sizes in which the company was producing the vessel by 1897 (see also cat. no. 94).[1] The pastel-colored roses that liberally adorn each of the four panels on its surface were a motif for which Morley was famous. His rose-decorated vases were featured in numerous advertisements published by the Ceramic Art Company, and roses served as his subjects on complete sets of service plates, each plate depicting a different species. On this vase, the predominant ground color is sea green, except in the reserves framed in scroll borders of raised gold, where the background is a soft blending of pale rainbow hues. The effect of immense grace and femininity conveyed, one characteristic of Morley's work, contributes an impression described in an article of 1911 as "happily colored light and shade."[2] The writer discussed Morley's work in terms whose period quaintness does not disguise their relevance to this object: "In a word, he has discovered the secret of soft grays and enhanced the value of all his other tones in their

use. Verily doth he make the roses so that one wonders if he has not in reality improved on old Mother Nature. And the garlands of roses . . . are done freehand and with as much care and attention to detail as is given the single large flower itself."[3]

1. *The Ceramic Art Co.* 1897.
2. Sophie Irene Loeb, "The Pottery that Points Nearest to Perfection," *Pottery, Glass and Brass Salesman* 3 (16 February 1911), p. 48.
3. Ibid.

94
Vase, 1903–4

Ceramic Art Company, Trenton, New Jersey
Decorated by Lucien Emile Boullemier
Porcelain; H. 18⅛ in. (46 cm.)
Signed at lower right of figure: Boullemier.
Marks (on bottom, stamped in green):
conjoined CAC within wreath / LENOX
Archives of Lenox China

This vase, of a conservative ovoid form and the smooth ivory body and shiny glaze perfected by Walter Scott Lenox, lends itself admirably to painted decoration. Its enlivening subject—a colorfully clad Turkish Gypsy—is presented within an architectural setting, with a suggestion of Mediterranean foliage in the background. The exoticism of the Near Eastern theme is maintained in the raised, jewellike dots of pink, red, turquoise, and white enamel that hang around the top half like an ornate necklace (ill.) and in the gold and enamel painting around the body.

The dating of the vase was determined by its stamped mark, consisting of the initials *CAC*—for the Ceramic Art Company—and the Lenox name, indicating that the piece was made sometime between 1896, when Lenox, having bought out his partner, Jonathan Coxon, became sole proprietor of the firm, and the beginning of 1906, when it was incorporated under his name. The artist who signed the vase was in Trenton for not more than two years, which allows for a more precise date. The signature in itself is a departure from standard practice in most American potteries, where decorators usually remained anonymous. Under Lenox's influence, the firm that he founded always focused on the artistic nature of its wares (in one instance, it was said to be more like an artist's studio than a factory), and Boullemier's signing his work was the privilege of the Ceramic Art Company's painters.

Lucien Emile Boullemier was the son of Antonin Boullemier, a French porcelain decorator who is known to have worked at Sèvres between 1859 and 1862.[1] In 1872, Antonin went to England and remained there for the rest of his life. He was employed at the Minton factory, where he specialized in figural subjects in the eighteenth-century-Sèvres style.[2] That was the environment in which Lucien Emile and his brother, Henri, who also became a porcelain decorator, grew up and, presumably, learned their craft. Lucien, working in his father's style, was employed at several English potteries during the latter part of the nineteenth century. Exactly when he came to America or was first associated with the Ceramic Art Company is difficult to establish. He was still in England in 1902, for in that year he is known to have been at the Worcester Royal Porcelain Works.[3] He must have visited America by 1903 or 1904, for it was he who painted the famous Trenton Vase (see cat.

94. Detail (reverse side)

no. 95) to be part of the Trenton Potteries Company's display at the Louisiana Purchase Exposition in Saint Louis in 1904. In the same year, his name appears in the Trenton city directory, where he is listed as an artist.[4]

In that period, during which Boullemier executed this vase, the firm probably had access to a number of accomplished regional artists, most of them European-trained, whom it could hire to finish its porcelain blanks. Boullemier's stay in this country must have been brief; in 1905, he is recorded as working at Shelton in Stoke-on-Trent.[5] He probably returned to England shortly after completing the Trenton Vase.

1. Faÿ-Hallé and Mundt 1983, p. 212.
2. Aslin and Atterbury 1976, pp. 10, 54, 57–58.
3. Sandon 1973, pp. 39, 85; pl. X.
4. I am grateful to Ellen Paul Denker for providing me with the directory information.
5. Twitchett and Bailey 1976, p. 218.

95
The Trenton Vase, 1904

Trenton Potteries Company, Trenton, New Jersey
Painted by Lucien Emile Boullemier; raised paste work by George Mardel;
shape by Peter Korzelius; design by John Wrigley;
porcelain paste by Henry Podmore
Porcelain; H. 54 in. (137.2 cm.)
Signed on reverse, at bottom of scene: after Pope / by L. Boullemier
Unmarked
New Jersey State Museum,
Gift of The Trenton Potteries Company (CH359a–d)

THE Trenton Potteries Company was formed in 1892 when five Trenton manufactories—the Crescent, the Delaware, the Empire, the Enterprise, and the Equitable—merged, though each continued to operate separately. This is one of an original set of four urns, or vases, actually made by the Empire factory but exhibited in the name of the Trenton Potteries Company at the Louisiana Purchase Exposition in Saint Louis in 1904.[1] The fair opened to the public on 30 April, but work on the urns had begun many months before. An account in a trade journal of the previous September, reporting that the Trenton Potteries Company had completed the manufacture of a vase five feet in height, continued: "It is estimated that the vase will represent an expenditure of something like $1000."[2] The embellishment had not yet begun: "A solid color will cover the surface, with panels on either side for the application of decorative subjects."[3]

In form and design, the set's four examples imitate the so-called Sèvres-style vases popular in both England and Europe in the late nineteenth century, a traditional form having a pedestal and a domed cover elaborately ornamented in gold, with painted decoration (generally landscapes or historical subjects; occasionally, floral bouquets) on front and back against a background of deep cobalt blue. Each of the four had a different theme and was referred to by a different name—the Rose Vase, the Woodland Vase, the Grecian Vase, and the Trenton Vase—but all belong to the standard design vocabulary of the day. The epic painting on the obverse of this example, Emanuel Leutze's *Washington Crossing the Delaware*, is as eminently suitable to an American chef d'oeuvre as scenes of the Napoleonic wars are to its French counterparts. Finished in 1851, the huge painting, depicting a pivotal event in America's War of Independence, has become an icon of American patriotism. (The point at which Washington crossed the river—near Trenton, the site of the maker's factory—undoubtedly influenced the choice of subject matter.)

Widely circulated in the second half of the nineteenth century in the form of lithographs, the work became one of the nation's best-known images. In 1897, the Leutze canvas was purchased for a large sum, donated to the Metropolitan Museum, and elevated to the unchallenged preeminence in the national lexicon it occupies to this day.

The view on the reverse of the vase—a winter scene of General Washington, possibly at Morristown or Trenton—is identified only by the inscription "after Pope." The original source is yet to be discovered, but may be traceable to the nineteenth-century American genre painter John Pope. Classical portraits of the general within oval medallions appropriately flanked by American flags carry the patriotic theme through to the square base.

The similarity of this decoration to that of the Sèvres type found on vases produced in England and on the Continent is understandable, since Lucien Emile Boullemier, trained in the style in England (see cat. no. 94), painted the scenes on all four vases of the set and directed the artisans who completed them.

1. The Trenton Potteries Company presented the Trenton Vase to the New Jersey State Museum in 1956. In 1969, its successor firm, the Crane Company, gave one of the other vases to The Brooklyn Museum (acc. no. 69.161) and one, also signed by Boullemier, to the Newark Museum (acc. no. 69.133). Both vases featured young maidens in flower-filled landscape settings. The location of the fourth is unknown.
2. "Among the Potteries: Trenton," *Crockery and Glass Journal* 58 (17 September 1903), p. 30.
3. Ibid.

96
Plate, 1904–5

Ceramic Art Company, Trenton, New Jersey
Decorated by Bruno Geyer
Porcelain; Diam. 10¼ in. (26 cm.)
Signed on front: B Geyer
Marks (on back): conjoined CAC within wreath / LENOX / TIFFANY & CO (stamped in gold); LENOX / OO (impressed)
Arthur V. Colletti

THE FASHION for decorating porcelain plates with portraits copied from oil paintings began in Europe in the early years of the nineteenth century and continued into the first decade of the twentieth, particularly at factories in Vienna and Berlin. Though the source of this exceedingly well executed depiction is as yet unidentified, the tradition can be seen in this example painted by Bruno Geyer, probably assisted by a specialist who did the gold work. The border of stylized flowers and leaves, recorded by the factory in 1904, is divided into eight panels by a continuous double branch whose sinuous curves are a characteristic of the prevailing Art-Nouveau style. The claret color, while relatively unusual (the favored hue was a deep cobalt blue), provides a felicitous complement to the warm palette.

Cabinet plates, made not for use but for display, were fashionable among European and American collectors during the late 1800s and well into this century. The subject of this entry was undoubtedly one of a set of at least twelve painted by Geyer. Its companions are currently unlocated; presumably, each featured the portrait of a different woman. Of similar sets of plates marked with the artist's signature, a set of twelve in the Archives of Lenox China is closely related to this example: its blue-bordered plates all feature raised gold-paste decoration identical to this. The original drawing for the border design, specified

as "Tiffany Special," included the notation that it was designated for the "Geyer Heads."[1] All the known portrait sets by Geyer are marked with the name of Tiffany and Company, indicating that they were made exclusively for the august New York City china and jewelry store.

Geyer may have executed the few sets of porcelain plates he signed as a free-lance artist. Apart from that, almost nothing is known about his career; his very presence in this country has not yet been documented.[2] He worked in the Austrian or German manner, but his place of birth is not recorded. There was an Austrian china painter named Josef Geyer who was active at the Imperial Porcelain Manufactory in Vienna in the early 1800s.[3] Bruno, possibly a relative of Josef's, may have been the Geyer who specialized in painting portraits on porcelain in Vienna in the third quarter of the nineteenth century.[4]

1. Design drawing B35, Archives of Lenox China, Lawrenceville, N. J.
2. Geyer's name does not appear in the city directories of New York or Trenton of that period.
3. Faÿ-Hallé and Mundt 1983, p. 60.
4. See Waltraud Neuwirth, *Wiener Porzellan: Original, Kopie, Verfälschung, Fälschung* (Vienna: Privately printed, 1979), p. 243.

97
Coffeepot, ca. 1906

Lenox, Incorporated, Trenton, New Jersey
Porcelain; H. 6⅝ in. (16.8 cm.)
Marks (on bottom, stamped in green):
conjoined CAC within wreath / LENOX
Mrs. Kenneth C. Heath

Its small size suggests that this charming object was originally part of a breakfast set. The matching pieces—a teapot, a sugar bowl, a cream pitcher, a teacup and saucer, and a coffee saucer—are shown in the original drawing (ill.).[1] The coffeepot, which belonged to the prolific Lenox artist William H. Morley and descended in his family, was probably a hand-painted prototype made before the set went into production. The gilding shown surrounding the lid opening and the spout and on the handle and the finial in the design drawing are not present on the actual object. The palette is limited to varying shades of pink and green. The lid is a replacement based on the one in the drawing.

The coffeepot is made of the white bone china added to the standard production of cream-colored porcelain about 1902, some four years before the company controlled solely by Walter Scott Lenox became incorporated under his name. The overglaze decoration in the Art-Nouveau style, characterized by the elongated, whiplash-curved stems, is a rare instance of the style's appearance in American ceramics. Frank G. Holmes succeeded Walter Scott Lenox as the firm's artistic director and served in that capacity for almost half a century. The subject of this entry, executed in the very early years of his tenure, is possibly the work of his hand.

1. The design, marked C32, and the shapes, 579–581, were recorded by the Lenox firm in 1906. A coffee cup was not included in the design drawing.

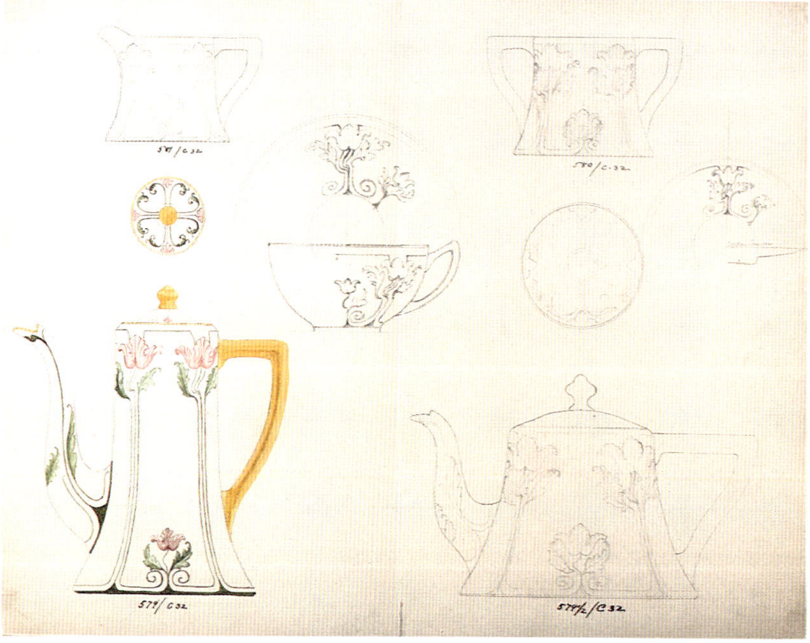

Possibly Frank G. Holmes. Design drawing for breakfast set, ca. 1906. Watercolor and pencil on paper, 14 × 18⅛ in. (35.6 × 46 cm.). Archives of Lenox China

98
Plate, 1906

Lenox, Incorporated, Trenton, New Jersey
Decorated by William H. Morley
Porcelain; Diam. 10⅜ in. (26.4 cm.)
Signed on front: W H. Morley.
Marks (on back): 15 (painted in purple); Cattleya / Mantinii / Trenton N. J. / Dec. 25th 1906 (painted in gold); L within wreath / LENOX (stamped in green); LENOX / OO (impressed)
Inscribed (on rim): CGR
Arthur V. Colletti

WILLIAM H. MORLEY made a specialty of decoration featuring flowers, birds, and fish for the Ceramic Art Company and for its successor firm, Lenox, Incorporated. He meticulously painted each cabinet plate in several large sets with a different species of orchid, carefully recording on the back its Latin name. This example, one of thirty-two plates made for Charles G. Roebling, is part of the famous first orchid set Lenox made. Its full documentation is recorded in its marks: it depicts one of the species *Cattleya mantinii*; the date shows that the service was undoubtedly a Christmas gift; within the acid-etched border is the patron's *CGR* monogram. Roebling, third son of John, designer of the Brooklyn Bridge, was passionately interested in botany and maintained extensive greenhouses at his Trenton residence. According to a Lenox company legend, Morley painted the subject of each of the plates after an actual specimen in Roebling's conservatory.

In 1906, the firm began a serious campaign to promote its richly embellished sets of cabinet plates, proclaiming in one illustrated advertisement, "We make a specialty of Individual Services, Monograms, and Family Crests [exhibiting] attractive designs in Acid Gold Borders."[1] The sets must have attracted considerable attention. In 1908, a journalist wrote: "American millionaires have now learned to appreciate this American porcelain and seek it for their tables. One of the finest things ever produced at the Lenox factory was the Roebling orchid set, which cost over three thousand dollars, and consisted of thirty-two plates decorated with orchid blossoms."[2]

1. *American Pottery Gazette* 3 (10 August 1906), p. 29.
2. "Fine American Table Porcelain," *Pottery and Glass* 1 (July 1908), p. 12.

99
Plaque, ca. 1906–10

Lenox, Incorporated, Trenton, New Jersey
Decorated by William H. Morley
Porcelain; H. 8⅛ in. (20.6 cm.), W. 11¼ in. (28.6 cm.)
Signed at lower right: W. H. Morley
Unmarked
Archives of Lenox China

FAMOUS for the plates he painted with designs of flowers or fish, William H. Morley was equally known for those depicting various kinds of birds and game, which the Lenox firm was advertising by 1906.[1] The plaque is a far rarer form. On this example, three ptarmigan (a species of grouse found in northern regions) in their pure white winter plumage are pictured in a snow-covered landscape. The same decoration also appears on sets of service plates, though varied in setting and plumage according to season. Scenes of winter are slightly less common. On the porcelain plaque, both the particularly rarefied composition and the muted palette subsume the body of the white bone china into the decoration, achieving an effect that approaches the delicacy of the renowned wares produced at Denmark's Royal Copenhagen factory.

1. For an illustration, see Lenox advertisement, *American Pottery Gazette* 3 (10 August 1906), p. 29.

100
Plate, ca. 1920

Lenox, Incorporated, Trenton, New Jersey
Designed by Frank G. Holmes; raised pastework by Robert Pfahl
Porcelain; Diam. 11⅜ in. (28.9 cm.)
Marks (on bottom, in gold):
1326/V.20.B. (painted); L within wreath/LENOX (stamped)
Archives of Lenox China

THE MOST EXTRAVAGANT use of raised gold-paste work ever executed at the Lenox factory may well be that of this plate. Frank G. Holmes, head decorator at Lenox from 1905 until 1952, probably created it specifically for display at the Fifth American Industrial Art Exhibition, held at the Metropolitan Museum from 15 December 1920 through 30 January 1921 and the first in which the Lenox company was invited to participate. (The plate is accompanied by his original design drawing [ill.].) The proprietors of the firm naturally wanted to produce an object precious enough to leave a lasting impression on the viewers, and they succeeded so brilliantly that Lenox was thereafter an annual participant. The Metropolitan had inaugurated the series of exhibitions in 1917 for the purpose of encouraging the country's manufacturers to use

F[rank] G. Holmes. Design drawing for plate, ca. 1920. Watercolor and pencil on paper, 9½ × 14 in. (24.1 × 35 cm.). Archives of Lenox China

museum holdings for design inspiration, not for mere mimicry but for the adaptation of old forms to new purposes.[1] Exactly what museum object Holmes chose as the basis of his concept for this plate has not been determined; possibly it was a piece of European metalwork.

Its genesis notwithstanding, the plate, divided into four quadrants by the elaborate raised gold-paste work on a deep cobalt-blue ground, is an example of the fine quality and rich adornment of the bespoke sets Lenox produced for its moneyed clientele in the last decade of the old century and the first decades of the new. In executing those commissions, the labor was divided among various specialists, for mixing the porcelain formula, for shaping the plate, for creating the design, for laying the ground color, and for applying and gilding the raised-paste embellishment.

To accomplish decoration that in this object almost overwhelms the viewer with its complexity and virtuosity of execution, a craftsman first ensured that the paste was of the required smooth texture, having the consistency of prepared mustard. He had previously traced the artist's design onto the body of the piece, for it was vital that the paste be applied steadily to maintain the smooth surface needed to receive the gold finish. The very high relief that appears on this plate was probably attained through a series of applications, each allowed to dry to exactly the proper stage, for paste that was too dry or too moist would result in cracking during its firing. The next step—covering the raised paste with a 24-karat gold solution—was exacting work. When it was done, the piece was fired again and the gold burnished to a lustrous finish.[2]

In 1920, the Lenox factory made a set of twelve plates of this design. It was likely the only set the factory ever produced, though duplicates were attainable at the price of twelve thousand dollars.[3]

1. For a thorough study of the history of the Metropolitan's design exhibitions, see Christine Wallace Laidlaw, "The Metropolitan Museum of Art and Modern Design: 1917–1929," *The Journal of Decorative and Propaganda Arts, 1875–1945* (Spring 1988), pp. 88–103.
2. The paragraph is a summary of a description of raised or encrusted gold paste taken from S. S. Frackelton, *Tried by Fire* (New York: D. Appleton and Company, 1895), pp. 53–57.
3. "Here Are a Few Examples of Modern China and Glassware Designed and Made in This Country," clipping from *Detroit News*, 12 October 1926, Archives of Lenox China, Lawrenceville, N.J.

101
Vase, ca. 1892

Ceramic Art Company, Trenton, New Jersey
Decorated by Kate B. Sears
Porcelain; H. 7½ in. (19.1 cm.)
Signed on side (incised): K. B. Sears
Unmarked
R. A. Ellison

The Belleek clay body developed in 1889 by the Ceramic Art Company was characteristically decorated over the glaze by polychrome enamel painting or by designs in raised gold-paste work. It was now treated to a new manner of embellishment under the hand of Kate Sears, who applied to the fragile medium a delicate method of carving. The small number of vases and bowls she turned out (see also cat. nos. 102, 103) date to the period of about 1891 to 1893. That information constitutes practically everything known of Sears or her career. Such work had never before been seen in American porcelain. Because her designs were exquisitely wrought on a plain white body, the objects she created were in striking contrast to those her contemporaries were adorning with elaborate painting. Sears's subjects are carefree, innocent scenes, possibly based on children's tales. While this particular vase is of a shape made for many years at the Ceramic Art Company, where the form was usually decorated in overglaze enamel and gold (see cat. no. 91), here it exemplifies the different character of Sears's treatment in its greater depth and intensified play of light and shadow. Carved in exceedingly fine detail is a group of rabbits frolicking in high grasses around a baby dressed in a rabbit costume. A companion piece in the Archives of Lenox China features baby girls in petal skirts, personifying dancing flowers.

One short notice in a trade journal dated 1 October 1891 gives a brief glimpse into Sears's work:

> The Ceramic Art Co. have just turned out a series of new pieces that may be put down as a radical departure from the usual methods of ornamenting pottery and porcelain. They have engaged a young woman of art, I can't say bachelor of arts, who is carving figures and flowers on the wet clay with a jack knife and she is producing some astonishingly beautiful effects in relief that rival Solon's pate-sur-pate in the treatment of light and shade. I think she must be a Yankee girl, and probably a descendant of the early whittlers. If she is, she has certainly improved on her inheritance, as her work is worthy of the highest consideration.[1]

The reference to whittling suggests that Sears was one of many women who took up the art of woodcarving during the 1880s, a pastime that sometimes led them on to ceramic ornamentation.[2]

1. "The Potteries," *Crockery and Glass Journal* 34 (1 October 1891), p. 31. The "Solon" referred to was Marc Louis Solon, a French decorator at Minton who perfected the pâte-sur-pâte technique.
2. For further information on a well-known group of women woodcarvers, see Kenneth R. Trapp, "'To Beautify the Useful': Benn Pitman and the Women's Woodcarving Movement in Cincinnati in the Late Nineteenth Century," Kenneth L. Ames, ed., *Victorian Furniture: Essays from a Victorian Society Autumn Symposium* (Philadelphia: Victorian Society in America, 1983), pp. 173–192; see also Frelinghuysen 1986, pp. 221–24.

102
Fern pot, ca. 1892

Ceramic Art Company, Trenton, New Jersey
Decorated by Kate B. Sears
Porcelain; H. 6¾ in. (17.2 cm.)
Signed near base (incised): K. B. Sears
Marks (on bottom, stamped in black):
conjoined CAC within wreath / LENOX
Archives of Lenox China

WHEN AN OBJECT of similar shape to this spherical bowl with its ruffled rim was illustrated in the Ceramic Art Company catalogue of 1897, it was called a "fern pot."[1] Probably intended for painted decoration, the form took on a totally new appearance under Kate Sears's inspired touch. A fern pot of her making, exhibited in 1893 at the World's Columbian Exposition in Chicago, was said to consist "of elaborate designs of lilies and child figures extending around a central zone."[2] Some years later, the author of an article on American ceramics lauded work that must have been Sears's, though he did not mention her name:

> Of purely artistic work, independent of color or gold, the carved belleek of the Ceramic Art Co. is a fine example. It would be hard to imagine anything more exquisitely beautiful than the completed articles of this kind of ware. Vases of pure outline in the soft, unglazed finish and the creamy white tint of the ware are adorned with figures in low relief. Flowers, vines and leaves, cupids, heads, figures with flowing drapery, and graceful scroll work stand out on panels of half transparent fineness. The shadowy leaves in the background are scarcely raised above the surface of the vase, yet so delicately traced and veined that they add much to the whole.[3]

1. *The Ceramic Art Co.* 1897.
2. Barber 1893, pp. 237–38.
3. "American Belleek Ware," *The Art Interchange* 36 (April 1896), p. 98.

103
Vase, ca. 1892

Ceramic Art Company, Trenton, New Jersey
Probably decorated by Kate B. Sears
Porcelain; H. 9¾ in. (24.8 cm.)
Unmarked
Archives of Lenox China

POSSIBLY one of a pair, each gilded on the interior of the leafy rim, this vase has Japanesque decoration of flying storks and swallows carved in low relief. Those motifs, popular during the Aesthetic movement of the 1870s and 1880s, are arranged in a manner found also on English relief-molded jugs, dating to the 1870s, of a pattern referred to as Yeddo, after the former name of Tokyo. The form is among the few in the Ceramic Art Company's repertoire utilized by Kate Sears. Several other of her versions of it are known, some of which are signed and dated either 1891 or 1892.[1]

Though the other vase of the presumed pair does not include oriental motifs, it too demonstrates that Sears was acquainted with Aesthetic design theory (ill.). She has formed the common cornstalk that is the prime element of her scheme into a geometric pattern repeated equidistantly five times around the vase. Not even the naturalistic rendering of the stalks and the touch of whimsy contributed by little mice appearing here and there disturb the symmetry of the design. The meticulous work exacted for the realization of each of the vases was recognized by a contemporary reporter: "The time put on a single one of these vases covers two months of steady work by the carver, and the result is something that the visitor turns away from reluctantly and comes back to again and again, each time finding some new attraction in the exquisitely modeled forms."[2]

Vase, ca. 1892. Ceramic Art Company, Trenton, New Jersey. Probably decorated by Kate Sears. H. 9¾ in. (24.8 cm.). Archives of Lenox China

1. A Sears vase of the same shape, inscribed CERAMIC ART CO. / K.B.SEARS / NOV 21, 1891, was formerly owned by Edwin AtLee Barber, whose daughter gave it to the Henry Ford Museum, Dearborn, Michigan (acc. no. 63.35); two others, each dated 1892, are in the Archives of Lenox China, Lawrenceville, N.J.
2. "American Belleek Ware," *The Art Interchange* 36 (April 1896), p. 98.

104
Vase, 1899

M. Louise McLaughlin, Cincinnati, Ohio
Porcelain; H. 6⅞ in. (17.5 cm.)
Signed on bottom (incised): MCL in monogram
Marks (incised, on bottom): 56/8 within box
Betty and Robert A. Hut

M. Louise McLaughlin was one of the first women to enter the field of American ceramics. In 1877, she gained recognition for her underglaze slip painting on earthenware in the manner found on Limoges pottery, a technique she described in her book *Pottery Decoration under the Glaze* (1880). Almost two decades later, in October 1898, she established her own small studio in Cincinnati, where she decorated forms she had thrown or molded herself from porcelain of her own making. In so doing—especially in entering the highly specialized field of porcelain—she was pioneering in a medium previously worked only in large factories. During the first year of her studio experiment, McLaughlin completed four full firings from her backyard kiln.[1]

This particular vase, which is among her earliest known porcelains, can be specifically dated to one of the two firings that she made from mid-November 1899 until the end of the year.[2] Consistent with her work of that period, the vase depicts flying geese incised in the white porcelain body and left uncolored, except for a few details in black and brown glazes. The remainder of the vase is covered with a mottled glaze of deep blue. (In the same year, McLaughlin was also using other oriental motifs, including dragons, storks, and various flowers that included peonies and poppies.) The sturdy, symmetrical Chinese shape—one of the earliest she developed—the blue-and-white palette, and the incised motifs show that she was still influenced by oriental ceramics, a tendency discernible in some of her underglaze slip-decorated earthenwares of the late 1870s and early 1880s. She would later give up this gentle incising for a more vigorous manner of carving, but she kept to the restrained palette as long as she continued to work in porcelain.

In 1898, at the beginning of her career in that medium, McLaughlin started to keep a journal of her production. M[ary] Louise McLaughlin's Losanti Record Book, called after a former name for Cincinnati, is an unpublished manuscript invaluable to any study of the artist's work in porcelain. In notes she made at the end of the year, she recorded that of the hundred and seventeen pieces she had done in 1899, only eight could be considered salable and only two were actually sold.[3] This vase, however, gives no evidence of the trouble she was then encountering in her work.

1. This information is contained in the unpaginated opening section of the Losanti Record Book, 1898–1903, Cincinnati Art Museum Library, Gift of Mr. and Mrs. James Todd.
2. Ibid. In the middle of 1899, McLaughlin began a new marking system for the work she was engaged on, incising each piece with consecutive numbers within a box under her monogram. That mark appears on this vase. When the series ended, in the beginning of 1900, she instituted another marking system that consisted of the same incised monogram, the Roman numerals MCM for the date 1900, and consecutive Arabic numerals for each piece.
3. Losanti Record Book, p. 70.

105
Vase, 1901

M. Louise McLaughlin, Cincinnati, Ohio
Porcelain; H. 5 in. (12.7 cm.)
Signed on bottom (incised): MCL in monogram
Marks (on bottom): Losanti. (painted in underglaze blue); II/281 (incised)
Alfred and Michiko Nobel

IN HER RECORD BOOK, McLaughlin described this vase as having a "carved scroll design."[1] The concept—a scroll design, carved in the unfired clay in high relief at the top and incised at the bottom so as to appear flat, finished with a translucent, colored glaze—has been borrowed from oriental celadon porcelains. In discussing her work in a letter to the editors of an influential periodical titled *Keramic Studio*, McLaughlin herself acknowledged that influence: "It probably does resemble the old Chinese soft paste more than anything else."[2] On this object, where the green glaze has been applied more thickly, its color deepens to emerald, accentuating the carved design and endowing it with a greater sense of depth. The laborious process that culminated in such an artistic triumph required several months' work.

In the records she kept between 1898 and 1903, McLaughlin referred often to this vase, which had originally been covered in what she called number 46, a thick white glaze she used often. She subsequently reglazed and refired the vase twice, introducing other elements into number 46, but she still found the finish unacceptable. In April 1901, several months after its inception, she glazed and fired the vase again, that time having found a successful combination of ingredients. Finally, she was able to record its "improved, beautiful glaze."[3] Her pleasure in her accomplishment can be measured by the several exhibitions to which she sent the vase. In May 1901, shortly after having completed it, she included it among the pieces of her work she showed at the Pan-American Exposition in Buffalo, New York, where she was awarded a bronze medal.[4] The objects she displayed were extremely well received by the public, and she sold more than half of them. That December, the vase went to the exhibition the Keramic Society of New York, held at the Waldorf-Astoria Hotel; at the end of the exhibition, McLaughlin consigned it to the New York firm of Taft and Belknap, which had offered to act as her agent and which forthwith sent a group of her porcelains to the International Exposition of 1902 in Turin, Italy. The vase's extensive exhibition record eventually included showings in Chicago and at the Louisiana Purchase Exposition of 1904 in Saint Louis. In an article on the exposition in which a group of her work was pictured (ill.), a reviewer called McLaughlin's work "creditable in the extreme."[5]

"Porcelains. M. Louise McLaughlin." Illustration, *Keramic Studio* 6 (March 1905), p. 251

1. The vase is no. 281 in McLaughlin's 1901 series. Losanti Record Book, 1898–1903, Cincinnati Art Museum Library, Gift of Mr. and Mrs. James Todd, p. 136.
2. "We just received an interesting letter from Miss M. Louise McLaughlin," *Keramic Studio* 3 (July 1901), p. 1.
3. Losanti Record Book, p. 136.
4. Ibid., unpaginated section.
5. "Louisiana Purchase Exposition Ceramics (continued)," *Keramic Studio* 6 (March 1905), p. 251.

106
Vase, 1902

M. Louise McLaughlin, Cincinnati, Ohio
Porcelain; H. 5 in. (12.7 cm.)
Signed on bottom (incised): MCL in monogram
Marks (on bottom): Losanti (painted in underglaze blue); III / 8 (incised)
Private collection

THIS DELICATE VASE, sent to the New York agents Taft and Belknap on 31 January, was among the first of the series that McLaughlin started in 1902.[1] That she had begun a new series is documented in the incised mark of the Roman numeral three; the Arabic number eight indicates that the piece was the eighth in the series. In her record book, McLaughlin noted the technical procedure she had followed: "Paeony design. Flowers at bottom made by spraying ground with Rouge S and slip, then incising the pattern and taking out ground. Stem running up to the top with leaves in Bailey green. Three coats of glaze 46."[2]

In 1901, *Keramic Studio* (a trade publication to which virtually every art potter subscribed) published an article on Copenhagen porcelains, which was illustrated with groups of vases from the Danish firm of Bing and Grøndahl.[3] McLaughlin, who had undoubtedly seen that issue of the magazine and may also have been acquainted with actual objects then being sold in the United States, seems to have been reacting to the influence of her Scandinavian contemporaries in her concept for this piece. The shape, with its bulbous base and cylindrical neck slightly flared at the rim, is all but identical to several Bing and Grøndahl examples; the low-relief carved decoration of floral motifs is typical of designs on Danish counterparts. Moreover, the muted palette of pale pink and green, slightly gray in tone and rendered even more delicate by the application of three coats of the thick, almost milky translucent glaze that McLaughlin favored, recalls some of the artistic work done in the late nineteenth century at the Royal Copenhagen Porcelain Manufactory.

1. Losanti Record Book, 1898–1903, Cincinnati Art Museum Library, Gift of Mr. and Mrs. James Todd, p. 183.
2. Ibid.
3. "Copenhagen Porcelains—Bing & Grondahl," *Keramic Studio* 3 (July 1901), pp. 60–61.

107
Vase, 1902

M. Louise McLaughlin, Cincinnati, Ohio
Porcelain; H. 5 in. (12.7 cm.)
Signed on bottom (incised): MCL in monogram
Marks (on bottom): LOSANTI (painted in underglaze blue);
II[I]/215 (incised)
Private collection

As do other vases made by M. Louise McLaughlin in the third year of the twentieth century (see cat. no. 106), this object utilizes some of the design ideas characteristic of the work of Bing and Grøndahl. The porcelain produced at the Danish factory was highly praised in an article in *Keramic Studio*, a widely circulated trade magazine: "Here the paste is everywhere incised, broken by open work decoration, thrown in powerful and striking shapes, and the color is only used to complete the decoration."[1] The article was illustrated with photographs of sculpted vessels that seemed to be made up of actual leaves and flowers. The same may be said of this vase. Save for the pale greenish tinge of the translucent glaze, which lends an overall creamy appearance to the form, it is devoid of color.[2] The entire design therefore consists of its carved and pierced work—the vase formed of flat, overlapping leaves; the neck, of open webbing filled in with glaze.

The essential technique, akin to that required for oriental rice-grain decoration (see cat. no. 84), was one that McLaughlin had experimented with two years earlier for a vase that she sent to the Exposition Universelle in Paris. From her description of it in her record book, where she listed it as number 11, it must have resembled the subject of this entry: "Carved design of leaves, perforated at top."[3] Nicola di Rienzi Monachesi, a period china decorator and author, particularly admired that feature of McLaughlin's work: "The designs are graceful, artistic, and professionally executed, especially those with perforations around the top of the vase, which represents clever manipulation of materials with the modeler's tools."[4]

McLaughlin herself deemed this vase "very good," and sent it to Taft and Belknap, her agents in New York City. She later recorded that it had been sold on 24 March 1904 to a Mrs. Louise Anderson for fifteen dollars.[5]

1. "Copenhagen Porcelains—Bing & Grondahl," *Keramic Studio* 3 (July 1901), p. 60.
2. McLaughlin described the vase as having a white glaze. For firing, she placed it in a seggar (the receptacle holding an object in the kiln) that had been coated on the inside with "Marsching's red oxide copper." Losanti Record Book, 1898–1903, Cincinnati Art Museum Library, Gift of Mr. and Mrs. James Todd, p. 248.
3. Ibid., p. 72.
4. Monachesi 1902, p. 11.
5. Losanti Record Book, p. 248.

108
Vase, 1902

M. Louise McLaughlin, Cincinnati, Ohio
Porcelain; H. 6 7/16 in. (16.4 cm.)
Signed on bottom (incised): MCL in monogram
Marks (on bottom): LOSANTI (painted in underglaze blue);
II[I]/232 (incised)
Private collection

In the record she kept of her porcelain production, M. Louise McLaughlin frequently mentioned scrolls as the design motif she was currently using. The scrolls on this vase are carved and interlaced so as to resemble stylized fern fronds and vine tendrils, and they emerge from the bottom of the vessel in a mannered fashion that adheres to the design tenets of the Art-Nouveau movement then prevalent in Europe. McLaughlin was certainly aware of developments in contemporary European decorative arts, which were published in American periodicals and were visible in examples exhibited and sold throughout the country. Nevertheless, she regarded the current vogues objectively: "But new ideas, when time shall have modified their eccentricities, will lift Art to a higher plane, and the element of novelty introduced into time-worn motifs of ornament is not to be despised. The movement known as 'L'Art Nouveau' will and must have influence, but it cannot be followed without reason or moderation, except to the detriment and degradation of the Beautiful."[1]

The decoration on this vase was executed with much care. Not readily apparent is that the interstices in the scrolls are carved so deeply that they almost pierce the walls of the vessel. Those areas, though subsequently filled in when the glaze was applied, are almost transparent when the object is viewed against the light. McLaughlin noted that because the glaze had not completely filled one of the spots, she had to mend and refire the vase.[2]

1. M. Louise McLaughlin, "Losanti Ware," *Craftsman* 3 (December 1902), p. 187.
2. Losanti Record Book, 1898–1903, Cincinnati Art Museum Library, Gift of Mr. and Mrs. James Todd, p. 252.

109
Vase, ca. 1905–6

Adelaide Alsop Robineau, Syracuse, New York
Porcelain; H. 4⅜ in. (11.2 cm.)
Marks (on bottom): RP in square (incised)/979 (in ink)
Betty and Robert A. Hut

ADELAIDE ALSOP ROBINEAU was the first artist-potter in America to produce porcelain objects that in both design and execution rivaled those from Sèvres and other French porcelain factories. Her early work consisted of designs she painted on imported porcelain blanks, but about 1903 she made the radical decision to delve directly into the difficult medium of porcelain. Experimenting with published formulas for producing the clay body and the glazes—especially the ones developed by the Sèvres artist Taxile Doat—Robineau perfected a porcelain made in part from American clays. She also developed crystalline and other glazes that had never before been seen to any extent in this country. Even in her first years of devising her own porcelain forms, her success exceeded her expectations. Doat, an acknowledged master of glazes, praised Robineau's "crystals," saying, "I do not know of any finer specimens."[1]

In an attempt to launch a commercial line of work in 1905, Robineau began to produce a number of little molded vases, which exhibit some of her first crystalline glazes. The simple forms gain added interest from the unusual pattern created by the glistening crystals floating on their surfaces, as demonstrated by this vase less than five inches in height. Strongly influenced by the ethics and teachings of such English reformers in arts and crafts as John Ruskin and William Morris, Robineau must have found that the mechanical aspects of her venture violated her principles. Because her integrity demanded that she hand throw her pieces, making each unique, she abandoned her attempts at a mass-produced line. Her misgivings were groundless: the quality of these early molded vases proves that her artistic standards were not compromised by her ambition.

Along with all Robineau's molded works, the subject of this entry is marked on the bottom with the initials *RP*, for Robineau Pottery. Its date can be determined from its early mark and also from its having been made from a mold. (She used her own conjoined initials on her thrown works.)[2] The vase is illustrated along with some of the artist's major pieces in one of the earliest articles published on her and her works.[3]

1. See *A Collection of Robineau Porcelains, Arms, Curios, and Medals . . . at the Syracuse Museum of Fine Arts*, exh. cat. (Syracuse, N.Y.: Syracuse Museum of Fine Arts, n.d. [1916?]), unpaged [p. 3].
2. For a detailed discussion of the marks on Robineau's porcelains, see Evans 1987, pp. 247–49.
3. Curran 1910, p. 366.

110
Lantern, 1908

Adelaide Alsop Robineau, Syracuse, New York
Porcelain; H. 8 in. (20.3 cm.)
Signed inside, near base (incised): AR in circular monogram
Marks (incised inside, near base): 1908/668
Everson Museum of Art, Museum Purchase (16.4.5)

THIS LANTERN and an eggshell-thin porcelain coupe (cat. no. 121) were the most famous of Adelaide Alsop Robineau's works in their own time, as they still are today. The lantern derives directly from hexagonal, reticulated Chinese forms dating to the K'ang Hsi (1661–1722) and Ch'ien Lung (1735–96) periods.[1] The same form also inspired production at late-nineteenth-century English potteries, including Minton, whose version of a Chinese lantern was illustrated in a contemporary publication Robineau may well have known.[2]

For the elements of her decorative scheme, Robineau drew on the previous decades' motifs and design theories, which had relied heavily on the vocabulary of the Aesthetic movement in America. In her carving, Robineau has exploited the natural floral motif to the greatest effect, working out her design in much the same manner she had observed in the earlier, china-painting stage of her career. The principal, relatively stylized device, possibly a combination of plum blossoms and leaves, appears in a different arrangement in each of six round medallions encircling the piece

and, pared down to an essentially geometric expression, is repeated on the narrow vertical and horizontal panels that punctuate the surface.

The primary importance of the lantern is its proclamation of technical bravura. It is a dazzling paradigm of the art of carving—incising, piercing, and excising (the background carved away, leaving the design in relief)—a practice that was to preoccupy Robineau for her entire career.[3] The design on the lower half has been excised, leaving a solid inner wall that once concealed a candle; the walls of the upper half are perforated to allow the light to shine through. The lantern was admired by all Robineau's peers. William Grueby, of the noted Boston art pottery, called it "the finest ceramic work ever made in this country."[4] To Taxile Doat, it was among the Robineau pieces he found worthy of "great collectors"; Henry W. Belknap, manager of the Grueby Pottery, echoed his sentiments, saying, "This perforated piece should be bought by the Metropolitan Museum and ought to bring at least $1000."[5] (Robineau did offer the lantern to the Metropolitan in 1909, but it was declined.)[6]

Considering it one of her most prized accomplishments, the artist consigned the piece to Tiffany and Company for a brief display. She continued to exhibit it: at the International Exposition of 1911 in Turin, Italy; in 1912, at the Paris Salon and at the Musée des Arts Décoratifs; at the Panama-Pacific Exposition in San Francisco in 1915, where it was valued at four hundred dollars in a catalogue of Robineau works that accompanied her display. It was among the thirty-two pieces of Robineau porcelains that entered the collections of the Syracuse Museum of Fine Arts (now the Everson Museum of Art), New York, in 1916.

Five years after Robineau had completed this lantern, she executed another, which she also exhibited at the Panama-Pacific Exposition.[7] The second example combined the basic Chinese form with decorative elements borrowed from Incan architectural sculpture. It descended in Robineau's family before being given to the Carnegie Museum of Art by Dana Robineau Kelley, the artist's grandson.[8]

1. See Eidelberg 1981, pl. 107, reproducing illustration in *Keramic Studio* 15 (August 1913), p. 78.
2. See Jewitt 1878, 2, p. 197.
3. Robineau's most extraordinary effort in that mode is her Scarab vase (Fig. 51, p. 63), made in 1910 and said to have taken over one thousand hours to carve. See Weiss 1981, pp. 24–26.
4. "A True Porcelain Art Pottery," *Glass and Pottery World* 17 (March 1909), p. 13.
5. Quoted in *A Collection of Robineau Porcelains, Arms, Curios, and Medals . . . at the Syracuse Museum of Fine Arts*, exh. cat. (Syracuse, N.Y.: Syracuse Museum of Fine Arts, n.d. [1916?]), unpaged [pp. 3–4].
6. See correspondence, Adelaide Robineau to Sir Caspar Purdon Clarke, director of the Metropolitan Museum, undated (probably March 1909), Archives, Metropolitan Museum of Art.
7. *High Fire Porcelains, Adelaide Alsop Robineau, Potter, Syracuse, New York*, exh. cat. (San Francisco: Panama-Pacific Exposition, 1915), no. 101.
8. Acc. no. 82.90.3. The lantern is missing its original cover. A photograph of the piece, which apparently cracked during the firing, appears in Robineau's journal inscribed "Spoiled in Refiring." Before sending the lantern to San Francisco, she salvaged it by reglazing. See Martin Eidelberg, "Some Robineau Porcelains," *Carnegie Magazine* 56 (September/October 1983), pp. 21-24.

111
Plaque, 1910

Taxile Doat, University City Pottery, University City, Missouri
Porcelain; Diam. 15 in. (38.1 cm.)
Signed on back: T DOAT
Marks (on back, in underglaze pink): A/UWC/L in cartouche; ~ THE FIRST OBJECT OF CERAMIC ART DRAWN FROM THE KILNS OF UNIVERSITY·CITY ~ 2 APRIL 1910 ~
University City Public Library, University City, Missouri

TAXILE DOAT, celebrated French ceramist working at Sèvres from 1877, came to America in 1909 at the invitation of Edward Gardner Lewis, who two years earlier had founded the American Woman's League at University City, Saint Louis, Missouri, an institution devoted to women's education and advancement.[1] One part of Lewis's grand scheme was to build a pottery where some of the best contemporary artisans would gather both to execute their own work and to hold classes in the skill. The presence of nearby kaolin clay beds was cause for including the manufacture of porcelain in the curriculum. In 1910, when the University City Pottery officially opened, the director appointed was Doat, master of the medium. Adelaide Alsop Robineau and Frederick Hurten Rhead, two noted American potters, soon joined the faculty. Doat's name had been introduced in America in 1903, when Samuel E. Robineau, Adelaide's husband, translated his practical treatise on the making of porcelain and ran it in installments in *Keramic Studio*, the widely read trade magazine the Robineaus published.[2]

When on 2 April 1910 the first kiln was drawn at the University City Pottery, this impressive plaque was among the objects fired. Designed by director Doat as an appropriate celebration of the occasion, it was documented not only by his signature but also by a legend commemorating the event (ill.). Stylistically, the plaque closely resembles the work that Doat had specialized in at Sèvres a decade earlier. The form, one he favored, typically featured an applied pâte-sur-pâte central medallion, often depicting a classical head. On this example, the device is a stylized lion and the rim is adorned with a series of raised bosses, each covered with a large crystalline sunburst. A formal photograph taken for publicity purposes shows the kilnful, dominated by the plaque, arranged on a table surrounded by the pottery's artists and technicians.[3]

111. Detail (legend on back)

1. For more information on the University City schools and pottery, see Evans 1987, pp. 286–91, and Frederick Hurten Rhead, "The University City Venture," ed. by Paul Evans, Weiss 1981, pp. 93–115.
2. In 1905, the treatise appeared in book form. See Doat 1905. A condensed version appeared in *Art et Décoration* 20 (July–December 1906), pp. 87–104, 153–63; ibid. 21 (January–June 1907), pp. 69–80.
3. See Weiss 1981, pl. 110.

112
Vase, 1910

Emile Diffloth, University City Pottery, University City, Missouri
Porcelain; H. 6$\frac{15}{16}$ in. (17.6 cm.)
Signed on bottom: ED in monogram
Marks (on bottom): 134 (painted in black); THE AMERICAN WOMAN'S LEAGUE. within circle enclosing U-C/1910 (stamped in green)
Private collection

WHEN EDWARD G. LEWIS approached Taxile Doat to take charge of the ceramics division of the American Woman's League, Doat stipulated that he be allowed to bring with him to University City two artisans, Eugène Labarrière, an expert thrower and foreman of a pottery near Paris, and Emile Diffloth, at the time superintendent at Kéramis, the Boch Frères pottery at La Louvière, Belgium.[1] Of Diffloth's few objects that survive from his brief stay in University City, most are vases having slender necks with narrow openings and bulbous, slightly angular bodies similar in shape to this one. They display a variety of glazes, some crystalline, others iridescent. Diffloth, a specialist in ceramic chemistry, had a particular affinity for glazes, a phase of his work that Doat had singled out in his comments on the Belgian display at the Exposition Universelle of 1900 in Paris (a vital forum for contemporary ceramists).[2]

Diffloth, as a participant at that event, had had ample opportunity to view the work of porcelain establishments from all over the world. One of them—Denmark's Royal Copenhagen Porcelain Manufactory—may have exercised an important influence on his own oeuvre. The Danish pottery had already earned an international reputation from its displays at the Exposition Universelle of 1889 and was noted for its proficiency in producing colored crystalline glazes.

In 1900, the work exhibited by the Copenhagen factory made a strong showing again. Insects such as bumblebees, dragonflies, or grasshoppers, usually having a highly glazed blue body and white wings, appeared as applied decoration on the handles or covers of vessels. Diffloth must have admired their imaginative use, for the applied three-dimensional bees on this vase are borrowed directly from them. His University City colleagues Doat and Robineau also succumbed to the Danish influence: in the preface to his treatise on the making of porcelain, which discussed the ceramic movement in Europe, Doat illustrated a glazed horsefly (remarkably similar to Diffloth's bees) from the Copenhagen porcelain works;[3] Robineau employed dragonflies and bees as part of the design on several of her porcelains.

Diffloth did not stay long in America. He was in residence at University City when the first kiln was drawn in April 1910, but his name was not mentioned in a pamphlet published that autumn to describe University City wares. William Bragdon was listed as chemist. Whether because the pottery was in financial straits or because Diffloth had lived up to his reputation for being unable to get along with the rest of the faculty, he was discharged, as was Labarrière. Diffloth's dismissal spawned a bitter dispute that raged first between him and Doat and then between Doat and Lewis and ended with Diffloth's bringing suit against Doat for unpaid salary and breach of contract.[4] The case was settled out of court. Diffloth then returned to France, where he continued to work and to exhibit. In 1929, he was awarded a gold medal by the Société des Artistes Français.[5]

1. Rhead 1910, p. 192.
2. Doat 1905, p. 25.
3. Ibid., p. 19.
4. According to Doat's handwritten précis of the proposed lawsuit, in the collections of the University City Public Library, Diffloth laid claim to six hundred and sixty-six-odd dollars in unpaid salary and five thousand dollars for breach of contract, on the ground that he had given up his work in Europe to follow Doat to America.
5. Brunhammer 1976, p. 474.

113
Vase, 1910

Adelaide Alsop Robineau, University City Pottery,
University City, Missouri
Porcelain; H. 6¾ in. (17.2 cm.)
Signed on bottom (excised): AR in circular monogram
Marks (incised, on bottom): 22 / U C / 1910
Bryce and Elaine Bannatyne, in association with P. G. Pugsley and Son, San Francisco

IN 1910, WHEN Edward G. Lewis established his pottery at University City, Missouri, he brought together four of the best ceramists of the time: Adelaide Alsop Robineau, who had begun studio work in porcelain about 1903 at her home in Syracuse, New York; Frederick Hurten Rhead, a talented art potter who had come from England in 1902 to work at various American factories and who was knowledgeable about American clays; Kathryn E. Cherry, an American whose specialty was china decoration; and the celebrated Sèvres ceramist Taxile Doat from France. The assembling of such talent was a unique experiment that undoubtedly resulted in a highly constructive exchange of ideas, though each artist continued to work independently. During the twelve months of Adelaide Robineau's stay in University City, she produced some remarkably varied results, especially in her continuing exploration of the uses of glazes. This vase is particularly unusual in Robineau's oeuvre, not only for its demonstration of varicolored, opaque glazes in a period better known for crystalline or matte earth-tone finishes but also for the starkness of the simple ovoid shape, both presaging the ceramic art of the future. The vase was a gift from Robineau to her University City colleague Kathryn Cherry in 1911. It descended in Cherry's family to her grandson before entering the collection of the present owners.[1]

1. See catalogue, *Collector's Spectrum*, Dave Rago auction, New York City, 17 May 1986, lot 115.

114
Vase, 1910

Adelaide Alsop Robineau, Syracuse, New York
Porcelain; H. 6¼ in. (15.9 cm.)
Signed on bottom (excised): AR in circular monogram
Marks (incised, on bottom): o / u / c / 1910
Everson Museum of Art, Museum Purchase (16.4.3)

THE INLAID-SLIP technique displayed on this Robineau vase requires a decorative design to be carved into the surface of a vessel and then filled with colored clay in its liquid state. After the surface is smoothed and a clear glaze applied, what emerges is a ceramic version of cloisonné. In an article published in *Keramic Studio* in 1908, art potter Frederick Hurten Rhead recommended the technique highly: "There are few kinds of pottery work which display the individuality of the potter to the same extent as this inlaid process."[1] It seems likely that Rhead influenced Robineau to experiment with the technique while the two potters were working together at University City.[2] Although Robineau rarely used it, this exemplary piece attests that she had obviously mastered it.

While the inlaid-slip process was an anomaly in Robineau's work, the design she chose to use was not. The pair of stylized poppy blossoms and foliage on both sides of the vase hark back to her china-painting days of the late nineteenth and early twentieth centuries. The flower in all its decorative potential was the subject of an illustrated article she wrote in 1901 for *Keramic Studio*.[3] In it, she drew heavily on examples of the flower's use in the work of the contemporaneous French painter and specialist in the graphic arts M. Pillard Verneuil.[4] Although some of the poppy-motif schemes she illustrated displayed the characteristically sinuous Art-Nouveau curves, in this object of her own making she has executed the flower in a flat, geometric design more in keeping with the tenets of the Arts and Crafts movement, which had then reached American shores.

Robineau exhibited the poppy vase in Turin in 1911, in Paris in 1912, and in San Francisco in 1915. In 1916, the vase was acquired by the Syracuse Museum of Fine Arts, now the Everson Museum of Art, New York.

1. Frederick H. Rhead, "Pottery Class," *Keramic Studio* 11 (November 1909), p. 160.
2. For further discussion on the technical elements of this vase, see Zakin 1981, pp. 134–35.
3. Mrs. Adelaide Alsop-Robineau, "Poppies," *Keramic Studio* 3 (October 1901), pp. 122–26.
4. For further discussion of Robineau's interest in French art, see Eidelberg 1981, pp. 52–60.

115
Two gourd vases, 1912–14

University City Porcelain Works, University City, Missouri
Designed by Taxile Doat
Porcelain; H. 7³⁄₁₆ in. (18.3 cm.) (1);
9⅛ in. (23.2 cm.) (2)
Unmarked
Betty and Robert A. Hut (1)
Private collection (2)

Around the beginning of the twentieth century, several potters working in France began to produce ceramics objects inspired by vegetal forms. Among the hundred and seventy-two examples of his work Taxile Doat brought with him to University City in 1910 were divers vases in the shape of fruits and vegetables he had made during his tenure at Sèvres. In a handwritten evaluation of the objects, which he hoped the American Woman's League would wish to acquire for the edification of its working potters and students, Doat described his collection of "artistic and technical ceramics: hard porcelain and grès flammés" (many of which he had shown at the international exhibitions) as "unique." He continued, "In a great number of them I have developed my own ceramic theories regarding the utilization of natural forms such as fruits and vegetables as compared with architectural or conventional forms."[1] Doat's forms were of particular interest to Frederick Hurten Rhead, one of the artists joining Doat in University City in 1910. As Rhead said in an article he wrote on Doat's work in that same year, "His principal decorations are in fruit-like forms."[2]

Doat's vegetal vases, including these gourd-shaped examples, date mostly to the period beginning in 1912, when what had begun as the University City Pottery was reorganized into the University City Porcelain Works. The pieces are not hand-thrown but molded, and though they were produced in a limited number of shapes, each had a totally different appearance that came from the dazzling and varied crystalline glazes that covered them. The range of colors on any one vase could fluctuate widely: in these two gourd forms, they change from white and cream to subtle shadings of browns, greens, and blues. In an undated promotional pamphlet the pottery issued (probably shortly before the Panama-Pacific Exposition of 1915 in San Francisco), it claimed that its crystalline pieces could not be duplicated, "each piece offered being an exclusive gem of the high temperature at which it is produced."[3] The pamphlet also contained a description that could apply equally well to these vases: "Delicate, iridescent effects, in which the glaze has burst under the process into thousands of crystals large and small."[4]

1. Taxile Doat, "Collection of the Artistic and Technical Ceramics: Hard Porcelains and Grès Flammés," undated holographic manuscript [ca. 1910–11], Archives, Saint Louis Art Museum, Missouri. The collection was purchased in its entirety by the museum in 1911, when it was named the City Art Museum of Saint Louis. As occurred in many similar organizations earlier in the century, much of the collection was deaccessioned and dispersed.
2. Rhead 1910, p. 191.
3. *Hard Porcelains and Grès Flammés Made at University City, Mo.*, undated, unpaginated promotional pamphlet, Library, Saint Louis Art Museum, Missouri.
4. Ibid.

116
Vase, 1913

University City Porcelain Works, University City, Missouri
Decorated by Mabel G. Lewis
Porcelain; H. 6 7/16 in. (16.4 cm.)
Signed and dated near base (incised): MGL in monogram / 1913
Marks (on bottom, painted in green): U.C / 1913
Inscribed (in cartouche, on reverse, near top, in pâte-sur-pâte): St. LOUIS / MO.
Martin Eidelberg

In addition to his expertise in crystalline glazes, Taxile Doat was highly accomplished in pâte-sur-pâte decoration. He lavished his skill on several objects of monumental scale, some of which have been preserved at the University City Public Library. Mabel G. Lewis, a student of Doat's and the wife of Edward G. Lewis, founder of the American Woman's League, which sponsored the University City Pottery, was an active member in the league as well as its vice president. When the pottery was reorganized in 1912 as the University City Porcelain Works, she became its president, Doat retaining his post as director. An eager learner, Lewis perfected the pâte-sur-pâte technique for which Doat was so widely renowned. This vase, with its air of lyric delicacy, unmistakably reveals the influence of the master potter. Its ovoid shape, having antecedents in ancient forms, is one Doat favored for pâte-sur-pâte decoration while he was working in France.[1] In composition and decoration, the Lewis vase is a simplified version of Doat's Sèvres vases of the previous decade, including the banding, the pâte-sur-pâte medallions and garlands, and the arrangement of horizontal panels created with slips of different colors. Doat held that subject matter in pâte-sur-pâte work should be based on some poetic theme or historical event, and Lewis was a faithful disciple.[2] On her vase, the appropriate subject is the patron saint of the pottery's host city. On one side is a regal profile of the canonized King Louis IX of France realized in white pâte-sur-pâte within a medallion on a blue ground; on the reverse, within a similar medallion, are the words "St. Louis, Mo."

Just when Mabel Lewis began to be proficient in the pâte-sur-pâte technique is unknown, but about 1914 she was said to be "producing works that give promise that she will take high rank in the art."[3] Another example of this branch of her work is a white-and-green vase, dated 1914, depicting the nation's Capitol in pâte-sur-pâte.[4]

1. See Irene Sargent, "Taxile Doat," *Keramic Studio* 8 (December 1906), pp. 172–73.
2. Doat's ideas on subject matter are contained in "Collection of the Artistic and Technical Ceramics: Hard Porcelains and Grès Flammés," undated holographic manuscript [ca. 1910–11], Archives, Saint Louis Art Museum.
3. *Hard Porcelains and Grès Flammés Made at University City, Mo.*, undated, unpaginated promotional pamphlet, Library, Saint Louis Art Museum, Missouri.
4. Collection of the University City Public Library.

117
Peruvian Serpent Bowl, 1917

Adelaide Alsop Robineau, Syracuse, New York
Porcelain; H. 2 9/16 in. (6.5 cm.), Diam. 6 7/8 in. (17.5 cm.)
Signed and dated on bottom: AR in circular monogram (excised) / 1917 (incised)
Unmarked
The Metropolitan Museum of Art, Purchase, Edward C. Moore, Jr. Gift, 1923 (23.145)

IN 1923, on a document connected with the Metropolitan Museum's acquisition of this piece, Adelaide Alsop Robineau entered "Peruvian Serpent Bowl" in the space provided for the title.[1] On the object, the heaviness of the strong, sober form is alleviated by the fine carving on the exterior surface. The inspiration for the ornament is in pre-Columbian art. Conforming to the rectangular shape of each of the vessel's six feet is an incised crouching Mayan grotesque surmounted by a serpentlike creature (ill.); the figures and creatures, though similar, all differ slightly. A snakelike motif, stylized for greater effect, is utilized throughout the piece: tightly coiled, it appears in the bowl's interior at the center of three consecutively broader concentric circles, each composed of diamond-shaped scales made of varicolored glazes. The same scaly pattern, carved in such fine detail that it must have been executed with tiny, needlelike instruments, forms the border on the exterior surface. The sort of highly compressed linear activity palpable in the incised rings that encircle the bowl appear on two Robineau vases—the Indian, made in 1913, and the Cloudland, made in 1914.[2]

The monochromatic bronzelike glaze that covers both the Indian vase and the exterior surface and the interior snakelike device of this bowl was one Robineau developed sometime between 1911 and 1913.[3] The opaque color is eminently suited to the sculptural concept of the work, while the glaze itself is so thin that it allows the fine details of the carving to be perceived clearly.

Robineau showed the bowl in Boston and Detroit at exhibits sponsored by the Society of Arts and Crafts in each of those cities, and in 1923 sent it to a traveling exhibition of American handicrafts organized by the Washington-based American Federation of Arts. The several venues at which it appeared included the Metropolitan Museum, whose collections it then entered.

117. Detail (foot)

1. Museum copyright form completed by the artist, 7 January 1923, Archives, Metropolitan Museum of Art.
2. The vases were both exhibited in San Francisco in 1915 at the Panama-Pacific Exposition and were purchased by the Detroit art collector George G. Booth. The Indian vase is in the collections of the Detroit Institute of Art, Michigan (acc. no. 19.101); the Cloudland is at the Cranbrook Academy of Art, Bloomfield Hills, Michigan (acc. no. 1944.131); both were gifts by Booth. For a discussion of the two vases, see Garth Clark, "Beauty in Balance: Two Vases by Adelaide Alsop Robineau," *Antiques World* 2 (February 1980), pp. 88–89.
3. In a letter, Samuel Robineau said that the bronze glaze had not been developed at the time of the artist's tenure at the University City Pottery. Robineau letter, 27 December 1916, quoted in Frederick Hurten Rhead, "Chats on Pottery," clipping from *The Potters Herald*, 1934–35, Robineau Archive, Everson Museum of Art, Syracuse, N.Y. Since Robineau left University City in 1911 and completed the Indian vase in 1913, she must have perfected the glaze during that two-year period. According to Richard Zakin, the finish was not so much a glaze as a waxy, semivitreous black stain with roots in Chinese stoneware, where it was used to simulate bronze. See Zakin 1981, p. 138.

118
Vase, 1919

Adelaide Alsop Robineau, Syracuse, New York
Porcelain; H. 2 in. (5.1 cm.)
Signed and dated on bottom: AR in circular monogram (excised) / 1919 (incised)
Marks (on bottom, painted in black): 3.
Private collection

THE JEWELLIKE QUALITY of this vase obtains from its diminutive size and from a rich blue glaze whose alluring dark gray crystals sparkle as if alive. In February 1927, Adelaide Alsop Robineau sold the object to Fenton Ross of Columbus, Ohio, describing it on the bill of sale as a "Miniature round vase . . . covered with a fine crystalline glaze, in which the crystals have arranged themselves like a 'Swarm of Gnats' in concentric circular movement from any point of view— Unique"; its price was thirty-five dollars.[1] Ross had approached Robineau regarding a possible purchase after having seen the George G. Booth collection of her vases then on loan to the Detroit Institute of Arts.[2] A letter Robineau wrote to Ross prior to his purchase reveals that though she had made the vase almost ten years earlier, it remained one of her favorite examples of its kind. She told him that she produced small-sized vessels from time to time "to fill in my exhibit & give variety in size and shape—& bits of color," adding, "They sell so quickly on account of their convenient size for cabinet display."[3] She sent Ross several different vases on approval and subsequently expressed her happiness at this choice of his: "It is one of the most unusual pieces I have made, a great favorite of mine and the only one of its kind I have had—or seen."[4] For an additional five dollars, Ross could have had a "carved black porcelain stand" on which to place the vase.[5] He decided against it.

1. The bill of sale is in the collection of the present owner of the vase.
2. Letter, Robineau to Ross, 3 February 1927, collection of the present owner.
3. Ibid.
4. Ibid., 23 February 1927.
5. Ibid., 3 February 1927.

119
Covered jar, 1919

Adelaide Alsop Robineau, Syracuse, New York
Porcelain; H. 7½ in. (19.1 cm.)
Signed and dated on bottom: AR in circular monogram (excised) / 1919 (incised)
Unmarked
Everson Museum of Art, Gift of Dr. Ethel T. Eltinge (82.33.1)

THE APPEARANCE of a root vegetable or a gourd that results from the spherical form and stemmed cover of this jar is intensified by the green-colored glaze. Unquestionably, Adelaide Alsop Robineau was familiar with the gourd forms created by Taxile Doat at Sèvres in France and at the University City Pottery in America. Though Doat's vases tended to be more irregular in outline and their texture more knobby,

they probably inspired her own attempts with the shape, including this less naturalistic example of perfect geometric form and tight, smooth surface. The piece is further distinguished by the excised scalelike decoration of the cover, which is finished in the thinly applied bronze-colored glaze that Robineau favored for much of her carved work.

The jar was originally owned by the longtime Syracuse resident Professor Arthur Van W. Eltinge, music teacher and amateur photographer. Probably to express her gratitude for photographs he took of her elder daughter, Priscilla, the artist presented him with several pieces of her work, this porcelain jar among them.[1]

1. History provided by Dr. Eltinge, Professor Eltinge's daughter, 23 September 1982, when she gave the piece to the Everson Museum of Art, Syracuse, New York. Accession files, Everson Museum of Art.

120
The Urn of Dreams, 1921

Adelaide Alsop Robineau, Syracuse, New York
Porcelain; H. 10⅜ in. (26.4 cm.)
Signed on bottom (excised): AR in circular monogram
Marks (incised, on bottom): I / THE URN OF DREAMS / 1921
The Carnegie Museum of Art, Pittsburgh; Gift of Dana Robineau Kelley and Family, 1982 (82.90.1)

BECAUSE OF Adelaide Alsop Robineau's great admiration for pre-Columbian art, its influence is found in several of her later works, including this vase named by the artist. On the urn, echoes of the Peruvian Serpent Bowl (see cat. no. 117) are found in three medallion-like designs enclosing carved figures, though here the figures resemble in shape and position the burden-carriers of Mayan culture.[1] Each of the urn's three feet is in the form of a carved Mayan-style demon mask supporting a grotesque caryatid, all three grotesques a similar, flatter version of the burden-carrier. Carved in the spandrels are leering genies whose outstretched arms encircle the vase. The Aladdin-like concept of those wish-fulfillers may have inspired the artist's choice of title; again, "urn of dreams" may reflect the mystical side of a woman who in that period was developing an interest in theosophy.[2]

According to family history, Robineau dearly cherished the vase, which she made for her younger daughter, Elizabeth. Elizabeth lent it to the Metropolitan Museum in 1929 for her mother's memorial exhibition. The vase was described in the exhibition catalogue as "carved in relief with grotesque figures of Peruvian inspiration. Grotesque masques as feet."[3] Elizabeth bequeathed the piece to her nephew, Robineau's grandson Dana Robineau Kelley, who presented it to the Carnegie Museum of Art, Pittsburgh, Pennsylvania.

1. I am grateful to Julie Jones, curator of primitive art at the Metropolitan Museum, for this comparison.
2. See Martin Eidelberg, "Some Robineau Porcelains," *Carnegie Magazine* 56 (September / October 1983), pp. 21–24.
3. *A Memorial Exhibition of Porcelain and Stoneware by Adelaide Alsop Robineau, 1865–1929*, exh. cat. (New York: The Metropolitan Museum of Art, 1929), no. 49.

121
Coupe, 1924

Adelaide Alsop Robineau, Syracuse, New York
Porcelain; H. 2⅝ in. (6.7 cm.), Diam. 5¾ in. (14.6 cm.)
Signed and dated on bottom: AR in circular monogram (excised) / 1924 (incised)
Unmarked
The Metropolitan Museum of Art, Purchase, Edward C. Moore, Jr. Gift, 1926 (26.37)

THE EGGSHELL-THIN PORCELAINS that Adelaide Alsop Robineau executed during her career are among the most virtuosic of all her work. Porcelain—in itself the most brittle of all the ceramic mediums—can be carved only in its dry state, a procedure requiring the utmost patience and skill. The challenge of throwing on a potter's wheel a form of the paperlike thinness of this coupe, and then of carving out the surface to leave in relief a design of some complexity, was considered almost impossible by most of Robineau's contemporaries. The artist herself is documented to have succeeded in making only three perfect examples.[1] The technical feat was extraordinary, for the risks at every stage of the process were almost insurmountable. The bowl had to be an absolutely true circle after it was turned on the potter's wheel; if it was not and, subsequently, if it was too hastily dried, it would surely warp. The coupe had to be flawless, since any irregularity would be visible after firing, when the body would become transparent.

Robineau had begun her experiments with ultrathin porcelain much earlier in her career, although most of her attempts were concentrated in the last decade of her life. In 1907, however, a tiny unglazed coupe similar in shape to the subject of this entry was included in a photograph of a group of Robineau porcelains that appeared in an issue of *Keramic Studio*. The description read: "[A] little covered tea cup, Japanese style, is of egg shell porcelain, of which delicate material only a few pieces have yet been attempted, this work still being in the experimental stage. It is carved with a little border of plum blossoms, the background being cut back so thin that even before firing the light shines through the clay."[2] That particular object probably did not survive the firing stage. It may have been the prototype for a coverless coupe, also having a border of carved plum blossoms, now at the Cranbrook Academy.[3] In 1910, a coupe was illustrated, "the first rough cutting of a dainty design in a delicate egg-shell bowl."[4] Its pierced foot and rim closely resemble the pierced pattern of this bowl, but it too was likely destroyed.

Although the shape of this masterpiece of 1924 is clearly Japanese in inspiration and its palette of subtle shades of yellow and blue has a delicacy oriental in origin, the stylized floral stamens between the perforations of the rim and the foot relate closely to Egyptian motifs. The coupe was apparently made at the request of Joseph Breck, curator of decorative arts at the Metropolitan Museum from 1917 until 1933, who was largely responsible for building the museum's collection of contemporary applied arts. The first mention of the commission is documented to 16 December 1922, when Breck wrote Robineau:

> As I couldn't sleep last night I spent the time making a few sketches which I send you herewith, of a little bowl which I can see, so to speak, in my mind's eye, as being made of paper-thin white porcelain with a narrow border carved in low relief on the inside, and possibly pierced here and there so that the light would shine through the glaze. I should think the diameter might be about 8 inches.[5]

In replying, Robineau must have expressed anxiety over that size, for in his second letter to her, dated 2 January 1923, Breck said, "When I suggested an eggshell porcelain bowl 8 inches in diameter I was not thinking of a stunt. I'm afraid it was just carelessness on my part."[6] Later that month, Breck's dream was realized when Robineau reported to him that the

bowl was finished. In a previously unpublished letter, she wrote:

> I am bringing to New York the completed egg shell coupe and would like to deliver it to you. . . . I shall be relieved to have it safely delivered. . . . I feel that the coupe is rather beautiful—and a tour de force—I feel that it represents the utmost skill that I possess. It is the largest successful egg shell that I have made—and to my mind the most artistic. The one in Mr. Booth's collection at the Detroit Museum is about four inches in diameter and one and a fourth inches high—neither the beauty of the design nor the difficulty of piercing could compare with this one. To obtain it I have spent over two years (my working time between teaching & bread winning) and partly finished and broken five coupes ranging from five to ten inches in diameter (unfired). You understand that this is thrown and turned on the wheel, not cast, as are most egg shells. The slight variations of the thickness show this—and the design in the center is carved out of the thickness—not built up in the easier pâte sur pâte. You can easily see the delicacy of handling necessary in executing—and the achievement of which I am (I hope pardonably) proud.[7]

After some lengthy discussions as to price, Robineau accepted the museum's figure. In so doing, however, she requested that if she were to surpass her achievement, the museum would accept that version instead and would make her a supplemental payment.[8] Indeed, she may well have created a better piece for the museum: in 1927, she took to Detroit to the annual meeting of the American Ceramic Society what she considered to be her largest and finest eggshell bowl, which measured about ten inches in diameter and weighed only three and a half ounces.[9] The last piece of eggshell-thin porcelain Robineau ever attempted, it was decorated with a "beautiful excised design of swans."[10] The bowl, breathtaking in its beauty, was marveled at by all those who saw it. Having miraculously survived all the treacherous stages of its fabrication, however, it was dropped in Detroit and shattered to pieces. Elizabeth Robineau, who accompanied her mother to the meeting but had not witnessed the accident, described her mother's account: "She told me—how she had shown the coupe . . . how she had repacked it with the greatest care in its little box, tied it with a string—how she had picked it up by the string. The string slipped, the box fell, and there was nothing of the coupe but fragments. Never before or after had I ever seen my mother cry, but she cried then, heartbreakingly."[11]

When the subject of this entry was exhibited at the memorial exhibition of seventy-one pieces of Robineau's work held at the Metropolitan in 1929, Breck wrote of it: "As imponderous as an apple blossom, with its lacy openwork and delicate relief carving—[it] is a masterpiece of which any ceramist of any age or any country might well be proud."[12]

1. Robineau destroyed all her eggshell-thin porcelains that she considered imperfect. The three that survived are the Museum's coupe, a coupe at the Cranbrook Academy of Art, Bloomfield Hills, Michigan (acc. no. 1944.154), and a coupe that was later accidentally dropped and shattered.
2. "Porcelains," *Keramic Studio* 9 (December 1907), pp. 178, 180.
3. For an illustration of the Cranbrook piece, see Eidelberg 1981, pl. 23.
4. Curran 1910, p. 366.
5. Quoted in Ethel Brand Wise, "Adelaide Alsop Robineau—American Ceramist," *American Magazine of Art* 20 (December 1929), p. 689.
6. Ibid.
7. Undated letter (late January 1923), Robineau to Breck, Archives, Metropolitan Museum of Art.
8. In a subsequent letter to Breck, Robineau noted that the coupe was slightly imperfect because of an unexpected reduction in the temperature of the kiln, which had caused tiny black specks to appear in the clay body. Those, she said, would be noticed only by an expert. Undated letter, Robineau to Breck, Archives, Metropolitan Museum of Art.
9. Carlton Atherton, "Adelaide Alsop Robineau," typescript memoir, ca. 1935, p. 18, Robineau Archive, Everson Museum of Art, Syracuse, N.Y.
10. Samuel Robineau, "Adelaide Alsop-Robineau," *Design* 30 (April 1929), p. 205.
11. Quoted in Peg Weiss, "Adelaide Alsop Robineau: Syracuse's Unique Glory," Weiss 1981, n. 29, p. 207.
12. Joseph Breck, preface, *A Memorial Exhibition of Porcelain and Stoneware by Adelaide Alsop Robineau, 1865–1929*, exh. cat. (New York: The Metropolitan Museum of Art, 1929), unpaged [pp. 1–2].

Bibliography

"American Belleek Ware." In *Art Interchange* 36 (April 1896), p. 98.

"The American Institute Fair." In *Crockery and Glass Journal* 4 (28 September 1876), p. 14.

"American Parian." In *Crockery and Glass Journal* 5 (22 March 1877), p. 15.

"American Porcelain." *New York Times*, 27 October 1872, p. 3.

The American Woman's League and the Peoples University. University City, Saint Louis: The Lewis Publishing Company, 1910.

The American Woman's Republic. University City, Saint Louis: American Woman's League, n.d.

"Another Honorary Member Has Passed Away: Mary Louise McLaughlin." In *Bulletin of the American Ceramic Society* 18 (February 1939), pp. 66–67.

The Art Academy of the Peoples University. University City, Saint Louis: The Peoples University Press, 1910.

Aslin, Elizabeth and Paul Atterbury. *Minton 1798–1910*. Exhibition catalogue. London: Victoria and Albert Museum, 1976.

Atherton, Carlton. "Adelaide Alsop Robineau—Master Potter." In *Ceramic Age* 19 (May 1932), pp. 232–34.

Atterbury, Paul, ed. *The History of Porcelain*. New York: William Morrow and Company, 1982.

Axel, Jan, and Karen McCready. *Porcelain: Traditions and New Visions*. New York: Watson-Guptill, 1981.

Bach, Richard F. "Papers and Discussions: Art in Industry." In *Bulletin of the American Ceramic Society* 3 (August 1924), pp. 277–88.

Barber, Edwin AtLee. *The Pottery and Porcelain of the United States*. 1893. Reprint (rev. ed., 1909). New York: Feingold and Lewis, 1976.

———. "Historical Designs on Tucker Porcelain." In *Art Interchange* 34 (April 1895), p. 106.

———. *Historical Sketch of the Greenpoint (N.Y.) Porcelain Works of Charles Cartlidge & Co.* Indianapolis, 1895.

———. "The Pioneer of China Painting in America." In *The Ceramic Monthly* 2 (September 1895), pp. 5–20.

———. "The Oldest American China." In *The Clay-Worker* 24 (November 1895), pp. 439–40.

———. *Marks of American Potters*. Philadelphia: Patterson and White, 1904.

Barnard, Harry. *Chats on Wedgwood Ware*. London: T. Fisher Unwin, 1924.

Barret, Richard Carter. *Bennington Pottery and Porcelain: A Guide to Identification*. New York: Crown Publishers, 1958.

———. *A Color Guide to Bennington Pottery*. Manchester, Vt.: Forward's Color Productions, 1966.

Belden, Louise Conway. *The Festive Tradition: Table Decoration and Desserts in America*. New York and London: W. W. Norton & Company, 1983.

"The Belleek Pottery." In *The Art-Journal* (London) 8 (1 May 1869), pp. 149–52.

Benjamin, Marcus. "American Art Pottery." In *Glass and Pottery World* 15 (February 1907), pp. 28–31.

Binns, Charles F. *The Story of the Potter*. London: George Newnes, 1898.

———. "The Use of American Wares by American Ceramic Decorators." In *Keramic Studio* 1 (August 1899), pp. 81–82.

———. "The Art of the Fire." In *Craftsman* 8 (May 1905), pp. 205–10.

———. "The Possibilities of Porcelain." In *The Clay-Worker* 45 (January 1906), pp. 90–92.

Bishop, J. Leander. *A History of American Manufactures from 1608 to 1860*. 3 vols. Philadelphia: Edward Young and Co., 1868.

Bishop, Robert, and Patricia Coblentz. *The World of Antiques, Art, and Architecture in Victorian America*. New York: E. P. Dutton, 1979.

Blake, William P. *Ceramic Art: A Report on Pottery, Porcelain, Tiles, Terracotta and Brick*. Catalogue, International Exhibition, Vienna, 1873. New York: D. Van Nostrand, 1875.

———. "Ceramics." In *Reports of the United States Commissioners to the Paris Universal Exposition, 1878*. 3 vols. Washington, D.C., 1880, 3, pp. 113–226.

Bogart, Michele Helene. "Attitudes Toward Sculpture Reproductions in America 1850–1880." Ph.D. diss., University of Chicago, 1979.

Brandimarte, Cynthia. "Darling Dabblers: American China Painters and Their Work, 1870–1920." In *American Ceramic Circle Journal* 6 (1988), pp. 6–27.

Brewer, Harriet E. "American Belleek." In *New Jersey Historical Society Proceedings* 52 (April 1934), pp. 96–108.

Brown, Joshua, and David Ment. *Factories, Foundries, and Refineries: A History of Five Brooklyn Industries*. Brooklyn: The Brooklyn Educational & Cultural Alliance, 1980.

Brown, Michael K. "Piecing Together the Past: Recent Research on the American China Manufactory." In *Proceedings of the American Philosophical Society*. Forthcoming (1989).

Brunhammer, Yvonne, et al. *Art Nouveau: Belgium/France*. Exhibition catalogue. Houston: Institute for the Arts, Rice University, 1976.

Cameron, Elisabeth. *Encyclopedia of Pottery & Porcelain, 1800–1960*. New York and Oxford: Facts on File Publications, 1986.

Carr, James. "Reminiscences of an Old Potter." In *Crockery and Glass Journal* 53 (21 March 1901), pp. 27–28; (28 March 1901), pp. 24–25; (4 April 1901), pp. 17–18; (11 April 1901), pp. 15–16; (18 April 1901), pp. 23–24; (25 April 1901), pp. 15–16.

The Ceramic Art Co.: Potters and Decorators of Belleek China, Indian China, and Artists' Specialties. Trade catalogue. New York: E. O. Wagner, 1891. Jerseyana Collection, New Jersey State Library.

The Ceramic Art Co.: Makers and Decorators of Exclusive Productions in Artistic China and Porcelains. Trade catalogue. Trenton: Ceramic Art Company, 1897. Archives of Lenox China.

"Ceramics at Philadelphia." In *American Architect and Building News* 1 (29 July 1876), pp. 244–45; (5 August 1876), pp. 252–53; (12 August 1876), pp. 260–61; (19 August 1876), pp. 267–69; (26 August 1876), pp. 274–75; (23 September 1876), pp. 308–10; (30 September 1876), pp. 316–17; (7 October 1876), pp. 324–25; (21 October 1876), pp. 342–43.

"Charles H. L. Smith." In *American Pottery Gazette* 8 (September 1908), pp. 23–24.

Claney, Jane Perkins. "Edwin AtLee Barber and the Robineaus: Correspondence 1901–1916." In *Tiller* 1 (November–December 1982), pp. 31–54.

Clark, Garth. *A Century of Ceramics in the United States, 1878–1978: A Study of Its Development*. New York: E. P. Dutton, in association with the Everson Museum of Art, 1979.

———. "Beauty in Balance: Two Vases by Adelaide Alsop Robineau." In *Antiques World* 2 (February 1980), pp. 88–89.

Clement, Arthur W. *Preliminary Notes for a Catalogue of Made-in-America Pottery and Porcelain assembled for exhibition at the Brooklyn Museum*. New York: The Court Press, 1942.

———. *Notes on American Ceramics, 1607–1943*. Brooklyn: The Brooklyn Museum, 1944.

———. *Notes on Early American Porcelain, 1738–1838*. New York: The Court Press, 1946.

———. *The Pottery and Porcelain of New Jersey, 1688–1900*. Newark: Newark Museum, 1947a.

———. *Our Pioneer Potters*. New York: Privately printed, 1947b.

Collard, Elizabeth. *Nineteenth-Century Pottery and Porcelain in Canada*. 2nd ed. Kingston and Montreal: McGill-Queen's University Press, 1984.

"Copenhagen Porcelains—Bing & Grondahl." In *Keramic Studio* 3 (July 1901), pp. 60–61.

Cox, Lucille T. "Isaac Watts Knowles." In *Bulletin of the American Ceramic Society* 21 (15 August 1942), pp. 151–57.

Cox, Warren E. *The Book of Pottery and Porcelain*. 2 vols. New York: Crown Publishers, 1944.

Crannell, Carlyn Gaye. "In Pursuit of Culture: A History of Art Activity in Atlanta, 1847–1926." Ph.D. diss., Emory University, 1981.

Curran, Grace Wickham. "An American Potter, Her Home and Studio." In *American Homes and Gardens* 7 (September 1910), pp. 364–66.

Curtis, Phillip H. "The Production of Tucker Porcelain, 1826–1838: A Reevaluation." In *Ceramics in America*, Winterthur Conference Report, 1972. Edited by Ian M. G. Quimby. Charlottesville: The University Press of Virginia, published for The Henry Francis du Pont Winterthur Museum, pp. 339–74.

———. "Tucker Porcelain 1826–1838: A Re-appraisal." Master's thesis, University of Delaware, 1972.

d'Albis, Jean, and Céleste Romanet. *La porcelaine de Limoges*. Paris: Editions Sous le Vent, 1980.

Degenhardt, Richard K. *Belleek: The Complete Collector's Guide and Illustrated Reference*. Huntington, N.Y.: Portfolio Press, 1978.

De Guillebon, Régine de Plinval. *La Porcelaine à Paris sous le Consulat et l'Empire*. Paris: Arts et Métiers Graphiques, 1985.

de Jonge, Eric. "Tucker China: America's Porcelain." In *Early American Life* 5 (December 1974), pp. 50–53, 83.

Denker, Ellen Paul. Typescript history of Lenox China, 1987. Archives of Lenox China, Lawrenceville, N.J.

Denker, Ellen Paul, and Bert Randall Denker. "Mary Louise McLaughlin." In Wendy Kaplan. *"The Art That Is Life": The Arts and Crafts Movement in America, 1875–1920.* Boston: Museum of Fine Arts, 1987, pp. 249–50

Diviš, Jan. *L'Art de la Porcelaine en Europe.* Paris: Gründ, 1984.

Doat, Taxile. Correspondence and papers, University City Library, Saint Louis.

———. *Grand Feu Ceramics: A Practical Treatise on the Making of Fine Porcelain and Grès.* Translated, from the French, by Samuel E. Robineau. Syracuse: Keramic Studio Publishing Company, 1905.

Dow, George Francis. *The Arts and Crafts in New England, 1704–1775: Gleanings from Boston Newspapers.* Topsfield, Mass.: The Wayside Press, 1927.

Doyle, Maude M. "Lotus Ware." In *American Antiques Journal* 2 (November 1947), pp. 4–5.

Dunn, Kimberly A. "The Losanti Ware of Mary Louise McLaughlin." Master's thesis, Indiana University of Pennsylvania, 1983.

Earle, Alice Morse. *China Collecting in America.* New York: Charles Scribner's Sons, 1892.

Early Arts of New Jersey: The Potter's Art, c. 1680–c. 1900. Exhibition catalogue. Introduction by Boris Erich Nelson. Trenton: New Jersey State Museum, 1956.

Eidelberg, Martin. "Art Pottery." In *The Arts and Crafts Movement in America 1876–1916.* Edited by Robert Judson Clark. Exhibition catalogue. Princeton and Chicago: The Art Museum, Princeton University, and The Art Institute of Chicago, 1972, pp. 117–86.

———. "Robineau's Early Designs." In Peg Weiss, ed. *Adelaide Alsop Robineau: Glory in Porcelain.* Syracuse: Syracuse University Press in association with Everson Museum of Art, 1981, pp. 43–92.

———. "Some Robineau Porcelains." In *Carnegie Magazine* 56 (September/October 1983), pp. 21–24.

Elliott, Charles Wyllys. *Pottery and Porcelain, from Early Times down to the Philadelphia Exhibition of 1876.* New York: D. Appleton and Company, 1878.

Ellis, Anita. "Late Victorian Revivals." In *The Antique Collector* 56 (November 1985), pp. 84–89.

"English 'Bone-China' Made in America." In *American Pottery Gazette* 1 (March 1905), p. 21.

Evans, Paul F. "American Art Porcelain—Two: The Work of The University City Pottery." In *Spinning Wheel* 27 (December 1971), pp. 24–26.

———. *Art Pottery of the United States: An Encyclopedia of Producers and Their Marks.* 2nd ed. New York: Feingold & Lewis Publishing Corp., 1987.

Everson Museum of Art. *American Heroes Portrayed in Ceramics: From the 17th Through the 20th Century.* Syracuse: Everson Museum of Art of Syracuse and Onondaga County, 1976.

Faÿ-Hallé, Antoinette, and Barbara Mundt. *Porcelain of the Nineteenth Century.* New York: Rizzoli, 1983.

"Fine American Table Porcelain." In *Pottery and Glass* 1 (July 1908), pp. 11–12.

"Fine Porcelain. The New Orleans Factory: The Pioneer of the Industry in America." *The Sunday States,* 26 June 1887.

Frackelton, S[usan] S. *Tried by Fire.* 3rd ed. New York: D. Appleton and Company, 1895.

Frelinghuysen, Alice Cooney. "Aesthetic Forms in Ceramics and Glass." In *In Pursuit of Beauty: Americans and the Aesthetic Movement.* New York: The Metropolitan Museum of Art, 1986, pp. 199–251.

Garrett, Brice. "Ohio's Lotus Ware." In *Spinning Wheel* 22 (January–February 1966), pp. 16–17.

Gaston, Mary Frank. *American Belleek.* Paducah, Ky.: Collector Books, 1984a.

———. *Haviland Collectables & Objects of Art.* Paducah, Ky.: Collector Books, 1984b.

Gates, William C., Jr. *The City of Hills and Kilns: Life and Work in East Liverpool, Ohio.* East Liverpool: The East Liverpool Historical Society, 1984.

Gates, William C., Jr., and Dana E. Ormerod. "The East Liverpool Pottery District: Identification of Manufacturers and Marks." In *Historical Archaeology* 16 (1982).

Geijsbeek, S. "The Ceramics of the Louisiana Purchase Exposition." In *American Ceramic Society Transactions* 7 (1905), pp. 289–355.

Gillingham, Harrold E. "Pottery, China, and Glass Making in Philadelphia." In *The Pennsylvania Magazine of History and Biography* 54 (April 1930), pp. 96–129.

"Glass and Ceramics at the Chicago Exhibition." In *Art Journal* (London). Supplement 1893, pp. 29–32.

Godden, Geoffrey A. *Victorian Porcelain.* London: Herbert Jenkins, 1961.

———. *British Porcelain: An Illustrated Guide.* New York: Clarkson N. Potter, 1974.

———. *Staffordshire Porcelain*. London and New York: Granada Publishing, 1983.

Goldberg, David J. "Preliminary Notes on the Pioneer Potters and Potteries of Trenton, N.J.: The First Thirty Years—1852–1882 (And Beyond)." Typescript, 1983.

Golden Periods of New Jersey Ceramics. Exhibition catalogue. East Brunswick, N.J.: East Brunswick Museum Corporation and East Brunswick Arts Commission, 1985.

Gottesman, Rita Susswein, comp. *The Arts and Crafts in New York, 1726–1776: Advertisements and News Items from New York City Newspapers*. New York: New-York Historical Society, 1938.

Greeley, Horace. *Art and Industry as Represented in the Exhibition at the Crystal Palace, New York, 1853–54*. New York: Redfield, 1853.

"The Growth of Pottery: Work of the Greenwood Company." *Trenton Times*, 10 November 1883, p. 7.

Hard Porcelains and Grès Flammés Made at University City, Mo. University City, Missouri, n.d.

Henrywood, R. K. *Relief-Moulded Jugs, 1820–1900*. Woodbridge, Suffolk: Antique Collectors' Club, 1984.

Herman, Lloyd E. *American Porcelain: New Expressions in an Ancient Art*. Forest Grove, Ore.: Timber Press, 1981.

Hillier, Bevis. *Pottery and Porcelain 1700–1914: England, Europe, and North America*. New York: Meredith Press, 1968.

Holland, Eugenia Calvert. *Edwin Bennett and the Products of His Baltimore Pottery*. Exhibition catalogue. Baltimore: The Maryland Historical Society, 1973.

Holmes, George Sanford. *Lenox China: The Story of Walter Scott Lenox*. Trenton: Privately printed, 1924.

———. "Walter Scott Lenox." In *Bulletin of the American Ceramic Society* 16 (April 1937), pp. 177–80.

Hood, Graham. "The Career of Andrew Duché." In *The Art Quarterly* 31 (Summer 1968), pp. 168–84.

———. *Bonnin and Morris of Philadelphia: The First American Porcelain Factory, 1770–1772*. Chapel Hill: The University of North Carolina Press, 1972.

Hughes, G. Bernard. *Victorian Pottery and Porcelain*. London: Country Life Limited, 1959.

Hughes, Kathy. *A Collector's Guide to Nineteenth-Century Jugs*. London, Boston and Henley: Routledge & Kegan Paul, 1985.

Hull, William, "Some Notes on Early Robineau Porcelains." In *Semi-Annual Bulletin, The Everson Museum of Art of Syracuse and Onondaga County*. Syracuse: Everson Museum of Art, 1960.

Illustrated Catalogue of China, Pottery, Porcelains and Glass [Collected by] the Late Edwin Atlee Barber. Estate sales catalogue. Philadelphia: Samuel T. Freeman & Co., 1917.

Industrial Trenton and Vicinity. Wilmington, Del.: George A. Wolf, Publisher, for the Trenton Board of Trade, 1900.

James, Arthur E. *The Potters and Potteries of Chester County, Pennsylvania*. West Chester: D. Edwards Biehn, under the auspices of the Chester County Historical Society, 1945.

"James Tams, Dean Among Potters." In *Bulletin of the American Ceramic Society* 17 (January 1938), pp. 35–36.

J[ayne], H[orace] H. F. "A Note on Thomas Tucker." In *Philadelphia Museum of Art Bulletin* 52 (Spring 1957), pp. 55–58.

———. *Tucker China: 1825–1838*. Philadelphia: The Philadelphia Museum of Art, 1957.

Jervis, W[illiam] P[ercival]. "Taxile Doat." In *Keramic Studio* 4 (July 1902), pp. 54–55.

———. *A Pottery Primer*. New York: O'Gorman Publishing Co., 1911.

———, comp. *The Encyclopedia of Ceramics*. New York, 1902.

Jewitt, Llewellynn. *The Ceramic Art of Great Britain*. 2 vols. New York: Scribner, Welford, and Armstrong, 1878.

Johnson, Rossiter, ed. *A History of the World's Columbian Exposition Held in Chicago in 1893*. 4 vols. New York: D. Appleton and Company, 1897–98, 3.

Kaplan, Wendy. *"The Art That Is Life": The Arts and Crafts Movement in America, 1875–1920*. Exhibition catalogue. Boston: Museum of Fine Arts, 1987.

Ketchum, William C., Jr. *Potters and Potteries of New York State, 1650–1900*. 2nd ed. Syracuse: Syracuse University Press, 1987.

Klapthor, Margaret Brown. *Official White House China: 1789 to the Present*. Washington, D.C.: Smithsonian Institution Press, 1975.

Kohlenberger, Lois H. "Ceramics at The People's University." In *Ceramics Monthly* 24 (November 1976), pp. 33–37.

LaGrange, Marie J., comp. *Pottery and Porcelain: An Annotated Bibliography*. Indianapolis: Indiana State Library, 1938.

Lenox Belleek. Trade catalogue. Trenton: Lenox, Incorporated, 1909.

Levin, Elaine. "Charles Binns, Adelaide Robineau." In *Ceramics Monthly* 23 (November 1975), pp. 22–27.

———. "The Ceramics of Adelaide Alsop Robineau." In *Arts & Antiques* 5 (January/February 1982), pp. 88–95.

"Louisiana Purchase Exposition Ceramics." In *Keramic Studio* 6 (March 1905), pp. 251–52.

Lycett, Lydia. "China Painting by the Lycetts." In *Atlanta Historical Bulletin* 6 (July 1941), pp. 201–14.

McCabe, James D. *The Illustrated History of the Centennial Exhibition Held in Commemoration of the One Hundredth Anniversary of American Independence.* Philadelphia, Chicago, and Saint Louis: The National Publishing Co., 1876.

McCrum, S. *The Belleek Pottery.* Belfast: Ulster Museum, n.d.

McKearin, Helen, and Kenneth M. Wilson. *American Bottles & Flasks and Their Ancestry.* New York: Crown Publishers, 1978.

McLaughlin, M. Louise. "The History of Porcelain Making. The Losanti Ware." Typescript, Cincinnati Historical Society, n.d.

———. Losanti Record Book, 1889–1903. Cincinnati Art Museum Library.

———. "Losanti Ware." In *Keramic Studio* 3 (December 1901), pp. 178–79.

———. "Losanti Ware." In *Craftsman* 3 (December 1902), pp. 186–87.

———. "Miss McLaughlin Tells Her Own Story." In *Bulletin of the American Ceramic Society* 17 (May 1938), pp. 217–25.

Maddock, Archibald M. *The Polished Earth.* Trenton: Privately printed, 1962.

The Metropolitan Museum of Art. *Handbook for the Use of Visitors Examining Pottery and Porcelain in the Metropolitan Museum of Art.* New York: The Metropolitan Museum of Art, 1875.

———. *A Memorial Exhibition of Porcelain and Stoneware by Adelaide Alsop Robineau, 1865–1929.* Exhibition catalogue. New York: The Metropolitan Museum of Art, 1929.

———. *19th-Century America: Furniture and Other Decorative Arts.* Exhibition catalogue. New York: The Metropolitan Museum of Art, 1970.

Mitchell, James. "The American Porcelain Tradition." In *Connoisseur* 179 (February 1972), pp. 123–31.

———. *The American Porcelain Tradition, 18th, 19th, and 20th Centuries: A Loan Exhibition from the New Jersey State Museum.* Exhibition catalogue. Shreveport, La.: The R. W. Norton Art Gallery, 1972.

———. "Ott and Brewer: Etruria in America." In *Winterthur Portfolio* 7 (1972), pp. 217–28.

Monachesi, Mrs. [Nicola di Rienzi]. "Miss M. Louise McLaughlin and Her New Losanti Ware." In *Art Interchange* 48 (January 1902), p. 11.

Morris, Alfred. "The Robineau Porcelains." In *Sketch Book* 5 (January 1906), pp. 228–33.

Moses, John. "American Potteries." In *1795–1895: One Hundred Years of American Commerce.* Edited by Chauncey Mitchell Depew. New York: D. O. Haynes & Co., 1895, pp. 285–94.

Myers, Susan H. *Handcraft to Industry, Philadelphia Ceramics in the First Half of the Nineteenth Century.* In Smithsonian Studies in History and Technology 43. Washington, D.C.: Smithsonian Institution Press, 1980.

Neuwirth, Waltraud. *Wiener Porzellan: Original, Kopie, Verfälschung, Fälschung.* Vienna: Privately printed, 1979.

Norton, C. B., ed. *Treasures of Art, Industry and Manufacture Represented in the American Centennial Exhibition at Philadelphia 1876.* Buffalo: Cosack & Co., 1877.

Official Catalogue of the New-York Exhibition of the Industry of All Nations. 1853. New York: George P. Putnam and Co., 1853.

Patterson, Jerry E. *Porcelain.* The Smithsonian Illustrated Library of Antiques, ed. by Brenda Gilchrist. New York: Cooper-Hewitt Museum, Smithsonian Institution's National Museum of Design, 1979.

Pollok, Robert. "Biographical Data re Charles Cartlidge." Undated manuscript. Photocopy, Department of Decorative Arts files, The Brooklyn Museum.

"Porcelain." In *Crockery Journal* 1 (9 January 1875), p. 1.

"Porcelains." In *Keramic Studio* 9 (December 1907), pp. 178–80.

Porcelains from the Robineau Pottery. New York: Tiffany & Co., n.d. [1906].

Post, Robert C., ed. *1876: A Centennial Exhibition.* Washington, D.C.: The National Museum of History and Technology, Smithsonian Institution, 1976.

Pottery. Trenton: Thomas Maddock's Sons Company, 1910.

The Pottery and Porcelain of New Jersey, 1688–1900. Exhibition catalogue. Newark: Newark Museum, 1947.

The Pottery and Porcelain of New Jersey prior to 1876. Exhibition catalogue. Newark: The Newark Museum Association, 1915.

"Pottery at the American Institute Fair." In *The Art Amateur* 1 (November 1879), pp. 126–27.

Prime, Alfred Coxe. *Pottery and Porcelain of All Times and Nations.* New York: Harper and Brothers, 1878.

———, comp. *The Arts & Crafts in Philadelphia, Maryland, and South Carolina, 1721–1785.* Topsfield, Mass.: The Walpole Society, 1929.

Ramsay, John. *American Potters and Pottery.* Clinton, Mass.: Hale, Cushman & Flint, 1939.

"Rarities in Tucker Porcelain in the Collection of Philip H. Hammerslough." In *The Magazine Antiques* 74 (September 1958), p. 241.

Reis, Heinrich, and Henry Leighton. *History of the Clay-Working Industry in the United States.* New York: John Wiley & Sons, 1909.

Reynolds, Mairead. *Early Belleek Wares.* Dublin: Elo Press, 1928.

Rhead, Frederick H. "Pottery Class." In *Keramic Studio* 11 (November 1909), pp. 159–61.

———. "America as a Ceramic Art Center." In *Fine Arts Journal* 22 (April 1910), pp. 183–93.

———. "Adelaide Alsop Robineau: Maker of Porcelains." In *Potter* 1 (February 1917), pp. 81–88.

———. "Chats on Pottery." In *The Potters Herald,* 1934–35. Robineau Archives, Everson Museum of Art.

Richardson, Ralph R., comp. Genealogical Record of the Cartlidge Family. Typescript, 1960.

"Rivaling English Ware: What Ott and Brewer Have Done." *Trenton Times,* 15 October 1883, p. 1.

Robineau, Adelaide A. "American Pottery: Artistic Porcelain Making." In *Art World* 3 (November 1917), pp. 153–55.

Robineau, S[amuel] E. "The Robineau Porcelains." In *Keramic Studio* 13 (August 1911), pp. 80–83.

———. "Adelaide Alsop-Robineau." In *Design* 30 (April 1929), pp. 201–9.

Robinson, Dorothy, with Bill Feeny. *The Official Price Guide to American Pottery and Porcelain.* Edited by Thomas E. Hudgeons III. Orlando, Fla.: House of Collectibles, 1980.

Romeyn, Carlyn Crannell. *The Lycetts.* Classical Gems of Educational Art Treasures Series. Vol. 6. International Porcelain Art Teachers, n.p., 1983.

Rose, Arthur V. "Porcelain Made in America." In *International Studio* 37 (April 1909), pp. 49–52.

The Royal Copenhagen Porcelain Manufactory 1775–1975. Copenhagen: Royal Copenhagen Porcelain Manufactory, 1975.

Ruge, Clara. "American Ceramics — A Brief Review of Progress." In *International Studio* 28 (1906), pp. 21–28.

———. "American Pottery." In *Pottery and Glass* 2 (January 1909), pp. 27–36.

Sandier, Alexandre. "La Céramique à l'Exposition." In *Art et Décoration* 8 (December 1900), pp. 184–96; 9 (January 1901), pp. 53–68.

Sandon, Henry. *Royal Worcester Porcelain from 1862 to the Present Day.* London: Barrie & Jenkins, 1973.

Savage, George. *Porcelain Through the Ages.* Harmondsworth, England: Penguin Books, 1954.

Sayre, Stuart. "The American Invasion." In *Pottery and Glass* 2 (May 1909), pp. 231–37.

Schwartz, Marvin D., and Richard Wolfe. *A History of American Art Porcelain.* New York: Renaissance Editions, 1967.

Shrimpton, Louise. "An Art Potter and Her Home." In *Good Housekeeping* 50 (January 1910), pp. 57–63.

Silliman, B[enjamin], Jr., and C. R. Goodrich. *The World of Science, Art, and Industry Illustrated from Examples in the New-York Exhibition, 1853–54.* New York: G. P. Putnam and Company, 1854.

Smith, G. M. *Belleek Porcelain and Pottery: A Handbook for the Collector.* Guernsey, Channel Islands: Toucan Press, 1979.

Stiles, Henry Reed, ed. *The Civil, Political, Professional and Ecclesiastical History, and Commercial and Industrial Record of the County of Kings and the City of Brooklyn, N. Y., from 1683 to 1884.* New York: Munsell & Co., 1884.

The Story of Lenox Belleek China. Trenton: Lenox, Incorporated, n.d.

Stout, Wilber. "Notes on Early American Porcelain." In *Bulletin of the American Ceramic Society* 17 (April 1938), pp. 177–78.

Stradling, J. G. "American Ceramics and the Philadelphia Centennial." In *The Magazine Antiques* 110 (July 1976), pp. 146–58.

———. "Dr. Mead and the French Connection." Typescript, 1987.

Stratton, Herman John. "Factors in the Development of the American Pottery Industry, 1860–1929." Ph.D. diss., University of Chicago, 1929.

Strong, Susan R. *History of American Ceramics: An Annotated Bibliography.* Metuchen, N.J., and London: The Scarecrow Press, 1983.

———. "University City Pottery and The Woman's Republic of 1910: The Publications by the Artists and Their Effect on the Ceramics Movement." *Journal of the National Council on Education for the Ceramic Arts* 6 (1985), pp. 64–67.

Sturgis, Russell. "American Pottery." In *Scribner's Magazine* 32 (November 1902), pp. 637–40.

Tachau, Hanna. "American-Made Pottery Exemplified in Lenox China." In *International Studio* 67 (May 1919), pp. 92–96.

Thistlethwaite, F. "The Atlantic Migration of the Pottery Industry." In *Economic History Review*. Series 2, vol. 11 (1958).

Thomas, Curtis R. "Drawn from the Kilns of University City." Master's thesis, University of Missouri, 1974.

Towner, Donald. *The Leeds Pottery*. London: Cory, Adams & Mackay, 1963.

Tucker Pattern Books. 2 vols. Library, Philadelphia Museum of Art, Rare Books Collection.

Twitchett, John, and Betty Bailey. *Royal Crown Derby*. New York: Clarkson N. Potter, 1976.

Tyndale, Hector. "General Report of the Judges of Group 2: Pottery, Porcelains. . . ." In Francis A. Walker, ed. *U. S. Centennial Commission. International Exhibition, 1876: Reports and Awards*. 9 vols. Washington, D.C.: Government Printing Office, 1880, 3.

Union Porcelain Co.'s Price List of House Trimmings. Trade catalogue. New York: Francis & Loutrel, 1861.

Vases Manufactured in the Celebrated Lenox Belleek. Trade catalogue. Trenton: Lenox, Incorporated, 1909.

Voorsanger, Catherine Hoover. "Dictionary of Architects, Artisans, Artists, and Manufacturers." In *In Pursuit of Beauty: Americans and the Aesthetic Movement*. New York: The Metropolitan Museum of Art, 1986, pp. 400–487.

Wallis, George. "Report on Porcelain and Ceramic Manufacture." In *General Report of the British Commissioners on the N. Y. Industrial Exhibition*. London: T. Harrison, 1854.

Watkins, Lura Woodside. *Early New England Potters and Their Wares*. Cambridge: Harvard University Press, 1950.

Weidner, Ruth Irwin, comp. *American Ceramics Before 1930: A Bibliography*. Westport, Conn., and London: Greenwood Press, 1982.

Weiss, Peg. "Adelaide Alsop Robineau: Ceramist from Syracuse." In *Heresies* (Winter 1978), pp. 52–53.

———, ed. *Adelaide Alsop Robineau: Glory in Porcelain*. Syracuse: Syracuse University Press, in association with Everson Museum of Art, 1981.

Whiter, Leonard. *Spode: A History of the Family, Factory, and Wares from 1733 to 1833*. London: Barrie & Jenkins, 1970.

Whitman, Walt. "Porcelain Manufactories." In *I Sit and Look Out: Editorials from the Brooklyn Daily Times by Walt Whitman*. Edited by Emory Holloway and Vernolian Schwarz. Brooklyn, 1932, pp. 132–38.

"William H. Bloor." *Bulletin of the American Ceramic Society* 16 (January 1937), pp. 25–31.

Williams, Susan. *Savory Suppers and Fashionable Feasts: Dining in Victorian America*. New York: Pantheon Books, in association with The Strong Museum, 1985.

Wise, Ethel Brand. "Adelaide Alsop Robineau—American Ceramist." In *American Magazine of Art* 20 (December 1929), pp. 687–91.

Woodhouse, Samuel W., Jr. "The First Philadelphia Porcelain." In *The Magazine Antiques* 24 (October 1933), pp. 134–35.

The Work of The Potteries of New Jersey from 1685 to 1876. Exhibition catalogue. Newark: The Newark Museum Association, 1914.

Yarnall, James L., and William H. Gerdts, comps. *The National Museum of American Art's Index to American Art Exhibition Catalogues*. 6 vols. Boston: G. K. Hall & Co., 1986.

Young, Jennie J. *The Ceramic Art: A Compendium of the History and Manufacture of Pottery and Porcelain*. New York: Harper & Brothers, 1879.

Zakin, Richard. "Technical Aspects of the Work of Adelaide Alsop Robineau." In Peg Weiss, ed. *Adelaide Alsop Robineau: Glory in Porcelain*. Syracuse: Syracuse University, in association with Everson Museum of Art, 1981, pp. 117–38.

———. "Aspects of the Work of Adelaide Alsop Robineau." In *Journal of the National Council on Education for the Ceramic Arts* 8 (1987), pp. 11–13.

Index

Boldface numbers denote pages containing illustrations.

C

D

E

F

G

H

I

J

K

L

M

N

O

S

T

U

V

W

Y

Z

Photograph Credits

All photographs in the book are the work of Schecter Lee, except for the following: p. 5, Courtney Frisse; p. 9, Photo Studio, The Metropolitan Museum of Art; p. 10, The Henry Francis du Pont Winterthur Museum; p. 12, Musée National de Céramique, Sèvres; p. 15, Photo Studio, The Metropolitan Museum of Art; p. 19, The White House; p. 20, The Henry Francis du Pont Winterthur Museum; p. 22 and p. 23, Fig. 16, The Brooklyn Museum; p. 26, Fig. 20, Helga Photo Studio; p. 26, Fig. 21, Henry Ford Museum and Greenfield Village; p. 27, Library of Congress; p. 31, The Bennington Museum; p. 36, Joseph Crilley; p. 38, Library of Congress; p. 41, Christie's, New York; p. 43, courtesy of Edith Shields Kersey; p. 54, Fig. 42, and p. 57, Tony Lee Associates, Inc.; p. 62, Figs. 49, 50, University City Public Library; p. 75, Hans E. Lorenz; p. 76, no. 3a, and p. 91, Eric Long; p. 98, The Historical Society of Pennsylvania; pp. 112, 130, Photo Studio, The Metropolitan Museum of Art; p. 143, Wadsworth Atheneum, Joseph Szaszfai; p. 157, Fig. 2, Cartographic and Architectural Branch, National Archives and Records Administration; pp. 163, 165, Eric Long; p. 219, Museum of Ceramics at East Liverpool; p. 297, Tom Barr.

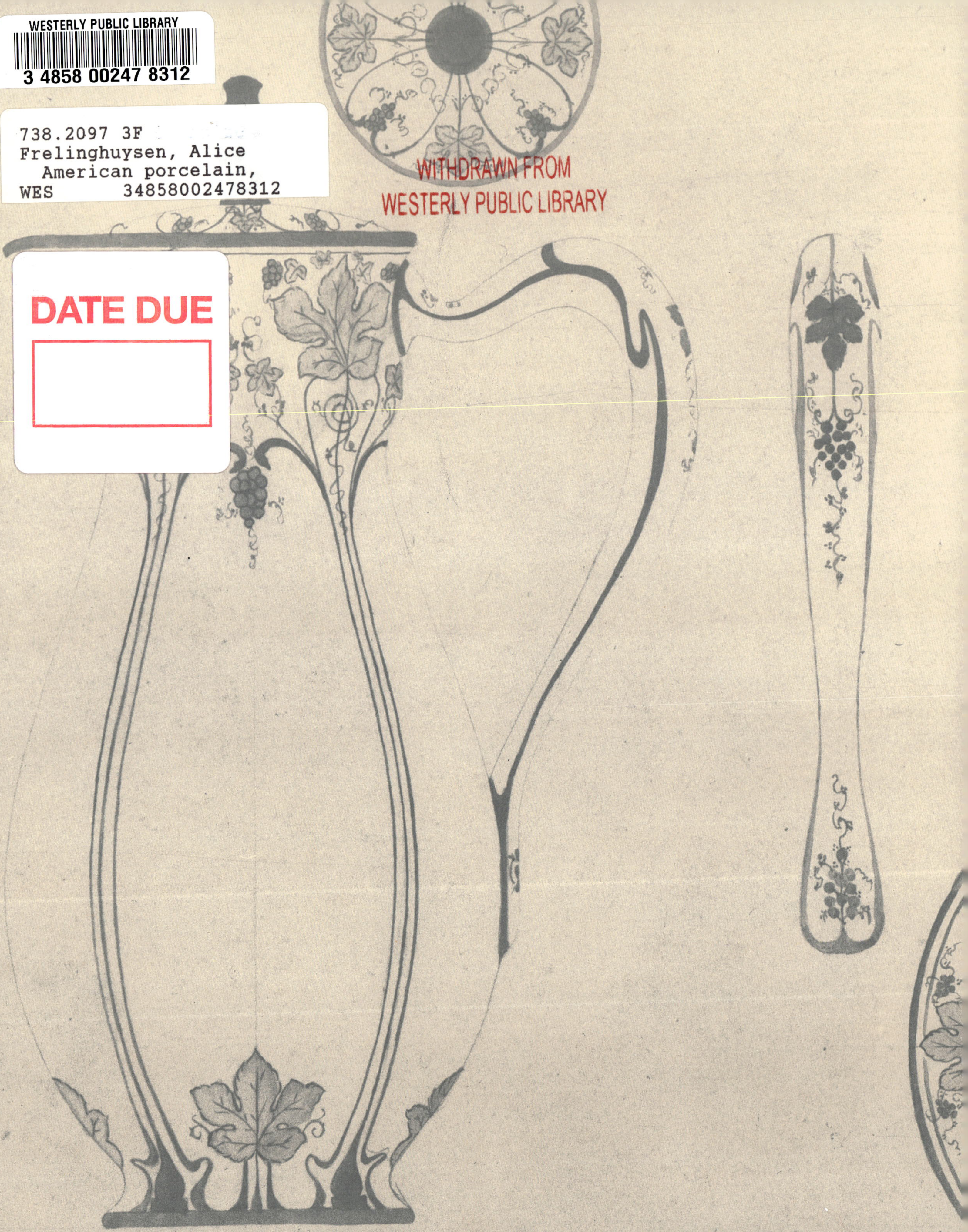